Transition to Adulthood During Military Service

SUNY Series in Israeli Studies
Russell Stone, Editor

A publication from the Center for
Study and Documentation of Israeli Society,
The Hebrew University of Jerusalem.

Transition to Adulthood
—— during ——
Military Service

The Israeli Case

Amia Lieblich

STATE UNIVERSITY OF NEW YORK PRESS

Published by
State University of New York Press, Albany

Printed in the United States of America

For information, address State University of New York
Press, State University Plaza, Albany, N.Y., 12246

Library of Congress Cataloging-in-Publication Data

Lieblich, Amia, 1939–
      Transition to adulthood during military service :
      the Israeli case / Amia Lieblich.
            p.   cm.   —   (SUNY series in Israeli studies)
      Bibliography : p.
      Includes index.
      ISBN 0–7914–0146–4.   —   ISBN 0–7914–0147–2 (pbk.)
      1. Draft—Israel—Psychological aspects—Case studies.
      2. Teenage boys—Israel—Case studies.   3. Men—Israel—Psychology—Case
      studies.   4. Soldiers—Israel—Psychology—Case studies.
      5. Psychology, Military—Case studies.   I. Title.   II. Series.
      UB345.I75L54   1989
      355.2′2363′095694—dc19   89–30041
                                                                          CIP

10   9   8   7   6   5   4   3   2   1

Contents

Acknowledgments

The list of people I wish to thank is long. From the first stages of planning the project to the final editing of the book, I was lucky to receive help and support from my family, colleagues, assistants, institutions and friends.

The idea of studying the psychological effects of mandatory military service in Israel was encouraged by many professionals, both from the military and the academic systems in Israel. Professors and administrators of the Hebrew University were helpful in announcing the call for volunteers for the study in classes and through the bulletin boards. The Hebrew University recognized the importance of the project by awarding me the Bird Prize for Outstanding Research, which provided the funding for paying the participants for their time, and several students for their aid in transcribing the tapes. For this stage of the research special thanks are due to Yoav Rinon, who performed most of the transcriptions and organized the project with great enthusiasm and warmth.

Further financial aid toward the completion of the study was granted by the Sturman Human Development Center of the Department of Psychology, the Hebrew University, and by the Israeli Schocken House, which published a Hebrew popular version of the same study, titled in Hebrew *The Spring of Their Years*. The Department of Psychology at UCLA, chaired at this time by Dr. Bert Raven, provided me with the necessary services for working on and typing the first drafts of the study during my sabbatical year in 1986.

Many of my colleagues read parts of the draft at different stages. The complete book was criticized in a most constructive manner by Anat Ninio from the Department of Psychology, and by Victor Azarya and Baruch Kimmerling from the Department of Sociology at the Hebrew University. The bibliographical work and the analysis was greatly aided by Meir Perlow, who also helped in improving my style in English. Hadas Weisman of the Department of Psychology provided valuable insight into some of the developmental processes studied in the book. Finally, Miriam Mantel performed the linguistic editing and helped in bringing the manuscript to its present form.

Needless to say, this project would not have been possible without the honest disclosure of the participants who were willing to be interviewed by me about their military service and war experience. Their outstanding willingness to open up to a stranger, and to talk about their painful as well as happy memories, has been a deep learning experience for me, for which I want to thank each one of them.

Finally, I would like to express my gratitude to the members of my family who, used as they were to my obsession with work and writing, have still been exceptionally supportive in the present project. My children Maty and Eliav were both patient with and proud of their busy mother. My own personal concern with the process of transition to adulthood during military service grew from my observation of and participation in the changes which took place in the life of my eldest son, Yuval, who served in the Infantry at the time of the research. This book is dedicated to the memory of my husband, Israel, a great admirer of the Israeli military force, who died in September 1986, while I was starting to write this book.

Jerusalem, October 1988.

Introduction

At an age in which young men in the Western world leave their sheltered homes for college life or for a job, in the spring of their years, young men in Israel begin three years of service in the military forces. This age span, known in psychological literature as late adolescence, youth, or the transition to adulthood, has recently become a focus of interest and research. The social conditions and life experiences which are undergone during these formative years have important effects on personality development, values, and the course of growth of these young men. This book investigates the psychological experience of these conditions: It documents the military service of a group of young men in Israel during the early 1980s (including the Lebanon War of 1982), and examines the influence of these experiences on the transition to adulthood. Although women also serve in the military forces in Israel,[1] the present study discusses only men's experience. Military service for Israeli men is longer and apparently more demanding. Only men participate directly in combat and continue to be 'soldiers' via compulsory reserve duty throughout the major part of their adult lives and the all too frequent wars. Therefore, the military experience touches men more profoundly, and affects their lives and identity to a greater extent.

Although a great deal has been written about the soldier who is psychologically damaged by combat, there is little systematic knowledge about men who, during their military service, showed no manifestations of psychopathology. Nor is there much information about military service as a stage of transition to adulthood, or about the effects of service in peacetime on personality development. The latter topics will be dealt with in the present study, taking the individual, subjective perspective.

The basic assumption of the book is that plasticity[2] is a central aspect of early adulthood, namely that at this age culture has its strongest impact on personality. Therefore, military service and wartime experiences during these formative years must have profound effects on the process of psychological development. Specifically, this book examines the formation of identity among young men who served in various roles and under different conditions in the army. Do they seem to progress or to regress on the route

toward adulthood? How are the requirements of the military system accepted by young men who possess the specific traits characteristic of adolescence? What happens to their relationships with their parents, women,
mentors, and peers? What are the effects of military service on their social
interests, values, and moral development? How does military service affect
their feelings of belonging to aggregates such as the Jewish people or the
State of Israel? Generally, how does military service affect the various concerns that seem to be typical of youth, such as the search for identity, intimacy, and stability? Or does the military service, due to its peacetime
demands, norms, and rules or to the special wartime experiences, create
some unique concerns which usually "belong" to other developmental
stages, such as the need to confront life and death? The in-depth examination of these and related problems will not only help to gain greater understanding of the psychological experience of this group of youth during their
military service, but will also shed some light on the more general question
of cultural relativity of life-span issues and the plasticity of early adulthood.

The study is based on individual, in-depth interviews (lasting from
three to twelve hours) with a group of thirty young men discharged from
the army a short time prior to the beginning of the research. Part I of the
book includes eight oral histories, or first-person narratives of soldiers;
these describe their own experiences during military service. The cases selected for presentation exemplify different occupations and courses of military service. They are representative of people with different backgrounds,
with different expectations and varying degrees of readiness to serve. They
demonstrate various crises and stages of military service, depict different
incidents that occurred during the war, and end up with a range of positive
to negative self-evaluations.[3]

The second part of the book provides a more formal analysis and
discussion of the psychological effects of military service. In order to explore the significance of the subjective material, I have chosen to analyze
and to discuss the Israeli experience of military service in two main contexts: in comparison to the experience of military service elsewhere, and as
a nodal period of transition in the life schemes of the participants. The
analysis focuses on three areas: courses of military service during relative
peacetime, the psychological effects of participation in war, and personality
development at the transition to adulthood in the context of military service
as previously described. The overall conclusion of this study may be stated
here in a general manner. The experience of military service at this nodal
point in the life of the young Israeli man constitutes a culture-specific version of the transition to adulthood differing from that of comparable age
groups elsewhere. Especially prominent in the Israeli version are the emphasis on the acquisition and elaboration of the young men's capacity for

actively coping with hardships and difficulties, and on the expansion of their personal boundaries in a variety of encounters with people, events, and values. This emphasis is in contrast to the themes prominent in Western literature, such as issues related to separation from parents, psychological moratorium, and heterosexual intimacy. In the last chapter of the book these differences are discussed, together with an exploration of the price paid by the Israeli youth in his encounter with the developmental tasks presented to him by his culture.

The military service emerges from the book as having not only negative aspects (as has been documented repeatedly in previous literature), but positive aspects as well. The present analysis identifies issues of personality development which are common to all the young men interviewed. At the same time it reveals the diverse ways in which military service influences individual development.

The Research Design

In planning the research project, I had attempted to select the most appropriate procedure for the attainment of two goals: to secure a detailed account of my participants' three to four year military experience, and to assess the psychological changes that occurred during that period. For the description of the military service, my focus was phenomenological, in that I recorded the experience as perceived and recalled from the participant's point of view. For the second goal, the assessment of the psychological changes that occurred during the service, I used a combined strategy. I asked the young men to describe in detail, and to evaluate, the psychological changes that they had experienced during their years in the army, and added on my own observations, interpretations and analyses.

I chose to adopt a retrospective approach, namely to interview the young men when they were civilians, following the completion of their military service.[4] Considering the type of data collected, I selected the open-ended interview, conducted in a series of meetings with each young man. This procedure allows time for trust to develop, so that meaningful and minimally biased accounts might be obtained. The present research belongs, therefore, to the tradition of qualitative studies (in psychology),[5] or oral history (in history)[6]—methods which, in recent years, have been quite well accepted and analyzed. Although problems of replicability, accuracy and bias cannot be completely solved using these methods, their advantage lies in the richness and depth of the material which they produce. For the subject at hand, the possibility of obtaining a number of diverse accounts was of central value. This follows my conviction that individual lives develop diversely, through a variety of paths.[7] Moreover, military service is indeed a very complex reality, and different individuals often witness separate aspects of it. To arrive at as complete a picture as possible, varied individual accounts are essential. When similar settings or events are described, however, the subjectively different experience is the focus of our interest. Rather than being considered a bias, or reflecting a lack of objectivity, this variability is precisely the object of our attention. The different perspectives of individuals regarding military service or war do not conflict with each other. They supplement each other in creating a rich, multidimensional picture. If one grants that social-psychological reality is exceedingly complex, then one may see the advantage of using this relativistic, subjective perspective.

For obtaining the oral history and evaluation of military service, it was decided to interview men who had graduated from high school before their military service, and who were, at the time of their interview, beginning their studies at institutions of higher education in Israel. This group of participants could be described as the elite of Israeli society, that social class which will determine the country's values and direction in the coming years. Due to their better verbal ability, I had expected this group to be more introspective and to be better able to provide comprehensive accounts. Yet, within these limits, I included individuals from a variety of backgrounds and military experiences. Although the military experience of the less privileged is likely to be quite different, even among this more educated group the variation in attitudes and course of development was quite significant. The in-depth study of those young men who completed the term of service without unusual complications has broad implications for our understanding of the impact of military experience on the transition into adulthood.

During the fall of 1984, and throughout the first half of 1985, I advertised at the various institutions of higher education in Jerusalem that I was searching for volunteers to participate in a study concerning their experiences during military service. The ads asked for the participation of young men who had not been out of the service for more than six months. They were offered modest pay for their weekly participation in a set of hour-long recorded interviews in my office at the Hebrew University of Jerusalem. Following a short screening meeting, aimed at selecting participants with a wide range of backgrounds and military occupations, thirty young men were chosen to participate in the study. The total number of sessions varied from three to twelve, depending on the time necessary for each individual to give his personal account. A total of 160 hours of conversation was fully recorded and transcribed verbatim for the study.

The men I interviewed ranged from 21 to 23 years of age. Half of them were freshmen in different fields at the Hebrew University of Jerusalem, and the other half were either in pre-academic preparatory studies (that is, candidates for higher education) or students at arts or music academies in Jerusalem. At the beginning of the interviews, they had been out of active service anywhere from a few days to six months. They had previously served in a wide variety of military fields, including the Armored Corps, the Artillery, Communications, Intelligence, Infantry, Fighting Pioneer Youth (Nahal), Medical Corps, Maintenance, Military Police, Navy, and the Air Force.[8] Twelve of the thirty had finished their service as officers, and therefore had served an additional, fourth year. Most of the interviewees were from urban backgrounds, but some of them were from kibbutzim, villages, or small development towns. All but one of the young men were born in Israel. Eleven of the thirty are of Sepharadic descent— that is, their parents or grandparents came from Moslem countries. The remaining nineteen were from European families. All were Jewish—a few were Orthodox, but the majority were nonobservant. In terms of their economic status, most of them were of the middle class, and a few were of the lower class, so they represent a wide variety of subgroups in Israeli society.

The first interview was dedicated to the young men's recollections of their background, and of their experiences prior to entering the army. I asked about their expectations regarding military service and about their physical and mental preparedness for it. The next stage of the interviews dealt with the military experience per se, recounted chronologically in as complete a way as possible, starting from the first day in the army to the very end of their service. The length and depth of the participants' accounts varied a great deal, depending on their experiences and their willingness to recall and to share them. Some, with very little encouragement from me, presented monologues, while others required much probing and suggestions on my part. Even so, for some of these latter participants only laconic accounts were obtained. The content of the accounts varied immensely. Some episodes came up repeatedly, however, representing the common background for the individual variations. After the chronological account had been obtained, each individual participated in a final interview, which concentrated on the psychological effects of the service, and on the individual's perceptions of the changes in traits, values and beliefs which he had experienced during that time.

As presented above, the accounts aimed at revealing the subjective, rather than the factual, level of experience.[9] No attempt was made to criticize or to correct the personal accounts from the point of view of their objective, or "truth," value. On the contrary, it is clear that some of the recollections were distorted due to the passage of time (although the time that had elapsed might be considered short when compared with some classic oral history accounts), the limited knowledge of the participants themselves *vis-a-vis* the exploits in which they had been involved, and their various political biases and personal motives. The personal viewpoint was most apparent in the war accounts, but it underlay all the remaining aspects as well, and emerged especially when painful episodes were recollected.

Most of the participants were pleased with the opportunity to recount their military, and especially their wartime, experiences. In spite of the fact that this was not our goal, several of them noted that the conversations had been therapeutic or cathartic, and expressed their gratitude and sent me their friends . . . All of them permitted me to use their accounts for the book, stating their belief that it contained an important message, particularly in helping prepare the younger generation and their families for military service.

Notes

1. Research on women in the military has become popular in the last decade, accompanying the growth of women in the United States armed forces. Interested readers may refer to Earl (1976), Binkin and Bach (1977), Chapkis (1981), Stiehm (1981), Holm (1982), Rogan (1982), Rustad (1982), Stephens (1983), and Stiehm (1985). Although some of these works mention the Israeli woman soldier, usually in comparison with the American case (see for example a brief note in Binkin and Bach, pp. 131–133, or in Rustad, pp. 40–41) little research has been published bearing directly on this subject. The two main sources for understanding women in the IDF are Hazleton (1977)—a popular, journalistic book on Israeli women, which includes a chapter on the military—and Bloom (1982) (in a book including several cross-cultural chapters, edited by Goldman), which is a more academic presentation of the subject. All the above writers agree that equality of women in the Israel Defense Force is, at this time, a myth. Women serve mostly in traditional feminine occupations, and are segregated from men. From the point of view of the military system, their roles are peripheral, completely distinct from the combat roles of men. Research on the integration of women into more innovative roles in the Israeli army was conducted by Eshkol, Lieblich, Bar-Yosef and Weisman (1987).

2. Psychological and sociological literature proposes that social influences, which are naturally active through the life span, are especially powerful at adolescence and during the transition to adulthood. This idea is formulated by Honzik (1984) as the "plasticity in the early adult years" (p. 327). A similar idea was expressed also by Hall (1904), who claimed that individuals are more prone to cultural influences during adolescence than at any other time. This idea will be further discussed in Part II.

3. A more complete collection of the oral histories obtained in this research appeared in Hebrew, in Lieblich, *The Spring of Their Years* (1987). In this book, twenty-one cases are presented, with very little analytical discussion.

4. An alternative design could have been to select a group of young men prior to their induction into the military, interview them at different points during their service, and conduct a final assessment after their release. Although follow-up studies of this type are very costly and quite time consuming, several notable psychological works have been carried out in just this way. However, conducting such a project within a military framework can be quite complicated. I suspect that the military authorities might not fully cooperate, given that the results of the study might not be favorable to the military system and its values. Even if they had been willing to cooperate, they would retain the right to have control over the selection of participants, and to maintain censorship of the material. Furthermore, for reasons of security, soldiers on active service, especially during wartime, are restricted in their freedom to discuss their military experiences much more than are civilians who are already out of mandatory service. As a result, the freedom of expression of both researcher and participants might have been severely hampered.

Research in developmental psychology utilizing the follow-up method may be exemplified by the studies summarized in Kagan and Moss (1962), Block (1971), Vaillant (1977a), and Eichorn, Clausen, Haan, Honzik and Mussen, eds. (1981). Special follow-ups of adolescents and young adults were also reported by Perry (1968), Offer and Offer (1975), and Bachman, O'Malley and Johnson (1978).

5. Qualitative methods in psychology were described and analyzed thoroughly by Runyan (1981), who refers to the Allport-Murray-White tradition of the clinical case study and the biography. Among the earlier contributions to this method in psychology, sociology and anthropology were Allport (1937, 1942), Murray (1938, 1948), Dollard (1935), Kluckhohn (1945) and White (1966). Some of the more recent important contributions include Bromley (1977), Denzin (1978), and Levinson *et al.* (1978). Bromley (1977) refers to the life history method as a "sadly neglected scientific method" (p. 164), the methodological development of which has been arrested as compared with the impressive progress of quantitative approaches in psychology. As the reader might already have gathered, our own work in the present investigation is not a single case study, but a collection of several such individual histories. Some of the content analyses will be at the group level, while most of the data presentation will be at the individual level (to use Runyan's terminology). One of the major messages of Runyan's work is that not all case studies have to remain descriptive, subjective or qualitative. Our approach in this study may be characterized as "idiographic" (to use Allport's famous concept), not in the sense of studying a single life, but in the sense of studying "particular subjective meanings of events and circumstances to the individual" (Runyan, 1982, p. 168). The idiographic-nomothetic debate flourished in psychology for years, especially in the 1950s and 1960s. See, for example, Allport (1942, 1961), Eysenck (1954), Meehl (1954), Holt (1962) and others mentioned in Runyan's chapter on the subject. Although several of these writers suggested abandoning these terms, they

seem to linger on in psychology and presently relate to a whole set of issues related to choosing a particular research strategy and focus.

6. One should be reminded, of course, that the field of anthropology has always used naturalistic observation, including informants' interviews, as one of its major research tools. See, for example, Spradley (1979a, 1979b), Hammersley and Atkinson (1983), and Burgess (1984). In Europe, social historians have been attracted to the 'new' method of research, and oral history has become an intellectual movement. The major contributions to this field are summarized in Thompson (1978) and Bertaux (1981). A more recent review can be found in Bertaux and Kohli (1984), who summarize the "continental view" on the oral history approach. Special journals deal specifically with research conducted using this method, *e.g.*, *Oral History, Oral History Review,* and *International Journal of Oral History.* It would be difficult to single out the few works in oral history that are important in the present context. Let me just mention those works which have most affected my own work in this area: They are Blythe (1969), Myrdal (1965), Thompson (1975), and most notably Studs Terkel's *Hard Times* (1970), *Working* (1974), and *The Good War* (1984). Motley (1975) published an oral history of the experience of black soldiers during World War II, which has some relevance to the present study. My own research in the oral history tradition is published as *Kibbutz Makom* (Lieblich, 1981). In psychology, there has also been a trend toward more naturalistic research methods. See for example Willens and Rausch (1969), Cronbach (1975), Epstein (1979), Wachtel (1980), Howe (1982).

7. This idea will be further elaborated upon in Part II.

8. Some additional information may be helpful at this point. The infantry participants came from three separate IDF infantry units: the parachutists, Golani, and an elite reconnaisance unit. The Fighting Pioneer Youth, or Nahal, combines service in agricultural border settlements with regular military assignments. I should point out that the Air Force participants were not former military pilots, but were technicians in various roles. Pilots serve much longer than the regular three or four years, and therefore are older when they enter the universities, and are thus out of the age range of the present study.

9. For readers who are interested in comparing our subjective accounts with more factual descriptions of the military service in Israel, as well as the Lebanon War, Gabriel (1984) and Schiff (1985) are recommended.

PART I

Personal Accounts

1

DAVID

I went to a vocational high school in Jerusalem. I was an athlete. Running and bicycle riding were my hobbies.

I am the eldest boy in the family, and so I had no first hand information about the army. But I knew that I wanted to be a combat soldier, and that I would do well in the army—for myself, not because others expected me to. It is a feeling you grow up with. Maybe it had to do with the fact that my uncle had been killed in the War of Independence. Somehow it all seemed related.

I volunteered for the paratroopers and I was accepted. Right from the start, at the induction base, I remember walking around proud of my red boots. I felt exhilarated. (smiling) As new enlisted men, they also gave us a nice sum of money, and in the evening I went to Tel Aviv with my new uniform, my own money—I felt really good. I had reached the place that I wanted to be in, and I knew that physically I was well prepared.

At the end of the week we were taken to the paratroopers' basic training camp. I remember the welcome we received there—"If you don't feel strong enough, go back to the bus and leave; you can still change your mind." Immediately you are in a completely new world. You have to run up the road in these new, heavy boots, you have to carry two heavy kitbags full of things, you get your work clothes for the first time and don't know how to put them on, and almost every soldier you meet yells at you and orders you around.

The fact that I was strong and fast helped me a great deal. I stood out as a runner. We circled the camp all the time, and I was always the first one to complete the round. My commanders noticed that I was highly motivated. In difficult moments I used to tell myself: That's what you wanted all along, so now you're here, go on, you can do it.

3

For the first week or so, we were waiting for the rest of the new recruits to arrive, so all we did there was clean the base and work in the kitchen. We were often harrassed by our leaders. Especially before meals. Standing at attention near the mess hall, if one of us moved a bit, we were ordered to circle the base, running, again and again. The whole unit was punished for every little thing done by one of the trainees. There were moments that I felt: Is that it? Is that what I volunteered for?

Then our basic training really began. We were divided into platoons and we met our staff, namely the squad leaders. They made a great show of being tough. The officer was at a distance, we never saw him. We were absolutely forbidden to talk to him. He was like God in our eyes.

The thing I remember most is the sense of uncertainty. You could never guess what might come next. You go to sleep, but you may be awakened in ten minutes for a forced march. Nothing is predictable.

Gradually you acquire military habits. After you've run back and forth 50 times, you finally learn not to move during parade. You learn that you're responsible for the others in your unit, and you have to help them— or else you'll be punished for their problems.

Thursday was the hardest day of the week. During the day we had a hike, and then when we returned, exhausted, we had to prepare for the weekly inspection which took place on Friday. The preparations lasted all night, and if you were lucky to get a vacation for Saturday, you spent the whole day sleeping at home.

We were too tired and busy to get to know each other. The only one you get to know is the leader, who keeps making fun of your weaknesses. The hikes got longer, with heavier loads to carry. For every hike we usually got some reward. You hike for the strap of your rifle, for the paratroopers' insignia, for your cap. Gradually you learn to love those night marches, and you get to know yourself really well. Your odor, the sound of your footsteps. You smell the soil, the farms around you, hear the dogs barking at night, recognize the silhouettes of your friends. You admire the performance of your squad leader—he walks, while you run, and you still cannot catch up with him. Gradually you discover that he knows *how* to walk— and you learn this too. People develop their marching style. After 14 months of training together, I was able to identify my buddies from a distance by their way of walking, you know.

I loved those marches. They were challenging for me, and I wanted to prove myself. At the same time I had an outstanding record in running. I received tremendous rewards for my performance. I was even chosen to represent the battalion in a sports event, and managed to skip part of basic training for that.

I was somewhat embarrassed when I saw my buddies being harassed, circling the base, while I left every morning to train for the games. I joined them again just as we were moving into the field, for the second part of basic training. It was winter by then. We built little tents in the field, and were soaked by the rain at night. We got used to being wet all the time, but we had to keep our rifles dry, and this was a lot of work. People got ill quite often. It was tough.

At that stage we were given our different roles in the platoon, and I became the communications man for the platoon leader. This is an important job. You have to follow the officer all the time, with his radio on your back. He usually walks ahead, so you are the second, right after him. If he has any messages, he sends you to run back and transmit them to the sergeant or the soldiers. You have to be on the alert all the time. You attend the officers' meetings, you hear what is going on. You get the chance to know things that other soldiers still don't know. Radio communication is an art—to be credible, and to convey confidence.

As a communications man, a special relationship develops between you and your platoon leader. It is a kind of romance, you know. After 14 months together, you know each other in and out. I originally had thought that he was a hard man, but I discovered that he was an actor, and very human underneath. When I went on action with him, I saw him as a human being, even afraid. Once he pushed me behind a tree, turned to face me and said: "Take care!" His voice was strange. I knew that he was concerned about me. But this was much later on.

Anyway, from that stage on, I was attached to the radio. I hated it. It hindered me in running and training. On rare occasions, when I managed to get rid of it, I felt free like a bird.

During the field stage of our basic training we started to get to know each other, to love and to hate men of our unit. We got to know the country, too, since we lived outdoors and hiked a lot. The staff was more considerate, we felt. One night they stole some chickens from a nearby farm and made a festive dinner for us. They got hot water for our showers. But generally they were strict.

One night a soldier disappeared. All night we ran through the hills, in the rain, calling his name. Actually, it was pretty clear that he had run home, but the leaders wanted us to search for him just the same, so that we would get the message: If you run away, your whole unit pays for it; don't do it to your friends.

Our exercises grew more complex, and we learned the use of various weapons. I remember the excitement of shooting for real in those exercises—your heart beats wildly and you're short of breath. People got better all the time. We could walk much faster, we could stay awake much longer, we could perform more difficult tasks. The good soldiers stood out from the lot, and I was one of them. In the army, those who are considered good soldiers pay dearly for it. You carry a heavier load on your back, while the weak soldiers are left alone.

At the end of this stage we marched to an Air Force base, for the parachuting course, with stretchers and all the gear. It was about 70 km to walk, and we did it on a rainy night. This was the first time that we felt our squad leaders helping us. They even helped with the stretchers. It was a kind of competition between them—whose platoon would arrive the first. I remember the pride I felt as we walked into the base. Jets were flying above us. We were all dirty and exhausted, entering the gate with our stretchers, while at the base, clean soldiers with clean jobs were arriving from their homes for work. We received a good meal and were given leave for the weekend. (laughing) On that Friday I took the bus to Jerusalem, and slept all the way through. That was nothing out of the ordinary for me. However, when we arrived the driver didn't notice he had me aboard, so he parked the bus and went away. Three hours later I woke up in the bus. It was night already, there was no public transportation, and I had to walk home.

There were all these frightening moments I remember from the parachuting course. The first time you free-jump from the tower, which we called the "Eichman." The first time you jump from the plane. I remember the silence on the airplane—it's a silence I will never forget. And then there is the silence when you're out in the air, and the parachute opens above you, and you slow down and see the ground getting closer.

Each jump was a nightmare all by itself. When you're in the plane, and you all stand in line, and the door is opened, the wind comes in, you're so tense you can hardly breath. Yet you must think, and you mustn't panic, or else you'll make a mistake. The jumps at night were even more frightening, and then my first jump with the radio . . . I was always in line right after the platoon leader, with the radio ready. The best part is hitting the ground. It's such a relief! First thing, I check my legs, move every part of my body, checking. Then I start to scream, cursing the whole world, getting the tension out of my system. There's a beauty to jumping, but it is terribly frightening. You never adjust to it. On the contrary, I think that every jump is more scary, and gradually you get more afraid and you hate it. But when we all gathered at the meeting point on the ground we behaved like big boys again. We had jumped.

We received our wings (paratroopers' insignia) and were supposed to resume our training. However, due to some kind of an emergency, we were moved to the Golan Heights for security duty on the border with Syria.

This was the first time I lived in a stronghold. It was a tremendous transition from the Air Force base. First of all, we had new squad leaders. One of them collected a group of the best soldiers, and developed some kind of a special relationship with us. I can't tell you if it was love or hate. He kept harassing us all the time, to make us tougher, so he said. Also, it was terribly cold there. We were freezing all the time, even though we received good boots and snowsuits. When we patrolled we put newspapers into our shoes, on top of our socks. And still we froze. Finally, we expected to be treated better by the staff, now that we were doing security duty. But this was not the case. We were punished for every little thing, we were really terrorized by our leaders.

Every morning we had to check the road, walking about 15 km in the freezing cold. At night we did motorized patrols, six hours each, back and forth along the border. In addition there were all the chores of maintenance of the stronghold, cleaning and cooking. Our routine was patrolling, cleaning, and patrolling again, with punishments in between. The most hated drill was the dawn alert. Every day, at dawn, we were awakened to practice defense of the stronghold against attacks from different directions. It's always assumed that dawn is *the* hour for attack, you know. I had to run with my radio, its antenna all open in the wind—it was tough.

The worst thing was this sadistic commander. During the second week, people were so tired and cold that they avoided going outside to the toilets at night. One night a soldier defecated in one of the remote alleys of the stronghold. When the commander discovered it, he decided that until one of us confessed, nobody would get leave to go home. A silent struggle unfolded between our unit of ten men and our commander. Nobody confessed. We stayed in the stronghold for six weeks with no furlough. This punishment was out of proportion. Other members of our platoon, serving in other strongholds, got home every two weeks. They used to bring us letters and parcels from our families.

A very strange atmosphere developed. We were the best men of the platoon, with this sadistic commander. We were disciplined all the time, in full view of the Syrians, and were not allowed to go home. As a result, we became very cohesive and tough. We were different than the others. I remember the day when I got out of the stronghold for the first time after six weeks, and suddenly discovered we were really close to the Sea of Galilee. It was like coming out of prison, you know.

During our security duty in the north, we often crossed the border into enemy territory on patrols or various missions. Once we were assigned a mission against the PLO in Lebanon. Only the best men were selected to participate, and I was proud to be among them. We worked hard for three weeks, training with models. We received new equipment and met men from other elite units, and the platoon leader trained with us. It was a pleasure to work together.

The mission itself went very well. That's when I had the incident with my commander, when I felt for the first time that he cared about me. When we completed our mission, a helicopter came to take us back, and as we took off we were shot at by the PLO forces. I remember this wonderful feeling—you see the red flash of bullets, and you are safe inside. But when we landed I noticed a stretcher covered by a blanket, and the red boots sticking out underneath. The wind blew the blanket away, and I saw this man's head all smashed. It was awful. How could this happen? This was the closest I had been to a dead soldier at that time.

After all this time in the north, we felt like old timers. We were not punished as much as before. We had interesting maneuvers, involving all kinds of weapons and vehicles, in coordination with the Armor, Air Force, and Navy. It was a great experience. I felt I was participating in the best army. In fact, I used many of the skills I acquired then later on in the Lebanon War. At the end of the maneuvers we had a long hike, of 120 km, carrying all our gear. This was the first time that the platoon commander opened up to us, and said that he was proud to have such men as his soldiers and that we had become real paratroopers. That's the feedback you get after 14 months of effort.

Most of us went from there to the squad leaders' course. It was a tough transition. You are a full-fledged soldier—and here they make you feel like a beginner all over again. We were given a very strict time schedule, and if we didn't make it on time, we were punished for every second. The worst thing was scrubbing the floors of the rooms. We had always slept in tents until then!

We started by parachuting at night, continuing straight into a long march. We didn't know our fellow trainees, and the staff was mediocre. It was boring. That was the atmosphere for the whole course. I wasn't as motivated as I had been before, and I tried not to stand out. But I did okay.

Well, you graduate and now you're a commander yourself. Actually, it's back to the hard life. You get up at dawn with your trainees and run with them on the hills. You work even harder than the recruits—but that's what always happens to the best soldiers. And I was one of them.

I wanted to get new soldiers, start with them right from the induction base. However, I was attached to the staff of a platoon leader whose soldiers were already at the middle of their basic training. Our platoon leader was an excellent man, who used to be my squad leader when I myself had been in basic training. It was a privilege to be in his staff.

I met my squad in the field. Gradually I learned to know and to love them. At the same time I developed my own style as a commander. It is difficult to describe the process. Essentially it is a big show, but a real one. Basically, you care about your men, but you don't show it. Your military appearance is perfect, you make a severe face, you never smile and you are strict with your men. You acquire a tough style, a threatening tone of speech—and the soldiers are afraid of you. Then you go into the squad leaders' tent, or the platoon leaders', and you burst out laughing, sharing your experience with your peers. This duality is pretty difficult. Gradually I got used to that. I used humor with my trainees, but have never laughed in front of them. I never talked to them in a friendly manner—always like a commander. I made some mistakes, but soon I found out that it was natural for me to be a leader, to be tough, to command others and get some results. But it was hard work. As young squad leaders we got up at dawn, worked with the men till they went to sleep, and had our meetings afterwards. It was exciting, though. Just two weeks earlier I was a trainee myself!

As I got to know my men better, I realized they were a good group. We taught them enough self-discipline so that we didn't have to check every detail all the time. Such things cannot be achieved by force. It is the result of education by a good team. I realized that the essence of leadership was to create a balance between the maintenance of a distance from your men, and, at the same time, making them know that they can trust you and come to you when they really hurt. I also learned that it didn't matter what my soldiers were thinking about me. They cannot make a proper judgment from their point of view. What mattered were my own and my superiors' evaluations. I had a wonderful relationship with our commander, and his personality had influenced me profoundly.

As a squad leader I received orders to officers' course a couple of times. I managed to avoid the course, without directly refusing to go, thinking that I'd finish my service as a sergeant. My tasks had become relatively easy, and I had nine months of mandatory service left. On the other hand, it was tempting to become an officer, to have my men and to run my own platoon. I felt it was time for me to become more independent. I knew that I could be a good officer, and I wanted to build my men according to my own conceptions. So finally I decided to go.

Again you lose all your standing—you are a trainee. But it was a serious course, with good cadets, and we learned a lot. I remember getting back from a successful navigation of 60 km on a rainy night. The feeling that I had mastered it, that I could lead myself alone, even continue for another 10 km if necessary, was exhilarating. After the week of navigations I felt that I had overcome my own limits, that I had opened a new page.

It wasn't easy. As our final exercise we each had to command a mission that we had planned all by ourselves. You organize the other cadets as if they are your men, you plan the attack, including communication, artillery support, logistics—everything. My performance in my exercise wasn't brilliant. Lots of officers came to watch me, but I blundered. It all started when one of my Armored Personnel Carriers got stuck during the attack, and from then on it was a chain of mishaps. I didn't fail, but the 75 points (out of 100) I scored was like a personal failure for me. I believed that had I ruined my chances to return to my battalion as an officer. But the war changed everything later on.

We were almost done with the course when the war broke out. We were actually officers already at the time. (He is silent for a long time, and his face serious.) When the war started, we were well prepared for it. The Officers' School went out to war as an infantry unit, and my platoon was assigned to lead the fighting column on the eastern front. I was placed in the commanding APC, and we drove in.

It was strange, driving into areas we used to observe from a distance. Everything was quiet around us, the terrorists had fled, and we advanced without any battle for the first four days. We used to observe the air combat above us, where the superiority of our Air Force was so evident. We felt secure; we were sure we were winning the war.

On the fourth night we had the feeling that the enemy was close. We kept advancing at night, and suddenly the first tank, which was just in front of us, was hit by artillery, its cannon was off. It tried to turn back, but was stuck. As we all started to retreat, a second tank was hit more severely, and went up in flames. I saw the missile hitting the tank, and bodies of our men in the air—it was unpleasant. We were all firing in all directions, and I thought: "Here we're all going to die." Later I heard from the others that we all had the same thought at that moment. Anyway, my commander sent me out to evacuate the men from the tank in front of us and get them into our APC. It was frightening. I knew we were trapped by the Syrians, and I felt that any moment might be my last.

Finally we managed to withdraw from there. We reorganized our forces, and prepared for the morning attack. At dawn, just as we were getting into the APC, all hell broke loose, a terrible bombardment started. I had just gotten into the APC when a bomb landed nearby, and Levy, my friend who was behind me, got hit in the head. Another cadet was also wounded. They both fell on me, bleeding, and I knew they were dying. It wasn't easy.

Our driver saw what had happened, and immediately turned around and drove to the nearest medical post. I helped carry them out. Levy's head was a mess, and I waited a moment to see what the doctor would say, but I realized it was all over for him. I had to go back to my unit. While we drove back, I tried to clean the APC of the blood and the mess. I remember that another cadet poured a whole bottle of after-shave to eliminate the smell . . . We were in shock.

I know it was my sheer luck that I entered the APC just a second before Levy. He was killed on the spot, but the other injured cadet was saved by the doctors.

It was a hard day. Levy had been a good friend of mine from the officers' course. But the battle went on, and we had little time to think about our casualties. We fought the Syrian commandos all day, and we were hungry, exhausted and afraid. We saw what they were able to do. It was a nightmare—it wasn't the kind of battle we were trained for. We felt helpless, trapped in our vehicles, unable to see what was going on, like targets for the enemy to shoot at.

At night the shooting stopped. We camped in a village nearby, got some food, and the commanders briefed us about the events of the day. We were told to prepare for battle against the Syrian command forces at dawn. Each one of us went separately to check his weapons and ammunition, to prepare the gear. I remember that I prepared myself psychologically as well. I knew that I would be right at the front line, and that my chances of being hit were high. This was—(trails off).

Then we heard the news on the radio, and it was announced that a ceasefire had been declared, and that as of the next morning the combat would stop. We were all very glad. Then the radio announcer read a list of our casualties, and Levy was among them. Second Lieutenant Levy, promoted in death . . . The silence, the ceasefire, and the name of Levy on the radio. These are moments you can never forget.

Afterwards we had about two quiet weeks of slight advances in the area, but nothing much happened. We found many weapons caches, many enemy bodies. There were plenty of mosquitoes, I remember. All the men who had been in combat together felt bound by their experience.

Later on I received furlough and went to visit Levy's parents. I also heard about many other casualties. I found that the men who had taken part in battle were engulfed in silence. I too, was silent most of the time, and I smoked a lot.

Afterwards we were given an additional two weeks to complete the officers' course. When we finished I was assigned my first job as an officer and was sent with my men to wait for the battle for Beirut. We received new equipment, we were briefed, and knew exactly what to expect. Now I had to lead my men, and I felt it as a great responsibility. I remember the feeling. To take care of myself, and at the same time to pay attention to the men behind me. In addition, there is the radio, coordination with other forces—all that I had learned.

Actually, the battle was a quick one, and we did very well. When it was all over, we were taken out of Lebanon and sent back to the training base. I was made a platoon leader.

It was very peculiar feeling to return to the induction base, this time as an officer in red boots, with the Lebanon war insignia on my chest. To be surrounded by all these fresh recruits! How amusing to hear their complaints about the easiest tasks! It was my turn to select the recruits I wanted. I picked my sergeant as well, he was a good friend of mine, and had also been in the war. In the day we worked with the teams, selecting our soldiers, and at night we drove to Tel-Aviv, to drink and have a good time. When I realized how short life might be, I felt a great need to enjoy it.

Doing the basic training as a platoon leader was a new experience for me. Meetings with my staff into the small hours of the night, supervising their work during the day. As the platoon leader in charge I had to maintain my distance from the men, yet know what was going on at any given time. Actually, I worked more with the squad leaders than with the trainees. I felt how the soldiers would eye me from afar, watching, apprehensive. I spoke with them only before their hikes, saying a few words of encouragement. But I will never forget the first hike I led personally, marching at the head of the column. I alone am the leader, and my soldiers follow me.

My philosophy was to be strict and make many demands at the beginning, so that I could enjoy the results later on. I wanted to instill my soldiers with self-discipline, so that they would carry out their duties without constant supervision. As training advanced, I had more and more work. When they started learning to shoot, I was terribly worried about their safety and taking the right precautions. As is often the case, we did have one firing accident, and I myself was injured. It was the result of a startle reaction of one of my men, who accidently shot me in the leg. I didn't faint, and I acted as if nothing happened. You should never show weakness in front of your men. But my sergeant saw what had happened, and drove me immediately to the medic's station. Anyway, I had to be out of training for about two weeks, something that severely interfered with the goals I had set for my men and myself.

I joined my men at the end of their basic training, when we were assigned to security duty in Beirut. At that time, the situation in Lebanon was tense, with lots of terrorist activities against the IDF. We lived in constant alert. I was worried about my men, and the responsibility for their safety was my greatest burden. These were young men, fresh out of basic training, and here they were having to decide when to open fire, or what is a suspicious vehicle. Our main job was to supervise an intersection, to patrol the area and deter subversive activity by our presence. I, however, often felt like a target for enemy hostility.

It was a difficult time for me as a commander. Men tend to disregard discipline when they are in the front line. All they care about is to be able to catch a few hours of sleep between their patrol duty and the next shift. On my side, I wanted them also to take good care of their gear, and not to become so self-confident that they make all kinds of errors. It might start with minor details, like forgetting to put on your flak jacket, and end with disaster. I tried to maintain discipline, and my men discovered that I was not going to be too permissive even when we faced a common danger.

It wasn't easy, you know. As a result of my work, I was pleased with my men and their performance, but I often doubted the kind of orders I received from above. It was a dangerous area. Frequently I felt that our lifestyle there bordered on madness. At times, I felt exploited, as if trapped in a no-win situation.

After six weeks, we were moved for an additional period of six weeks to a stronghold on the eastern front, facing the Syrian Army. This was a completely different experience. Life wasn't so tense and dangerous, and I felt that commanding a stronghold was the essence of my profession. I think that that's where I really succeeded as an officer. It wasn't easy, mind you. I never slept more than three hours a night, but we built a model stronghold, ran it very smoothly, and even managed to conduct some training for the men in addition to all the security activities. My sergeant and I worked in harmony, and ranks were forgotten. Whoever had time took care of what needed to be done. We were no longer a lieutenant and a sergeant, but two friends and the men they were in charge of. (excitedly) I was happy that I had him to share this experience with. We also became much closer to our men, since living so tightly together we got to know each other really well. The peak of all this was the night of Passover which we organized and celebrated together in the stronghold. It was an incredible night for me. I felt that I had actualized myself.

When we returned to the south for training, my unit was functioning so well that they needed very little discipline or supervision from me. I trained with them for three months, and then they went to the squad leaders' course. I felt that I had done my share, and I was ready to get out of the army. My superiors wanted me to sign up for additional service, and they promised to promote me, but I had had it. Both my sergeant and I were due to be released in a couple of weeks and we just wanted to enjoy ourselves at last. I got an easy job, and visited my soldiers often in their course, but most of the time I managed to be on leave, helping my sergeant with the summer harvest at his parents' farm. That's it, my four years in the army were finally over.

2

ALON

I grew up in a small town. I enjoyed my friends and the Scouts. I loved motorcycles and girls—like any kid my age. On the other hand, I was a loner. I used to draw pictures, make up stories, invent all kinds of gadgets—things I buried in my drawers. Ever since I can recall, I lived in a world of my own, thirsty for the unknown.

I didn't like studying in school, but I had no problem finishing high school. My parents never got along well, and I used to have problems at home. I was always fighting them. I couldn't wait to go to the army, just to be away from home.

There were two different plans I considered when the time came to go into the army. When we were seventeen, we founded a Garin[1] to go to the Nahal[2] together. I had many good friends in the Garin, among them my girlfriend. Basically, I knew I was not the kind of person for military service. I am sensitive and vulnerable. I prefer to be free, on my own. At eighteen, I considered myself a pacifist, was leftist in my views, one of the first followers of the peace movement. I knew that the army was a harsh, strict organization, full of rules and regulations, definitely not what I needed. So I figured that if I had to serve, the Nahal seemed the best choice for me, because there I could find warmth and human relationships—more than in any other military unit. Today I know how right I was. I don't think I would have made it in any other unit. I needed the support of my Garin.

On the other hand, I was flattered to be accepted for pilot training in the Air Force. I got swept away by this fantasy of 'superman of the sky', and decided to try my luck as a pilot. After all, I knew I could return to my buddies if I failed the course. Today I realize that such an attitude is not very helpful if you want to finish the pilot training course successfully.

15

Basically, I was afraid of military service. I had heard scary stories about the forced marches, the harassment, about basic training. But it was clear to me that when the country calls, you come and serve. There was no question about it, no looking for a way out. I was not too good at preparing myself, either. (laughs) I would tell myself every night: Tomorrow you'll get up early to jog and work out. But I never did.

Our first period in the kibbutz was delightful. For the first time I lived together with my girlfriend, and I enjoyed my job, driving a tractor all day. I liked the others, and they liked me.

Socially, we were a curious bunch. Half of us were city kids, from good homes, and about half you might call slum boys, from poor, new immigrant towns. At first we did not mix, but soon some of the "snobs" left, and we all became buddies and forgot our origins. It turned into a joke between us, how foolish we were at first.

After four months at the kibbutz, it was time to start our military training. I went to the pilots' selection process, while the others were supposed to start their basic training in the Infantry about ten days later. The selection lasted more than a week, I remember. We had long hikes, we were given a hard time, and, at the same time, had to undergo all kinds of tests and interviews. They were trying to see how we functioned under extreme stress.

Surprisingly, it was not difficult for me. I had heard so many horror stories about it! And at the end, I passed. I went to the kibbutz to share the happy news with my friends. I remember the looks of envy in my friends' eyes.

But I was not a great success in the course itself. I managed to survive for three and a half months. At first, it was like college, with severe discipline. Then we started to fly Piper-cubs. I wasn't bad, but when on one Saturday we were supposed to be studying and my girlfriend came for a visit, I chose her over my studies. I missed my friends. I began to find the strict discipline hard to take. Gradually I realized that I was not that keen on becoming an "airplane driver." I had not come to the course with the right motives.

When the first flying stage was over, I was dismissed from the course. I don't know the reason for sure. Suddenly I felt deeply disappointed. I went back to the kibbutz, taking a couple of days' leave. My girlfriend comforted me, and in two or three days I recovered.

In the meantime, my buddies were half done with the Infantry basic training. I was supposed to join them there. I remember the feeling of going back to the military after my leave. It was the same feeling I had later on, whenever I returned to the army from furlough. You feel as if you are jumping into a dark pit, of your own volition—a terrible transition. I arrived in the Infantry during the hardest week of basic training. I was in a real state of shock. I didn't even know how to use a rifle. But soon I found that the discipline there was not too harsh, and my friends helped me a lot. They instructed me, they prepared my gear, and—the main thing—they taught me a lesson in evasion, how to "get around" the difficulties. They were good at that, let me tell you. So in a short time we finished basic training together, all the combat soldiers of the Garin, and we went to join the others in our new military agricultural outpost.[3] It was then that I stopped feeling sorry about flunking the pilot training.

Our outpost was on a white dune, not far from the beach of Rafah, in the Gaza Strip. Blue water and palm trees, a real dream. We loved it. We never wanted to go home on leave. Socially we were already very cohesive, and I became sort of the "big chief" of the lot.

I wouldn't say we worked hard . . . Our commanders were just before their release from their own military service and they couldn't care less about what we did. We got up at noon, did some sort of work, and at night we came alive. We learned to drink, to smoke hash. We had our own music. Sodom and Gommorah till 3 or 4 in the morning.

There were two things we did take seriously during those six months. We cared for the gardening of our outpost, because we loved the place so much, and we had our security tasks, which we performed to perfection. We continued our training, we went down to the Arab towns for daily patrols, and we took turns guarding our own outpost.

I am not sure whether it was the murder of Sadat or something else that stirred up riots in the Arab towns nearby. Anyway, one morning, six of us went down as usual on our infantry patrol in Rafah, when suddenly we were surrounded by an angry Arab mob. They were throwing rocks, burning cars—a serious riot. First of all we had to defend ourselves. We didn't want to shoot civilians, so we kept to 'cold' weapons, hitting them as much as we could. Suddenly I saw some burning tires being rolled toward us. I screamed at the officer: "Look out! Look out!" All of a sudden he was silent and helpless. I remember that it was a shock for me then—"An officer! Second to God, he can solve any problem!" Well, that's what I thought till then.

Then someone suggested blocking the intersection with cars. We started commandeering Arab cars. I recall one who refused. I fired at his tires and he came out of his car, mad as hell, trying to hit me. At that moment I was about to shoot him. My rifle was loaded, and he was facing me not more than two feet away. But I didn't shoot. Some of my friends jumped him from behind, more soldiers arrived, and the moment passed.

That's a scene I remember vividly. Often I think it all over. Why didn't I shoot? Would I have hesitated to fire two years later, after I had been through the war? I don't think so, but you never know.

Anyway, the riots continued all over town, and I'll tell you the truth, I was not a paragon of human kindness that day. I was amazed at how I struck people, even children. We were patrolling a street when a girl threw a rock at us from a window on the second floor. I rushed upstairs and I hit her with my hands, my boots, with my rifle. I found that I enjoyed this tension and release, somehow. From then on I understood how soldiers could behave like animals, as they had in Vietnam. I behaved that way too, as if I were a different Alon for a couple of hours. And then it was over. As if by the push of a button I was back to my old self.

We spent all that night patrolling, trying to return some order to the town. We returned to our post at daybreak, right on time for the morning inspection. Everyone stood at attention, and the commander inspected our guns. He was angry—"Why didn't you clean your rifles?" Of course they were dirty—we had used them all night long! I remember that moment as part of a psychedelic scene: the white sun, the mosques at a distance, smoke curling up from the burnt tires—and us, up on the dune, "Why didn't you clean your rifles?"

Two months later, after some more training and security duty on the northern border, I was sent to a medics' course. I had always wanted to become a medic. It was a good course, and I learned a lot, but there were two traumatic events for me during it. One day, one of the trainees killed himself, shot himself in the head. He seemed to be so normal, smart and successful. I couldn't figure out why he did it. It threw me for a loop. Suddenly I realized how we all walk the tightrope here . . .

Then, I had a problem with my girlfriend. As I told you she was my first true love, she was a virgin when I met her, and all that. Well, in the kibbutz there were too many single men around our girls, and we were away, busy at our duties. So, finally, she had an affair with another man. I was deeply hurt. I knew that she still loved me, and that she wanted us to continue as before—but, for me, something broke inside. After that, I did poorly in the course.

We never completed the medics' course, however, because three weeks before it was scheduled to end, the Lebanon War broke out. All the trainees of the course were moved to the Golan Heights and attached to various reserve units as medics. We just waited. Meanwhile my buddies were up in Lebanon, in battle.

In the third week, I received a 36-hour leave. I can still see it, like a movie before my eyes. I walk out of the camp, in uniform of course. The first civilian car that passes stops and takes me to the kibbutz where the girls are. I go to their rooms, no one is there. I walk to the kindergarten, where my girlfriend used to work, but I see only older women. I ask the teacher—Where are the girls from my Garin? And she stares at me and says: They have all gone already, don't you know? I ask her: Where? And she answers: To the funeral—didn't you know? Erez' funeral.

That's how I found out that one of my Garin members had been killed. Out of the blue.

I went to the bus station, and met many soldiers there. Then I heard it was not just Erez, but a whole list of men. Three or four I knew quite well. It was an accident, they said. One of our own planes bombed a convoy of our men.

I remember arriving at the cemetery. So many people were there. A fat sergeant stood like a conductor of sorts, with a long list. "Yea," he says, "You're right on time. A taxi is just leaving for Erez' parents' home. Hop in and go."

Erez was one of the slum boys. At his parents' house I saw all the girls from the Garin, and the non-combat soldiers. The combat soldiers had not been released for the funeral—the war was still going on. Erez was not one of my closest friends, but I cried a lot. It was the release of tension, I think—being away from my buddies, being cut off and not knowing what had happened to them.

Later we talked. I remember saying even then that the war was going to become a catastrophe for us all. Nobody realized this that early.

I wanted to join the men from my Garin in Lebanon, but being a disciplined soldier, I went to the medics' training base to receive my orders. There I was told that I had to complete the course first. I was sent to a hospital for additional training, practicing in emergency treatment and surgery for three weeks, and then I joined my buddies in Lebanon.

It was so strange to drive a car into Lebanon, to see the other side of the Beaufort Castle. It is a beautiful land. At night I found my Garin, stationed in an old schoolhouse. All the men were sleeping on mats on the floor, crowded together against the cold night, and I will never forget how I was pulled down to join them, in an embrace. To this day I remember that wonderful feeling. Zvika was on guard duty downstairs, and I went down to see him, too. We sat in the dark and he told me all they had gone through.

A few days later we were moved to the Eastern front. We drove our convoy of APCs across the country, like a convoy of gypsies. On the outside of every APC we tied cooking utensils, sleeping bags, personal belongings—it was a funny sight. That seemed to be our main occupation, driving around, east to west, to Beirut, I can't tell you how many times. I liked driving, it was wild. The roads were too narrow for our vehicles, and if a car was parked in our way we bumped into it, there was almost no alternative. It seemed natural then. No pangs of conscience about what we left behind us. "Get out of my way." That was the atmosphere.

I never stopped speaking against the war. But, like the others, I was more than careful about all the military requirements, ready for action any minute. This was simply for survival. My medical kit was ready down to the last possible detail. We knew that the fight over Beirut was at hand.

But the battle of Beirut was delayed again and again. Finally, after about two months of wandering around Lebanon, we were given furlough for a week. But we were not supposed to go home. We were sent to Acre for an organized military vacation, together with our girlfriends. All day long we lay on the beach, and at night we got drunk in the local pubs, paying or not paying for our drinks—there were many pranks there. After a few days we were suddenly ordered back to Beirut. It was so dramatic, like in the movies. Some buses came for us, the girls were there, in tears, and the boys went to war.

We arrived in Beirut, and were greeted by heavy fire. Too much fire. I never heard so many RPGs[4] before. We put on our flak jackets, filled the canteens with water, and drove into the combat zone. We never received any detailed briefing about the battle plan or anything. And I had absolutely no experience with first-aid in action.

I drove the APC into the streets of Beirut, with my buddies behind me, and my medical kit outside above. Then we were ordered to attack. My buddies left the APC, and I, as the driver, was told to stay put. I screamed at my platoon leader: "I can't stay here, I'm a medic, not just a driver." I remember the heavy fire, the men running right into it, an RPG hitting close by. I grabbed my medical kit, and pointed to a friend, Nicki, saying: "He's a driver, too. He can replace me." I will never forget the expression in Nicki's eyes as he was forced to replace me, while I joined my friends. "Pig," is what his eyes said. But I didn't care.

Amia: *Why did you want to run in?*

Look, it wasn't heroism or anything like it. All I thought of at the moment was that I wanted to join my buddies, and perhaps that I wanted the experience of combat, just for myself. Anyway, our unit was running into this street. I remember seeing Zvika running with his machine gun to cover us from the rear. The air was full of dust and smoke and I couldn't see too well. That's the last picture of him that I have in my mind.

Our company was going forward, throwing smoke grenades, covering each other, and advancing under fire. We were totally cut off from the rest of the battalion, so it seemed. I remember piles of garbage in the street, high buildings, and people firing at us from all the windows above. Grown-ups were shooting, children were shooting. I remember looking up to try to locate the window where this RPG fire was coming from, and I saw a woman standing there, beating her carpets. Crazy.

Well, pretty soon we had our first two wounded. They weren't seriously injured, and I stayed behind, in the lobby of a house, to dress their wounds. In the meantime the company commander, with my unit, advanced toward another building and I heard him on the radio calling for help. He had stumbled onto a large enemy force, and had many wounded. At that point I took charge in the building where we were. I called the other three medics, we took over a flat on the first floor and started setting up beds and preparing infusions—in short, organizing a small field hospital. When we were ready, I sent men over, with stretchers, to bring in the wounded, while I ordered other men to cover them from one of the top floors. Our men were not more than 50 meters away from us, but the fire was so heavy it was almost impossible to bring them in. Finally we had all the wounded in. That's when I saw severely injured people for the first time in my life. I reacted . . . outstandingly. I was cool. Professional. In control of the situation. It was as if I were a different person there, with a fantastic ability not to panic, to cope under stress. I think that never before or afterwards could I be that man.

Well, one soldier lost his sight, and another lost an arm. Our supplies were running out, and there was no question of evacuating anyone from there. We were completely surrounded by the enemy—we didn't even know who they were. Finally I had only two infusion kits left, and time was running out for the seriously wounded. One seemed to be suffocating—and the other medics were arguing with me about the right thing to do. I remember our commander sitting in the lobby of the building, talking nonstop into his walkie-talkie, but being absolutely useless to us otherwise. I felt totally alone, and again forced my opinion on the others, who obeyed—I don't know why.

Later, we decided we had to make an attempt to evacuate the wounded to a hospital, and we ordered one of the few Arabs who remained in the building to prepare his truck and drive us out of there. I volunteered to go with the injured.

As we started out of the parking lot, immediately I saw a mob. There was an RPG launcher right in front of us, and I realized that we were driving into a trap. It was hell. I was shooting into the mob and, at the same time screaming at the Arab driver to turn around. He kept driving forward, promising to bring us through safely. In the meantime, everybody in the truck was wounded again. I was the only one who wasn't hit. There was screaming in the truck, the infusions were all torn out—don't ask. I threatened the driver with my gun, and finally he took us back in. We had been out just a couple of minutes, but it felt like forever.

At that point, I lost control. I went out into the street and started shooting like mad, firing in all directions. When the commander realized what I was doing, he ordered me to come back. I had almost no medical supplies left. I bandaged the wounds all over again, injected morphine—there was not much else to do. Our Arab driver came to me, sobbing, too—he had an ugly wound in his knee. I didn't feel like helping him, but I bandaged him as well, and told him to go to the hospital.

Much later that night, a Lebanese policeman of sorts suddenly materialized in the lobby. He introduced himself as the local "sheriff," and told us that all the fighters of the neighborhood were under his command. Our commander suddenly awoke from his stupor, and together we explained to the Lebanese policeman that we had several severely injured people that we had to take immediately to the military hospital. This would be his task. If, in ten minutes we did not hear from the hospital—which was just down the street—that they had arrived safely, we were going to take one of the families that lived in our building and shoot them all on the spot. Hostages. We were theatrical enough in our threat, apparently, and the policeman was stupid enough to believe that Israeli soldiers might do such a thing—so it worked. First he took the blinded soldier in his own car, then he returned with a truck and evacuated all the other wounded soldiers—there were about six of them. And that was it.

That night we were allowed to sleep. I was exhausted. When I got up, our unit was already in contact with other forces, I received some new medical supplies, new ammunition, and we were told to proceed. (Alon sounds distracted and confused at this point.) Then the whole Army arrived, with tanks. Things looked completely different.

That was the day I heard that Zvika had been wounded. Not seriously, they said. I remember joking with Shlomi—Good for him, he is back home already.

I think that the next night was the Jewish New Year's Eve. The whole platoon joined together on the fourth floor of a building somewhere, and we relaxed, feeling that we deserved rest after what we had done. On the radio, the company commander wished us a Happy New Year. He also said something like—it was hard, but we've made it, and it'll be okay from now on. That was the atmosphere. (Alon is silent for a long while.)

I think that up to that moment, and all through the battle, I was completely lucid and in high spirits. From that night on—it was depression time for me.

The next morning we were ordered to retreat. We did not understand why, there was still so much to do. We were posted in an abandoned bank, guarding the intersection nearby. This was when the massacre of Sabra and Shatila[5] took place. But we didn't know a thing about it then.

One morning, at the intersection, a friend of mine asked me: "Did you hear that Zvika is dead?" "No," I said, "and you didn't tell me either." I ignored the news for three or four hours, not repeating it to any of my friends. Later, our commander called us all in, and told us that Zvika had died in the hospital, and that the funeral would take place the next day. I was under control. I didn't scream or cry. I informed those who came late and did not know. Actually, I was disappointed at myself for being so calm, while others, who were much less close to Zvika, reacted so intensely.

I remember the night after we heard the news. We were lying on our mats on the floor of the bank, telling jokes. We passed the night laughing our heads off. You see, ours was a peculiar reaction to death. We made a joke out of it, a huge macabre joke.

The funeral itself was tough, very tough. I remember that we threw our Army insignias into the open grave. We all cried. But I have no words to tell you what we felt.

After the funeral, the company commander told me that I would receive a citation for my behavior in Beirut, and so would Zvika.

We were given a week off to visit with the bereaved families. The first day I went to see the wounded soldiers in the hospital. I wanted some sort of special attention from them, thanks perhaps, appreciation for what I had done. Maybe I was expecting too much at that stage. They greeted me as they did all the others. It made me feel very distant all of a sudden.

Most of the time I spent with Zvika's parents. His father reacted like a real hero, even helping the rest of us to cope. His mother—bless her, she died of cancer a year later—she wept with us.

You know, there is a song of death, a kind of oriental lamentation. Old women chant it—there is nothing more horrible. Once I heard a woman chant it on a bus, when she suddenly heard on the radio that her nephew had been killed in the war. The second time was Zvika's mother at the funeral. It is something I will never forget.

My girlfriend tried to help. She went with me to my parents, accompanied me everywhere. I could not even make love to her, although the whole time we were in Beirut I kept dreaming about making love to her. Only the soldiers from the Garin, who shared the same experience, could provide some support for each other. I felt that only they understood.

Amia: *Understood what?*

The business of war. The mourning beneath our laughter, and the depression which started to take its toll, from each of us in a slightly different way.

Well, I never received my citation, nor did Zvika. The recommendations were forgotten in some drawer until it was too late. I was deeply disappointed. I wanted people to know, to say: "Alon was cited for his courage in the war." It was very important for Zvika's parents as well. But, well—(leaves off).

After the week of mourning we were sent for security duty in Jesin, east of Beirut. We were a small unit then, after all our casualties, and we felt we deserved special treatment. Our only obligation was to man the roadblock at the entrance to town. Otherwise we were free from training or duties, and were left on our own—to recover, so we believed. We used to laugh a lot, play whist and we drank quite heavily. Although it was easy to get, we didn't smoke hash; we never used drugs in Lebanon. We didn't discuss the war or what had happened to us. The only thing that mattered was to visit Zvika's parents as often as possible. They became our pals, it was relaxing to be with them.

I used to have many dreams about the war then, psychedelic dreams, very unreal. Often I dreamt about Zvika, as if he were still with us. But once I had a special dream, in which I knew that Zvika had died, but he had come back to talk to me. We were at the kibbutz in that dream. At first I was very afraid. I touched him and his arm was metallic, like a metal pipe of sorts. The kibbutz was getting ready to go to a peace demonstration and we sat outdoors and talked, watching the activity. He wanted to know what he had missed since he had been gone, and I told him. Then he said, gesturing in his typical way, "Look, look at this world. What is there to come back for anyway?"

This dream deeply affected me and I was afraid to share it with my buddies. I felt that if I could keep it to myself, Zvika might continue to return to me in my sleep, and we could talk again. But it never happened again, therefore I can tell you about it today. I tried to decipher his message to me. What was he trying to say?

There were also these slips of the tongue we often had, calling someone "Zvika" from afar. We used to freeze whenever that happened.

Well, that was our stay in Lebanon after the war. I think they acted wisely in leaving us up there for that period. We kind of withdrew from the scene gradually, which was probably better. Although we did not discuss politics, we all agreed that it was time for us to move out of Lebanon altogether. Personally, I was quite angry about the whole chain of events. No matter what they said, I was convinced that the battle of Beirut was an act of revenge for the murder of President Bashir Gemayel and was planned to allow the Christians to take revenge against the Moslems for murdering him. That, essentially, is what happened in Sabra and Shatila, right after we entered Beirut. Furthermore, I knew that the men who had fought against us in that street battle were quite marginal in the political scene; I don't know what we wanted from them, they were neither terrorists nor Palestinians. It was just a mess, and in this mess I lost my best friend. The newspapers said that we "cleaned the city of terrorists," but I'm not stupid. We are not the kind of soldiers that you can send to combat and then tell them stories later.

But I missed Zvika, truly I did. That whole time I was sick with longing for him.

About a month later we were moved out of Lebanon. We were all so happy. For the next six weeks we were sent to do guard duty on Mt. Hermon. It was a rough winter, and we were all very depressed. We were afraid of being alone, afraid of guarding the post from inside this kind of glass cage they had built around it against the snow. Our luck was that we were together, never leaving any single member alone, holding each other above water, one might way. I never would have made it otherwise.

Finally, our time came to return to the kibbutz. The girls had already prepared our quarters. My girlfriend prepared a room for us to share, but that was when I told her that it was all over between us, and I moved in with the men. It was a blow for her.

Together with the women, we were 22 members in the Garin then, a pretty large group. We enjoyed our jobs in the kibbutz, and we worked very hard, so nobody could complain. But after work hours—we were something else. Partying every night with loud music, drinking and smoking. The kibbutz members didn't like it and didn't quite know what to make of it. They thought it was due to Lebanon, that we had returned from the war somewhat deranged. But we worked well, and they wanted us to stay, hoping, perhaps, that this period would pass over. For our part, we did not care a bit what they, or anyone else, thought about us.

At that time I suggested that we start a pub in the kibbutz in memory of Zvika. The kibbutz did not reject the idea, but promised to fund it the next year.

Six weeks before the end of our second stint at the kibbutz, all the combat men were suddenly called up for duty in Lebanon. There was some kind of emergency there. For some reason, I was not on the list—probably because I had joined our unit later the last time we were in Lebanon. This time, however, I didn't volunteer to join them. I figured that this was a false alarm, and if anything serious developed they would come and get me too. In the meantime I stayed and worked in the kibbutz, and gradually I grew apart from my buddies.

Like the others, I had one more six-month period of active military duty before me, and figured that I should look for something easy to do, so that I wouldn't suffer too much. I requested an interview with the central command of the Nahal, and to my amazement, I found that I had become a sort of celebrity after the war. I used my reputation to get myself assigned to a good job as a medic on one of the bases well in the center of Israel. They put me in charge of seven or eight medics, so that I myself had very little to do. I used my free time to travel around and visit my buddies wherever they were posted.

I think that all our men were in a state of shell-shock from the war. When the Nahal was given security duty in Lebanon again, they did not take my Garin. They were sent to the Hermon instead. They had an awful reputation in the army, but there is really no way to discipline a soldier who is going to be released in six months.

I myself was not in good shape, either. I had separated from my girl-friend, and I was sad most of the time. On my frequent leaves I used to wander around, not feeling at home anywhere. I had a very simple philosophy then—if you're feeling, go where there's laughter. That's why I was attracted to my buddies,who horsed around a lot, although they were worse off than me.

When we returned to the kibbutz for our last stay of six months, the women had already finished their service and had left. We started to feel the end, and it was very heavy. Everything would soon be over, our group would be broken up. Each one was going his own way, some to the university and others planning trips abroad. We saw our fantasy of living together forever, stoned all the time, vanish before our eyes.

The kibbutz gave me permission to start 'Zvika's' pub. I drew up a whole plan, turning a bomb shelter into a disco-and-bar. All my requests were granted and I was given a free hand. It was a rare opportunity. I had never been in charge of any such thing before, and I felt that the kibbutz members respected me for what I was doing.

The only trouble was that I did not feel as close to my buddies as I used to. They said it was all my fault, that I didn't share my project with them. I felt that they didn't try to take part. What kept us together was our common concern to hide our hash away from the kibbutz members, who were very annoyed with us because of the drug problem.

So, that's how my story comes to an end. We were nine guys and one girl in the Garin at the end of our military service. We planned a final trip together, without outsiders, and managed to revive our old feelings for each other for a while. Or perhaps it was the result of all that hash.

Interestingly, each one of us left the kibbutz separately. Yuval and his girlfriend remained as members, and the others left one by one. I stayed four months after my release from the army, because I wanted to complete the pub, and had nowhere to go until the beginning of my studies in Jeru-salem. The pub turned out as beautiful as I had planned. But I had dreamt of making it a social center for young members from all the neighboring kibbutzim . . . (pondering) I didn't succeed in that. Anyway, I am glad when I hear that the kibbutz youngsters like my place.

Four months later I started a new life as a university student in Jerusalem. It wasn't easy, but that's another story, I guess. Or perhaps it all follows from what I went through in the service.

Notes

1. Literally—kernel, a group of youths who plan to serve together in the Nahal (see fn 2) and settle in a kibbutz.

2. Literally—Fighting Pioneer Youth. The Nahal is part of the IDF. The three-year army service in the Nahal normally consists of cycles of six months in the kibbutz and six months in active military duty. There is usually one particular kibbutz that the unit is attached to, and it is presumed that most members will settle there after their release from the army. One of the early six-month periods is usually spent in a military agricultural outpost in a border area.

3. A Garin normally consists of three groups of people: combat soldiers (men), noncombat soldiers (men), and women soldiers. Based on medical profiles, the vast majority of men are assigned to combat units—usually the infantry. The men's mandatory service is three years, and the women's is two years. As a result, women of the Garin are released from their military service about a year before the men. They are supposed to stay in the kibbutz, however, since all Garin members are, formally, preparing for membership in the kibbutz. In actuality, most Nahal soldiers leave the kibbutz at the end of their military service.

4. A Russian portable antitank grenade launcher, popular with the terrorist organizations, as well as with Russian-supplied Arab armies.

5. Palestinian refugee camps, known as headquarters of the PLO, south of Beirut. A massacre of the Moslem inhabitants by the Christian Lebanese took place several days after the murder of President Bashir Gemayel.

3

YOCHANAN

I grew up in a farmer's family in a village in the Galilee. I went to an agricultural high school. I liked to hike by myself and to take pictures of the views and the flowers.

I never gave any thought to my approaching service. I had a few weeks between my high school exams and the army, and I went on a long hike all by myself. Actually, I knew that I had a physical handicap, that I have no hearing in one ear. As a child I had dreamed of driving a tank, but I knew that my disability would not allow me to do so. I was so naive then, it didn't worry me what would become of me during my service. I guess I grew up in a home very remote from military concerns.

I vividly remember the day I was drafted, a hot day in August. I left my home in shorts and sandals and took the bus to the base. I was given boots and a uniform and felt I was suffocating. At the selection office, to my sudden horror, I discovered that I could go either into transportation or maintenance, but that was all. I chose transportation since I loved trucks. Next thing I knew I was at the "slave market," my name was called out, and I was assigned to the Military Police. There were others with me for the same job. Some of them were quite content to become MPs, a sadistic type of people. I was disgusted. I went calmly to the squad leader who had been calling our numbers and I said: "I am not going to the MP." I think I sounded determined, while he said, imploringly: "Please don't cause any problems for me, I just read the list. On the bus to the MP base, that's when you can cause problems."

Near the bus, there were indeed four draftees who refused to go on the bus. I joined them. The sergeant yelled a bit, and one changed his mind. "If you refuse my order," he said, "you will be arrested." We were ordered to take out our shoe laces. This was humiliating. One more recruit

29

boarded the bus. The bus left, and the three of us were put under arrest. In the prison, we were given back our shoelaces and were briefed about the court martial. "You have to march into the room. Answer only 'Yes, sir' or 'No, sir.' Salute if you are acquitted and not if you are sentenced," etc. The commander set my beret straight with his stick. It was unpleasant. I went into a room. It had a desk half a mile long. I stood at one end, and the officer, in a red beret, sat at the other. He read the charges against me and asked if I confessed to them. I said, "Yes, sir," and, at his request, explained my reasons. He wrote them down, but I could feel he was not interested. I was sentenced to two days in jail and fourteen days of probation. In two days I would be given another chance to go to the MP, and if I refused, I would be in jail for fourteen days. If I refused further—for 28 days, and so on.

I was insulted by the fact that he didn't listen to me. I told him I came to the army enthusiastic to serve and contribute, but I was not the kind of person to become a military policeman. In the prison I was ordered to stand at attention near the flag, outside in the sun, for a long time. I was almost dehydrated. Then I was brought into a cell, a little cage of two by two meters, with iron beds and a tiny window high up. I remember the iron door. The other objectors were brought to the same cell. We talked a lot. Together we decided to stick to our position to the very end. We shared fantasies about revenge or about leaving the country for good. I felt terrible.

Next morning, I was ordered to dress and shine my shoes for an interview with the base commander. This is what had saved me: two days previously, on my first day at the absorption base, I was full of criticism regarding the routine of the camp. I saw a complaint box, and I wrote down my comments. As a result, the commander of the base wanted to see me. Finally, there was someone willing to listen to me, and I explained my problem. He asked me whether I would be willing to serve in the Armored Forces. I told him I would be happy to, but when he heard how low my medical profile was, he said it was impossible. Then he suggested that I become a military youth leader at the Gadna[1] and, of course, I agreed. I was released from prison and sent to basic training. Right away, in order to change my image, I made up my mind to become an outstanding trainee. Basic training (for soldiers with physical limitations) was easy, but I was not selected as the outstanding trainee. From there, I went to the youth leaders' course.

A military youth leader works with high school students at school or at special camps and activities. There were both men and women soldiers on the course, learning different military skills as well as how to work with youth. It was an interesting course and except for one episode well organized. Remember that this is a job to which men are usually assigned if they have some kind of physical problem. One week was dedicated to field skills, and we had several hikes with a sadistic squad leader. He was especially mean toward the unit's most incompetent soldier. During a night hike this man strained his ankle and was carried on a stretcher for the rest of the way. Another man had an asthma attack, and we had to take care of him. At the end there were only four of us to bear the stretcher, in addition to our gear, with no one to relieve us. Yet the squad leader ignored the situation and ran up the hill, disregarding us. After a while, I told the other men to put down the stretcher, and I had an unpleasant confrontation with the leader. What did he think—that we were infantry soldiers in basic training? I was court-martialed again, and afraid, because of my previous probation, but luckily they were short of youth leaders, so I was just reprimanded for my behavior.

This episode is significant in my military service. I was willing to volunteer and to contribute, but I had a quick temper and I could not stand injustice. I would not keep my mouth shut. This attitude is not exactly appropriate for a soldier. Indeed in all my future evaluations I was regarded as highly motivated but at the same time as having disciplinary problems.

My first job was at a military youth camp in the south, where youngsters come for a week of premilitary training. We taught them field skills, firearms, some topography and navigation, and *yediat haaretz*.[2] It was a satisfying job. I had enough freedom to work with the kids as I wanted, and it was nice to see the immediate outcome of my work. Sometimes we got classes of children from underprivileged communities, or new immigrants, and we did first rate educational work, teaching them to love the country, love nature—all the sabra[3] values I believed in. At the same time it was very demanding, full days and weeks, with rare leaves to my village far to the north. On my free weekends I took solitary desert hikes, and I studied the land. It was a good period.

After about seven months, however, I started to think that in fact I was a healthy young man and all I was doing in the army was playing with kids. This became evident to me one Sunday, when I returned late in the day from my weekend at home, and the youngsters had already arrived and were drilled by a female youth leader. I watched the drill exercises and suddenly it became so ridiculous in my eyes, so utterly unimportant. I decided to look for something else to do. Soon afterwards the Lebanon War broke out, and I felt far worse. It was terribly frustrating. My job was to console the girls whose boyfriends were fighting at the front.

Right after the first battles, during the school summer break, the Gadna command sent me to an aviation summer camp for high school students. The camp was located at an Air Force base, and the kids attended it for two weeks at a time. They learned about aviation, and also flew some light planes, while I took care of their camp and their military appearance, gave them firearms training and drilled them a bit. They were nice kids, but the base was in a high state of emergency and the combination was absurd. One day a helicopter from this base was shot down—while I was playing military games with children. Not only was I frustrated, but the pilots, too, complained about the summer camp in the middle of the Lebanon War. In my free time, I volunteered to help load the planes with bombs and ammunition. What a job! I experienced how real, useful soldiers were spending their time in the army.

I set my mind on changing my job in the army. I decided to become a medic. I applied to the medical authorities to get a higher health profile but was rejected. I asked for a transfer from Gadna, and was refused. I asked for an interview with the Gadna commander and gave my reasons for requesting a transfer. He said: "Had you been a bad youth leader, I would have agreed. But you are good, therefore you'll stay." The whole thing was so absurd. Here he was, and many more officers, with secretaries, cars and drivers, and what were all their efforts for? Especially at a time like this!

I was given another job with youth, this time at a village on the Lebanese border. The area was full of combat soldiers going back and forth to the front. We had to train the village youth in the use of firearms so that they could help the few men who had not been mobilized in guarding the place. In addition, we provided various activities for the children so that they would not wander around. When I went home, hitchhiking on the road, everybody treated me like a combat soldier, and I felt bad.

I kept trying to get out. On one of my attempts, I went for an interview with the chief military physician, and convinced him that my hearing handicap would be of no consequences in the role of military medic. He was willing to give me a document testifying to this effect, and with this letter I went back to the Gadna command. Still they objected to releasing me. Finally we agreed that I would serve an additional nine months as a youth leader, and at the end of this period I would be permitted to go to the medics' course. I won, but I had to pay for it: I was "deported" to the farthest Gadna camp up in the forests of the Galilee.

It was a forest where youth movements used to have summer camps during school vacations. We were given the job of building a Gadna camp for the school year, where children would come for weekly activities, especially for volunteer work in military supply bases in the area. We started by building the camp, and then began our educational program with the young trainees.

It was a very special period for me. In this far-away camp, all military formality was totally dropped, and we led our lives according to our own rules. We had only primitive utilities, it was terribly cold during the long winter, but we were a group of unusual soldiers—all punished for something by the military authorities. I found wonderful friends there and retain warm memories from the place. One of us was an archeology expert, and, with the help of the children, started to dig in the area. I myself developed creative landscaping with rocks and tree trunks. We discovered hidden caves and turned them into hideouts, and we taught the kids about ecology and nature preservation.

I liked my work. I remember the day when one of the commanders came for a short ceremony in which I was given the rank of a sergeant. I felt that although I had been sent off to this far spot, my superiors knew that I did a good job. But I was still determined to do something more useful during the second half of my time in service.

There is another episode I remember from that stage. One day we were ordered to come to headquarters in full uniform to receive decorations for participation in the Lebanon War, like all the soldiers who had served during this period. Since I had not taken any active role in the war, I decided I would not use the decoration anyway and did not come to receive it. For some reason nobody acted against me on that account.

Toward the end of the allotted nine months, I started to push for my release from the Gadna, and after some additional complications and another rush to the chief military physician, I finally got to the medics' course. The separation from the forest was not easy. Due to our isolation I had become very close to the other men there. However, at the medics' course I also found a wonderful group of soldiers, all Infantry men.

In the course I had to readjust to military discipline. I was not my own master anymore. By rank I was a sergeant, yet my immediate commander was a corporal. I did my best not to interfere with his authority. I played down my rank and behaved like all the other trainees, who had been in service only three months. The whole course was somewhat like a nursery school. The level of studies was not high, and on Friday, before giving us permission to go home, the commander read a list of all the men and their minor offences of the week. "Yochanan was okay all week. Very nice, sit down." It was funny, but I remember that even when the demands were ridiculous, I controlled my tendency to rebel and I didn't stand out. Still, the course opened a new world for me, particularly during the week of training in hospitals and emergency wards.

During the course we were sent for one week of security duty in the occupied territories. This was a completely new experience for me. On one hand, here I was a real soldier at last. On the other hand, I disliked the role of an occupying force, I didn't like the behavior of the border patrol, and, for the first time, I felt what it meant to face a hostile population.

We received our diplomas as medics. Some of the trainees in the course didn't deserve it, but the army needed them all. As for me, I felt I was fitted for the job, and I dreamt about service as a combat medic in the Armed Forces. I asked to be placed there, but I received a different order: "You will serve as a medic in the military prison."

I was shocked; I was unprepared for that. But the commander said it was a challenge, it was a really difficult job, and they needed a medic there. I told him that I had run away already from the Military Police, and that I wanted to reach a combat unit. But I could not change the order, and our agreement was that I would go to the prison for a month.

Although I had previously spent two days before in detention, prison was a new experience for me. Every time I entered or left, the gates were locked behind me. I was jailed too. Our unit included one medic, completely burned out, a doctor and the clinic sergeant. My role was to reduce some of their pressure.

I will never forget my first evening at the infirmary. Suddenly they called me to the "ward"—this was the name of the toughest jail department, with the exception of the solitary cell. This ward consisted of tiny cells, with four inmates in each, living on a concrete floor, with a chemical toilet in the corner. Each of the cells had a peephole, through which the prisoners could be watched. A cage, really. I came to the cell, where a very young man was sobbing, handcuffed, a chain on his feet. A sergeant was harrassing him, and all his personal belongings were on the floor. "He says that he has a terrible headache," said the sergeant. I pushed him away from the man, and said: "Let me talk to him for a moment." Then I rushed to the infirmary, brought back a pill, and gave him some water from a cup I found nearby. The sergeant yelled at me: "Why do you give him a personnel cup? Don't you see he is a prisoner?" I was so mad I almost hit him, but I exerted control over my temper, and calmed the boy instead.

In the morning I came back to the cell to see how he was getting on. He was sleeping on a thin blanket on the floor, chained. He had wet his pants during the night, and the other guys said that he had not stopped sobbing the whole night. Later on I found out that he was a good man, from an elite unit, who had lost his nerve after his pal committed suicide. So instead of sending him to a mental ward, he was jailed. It was a difficult experience to watch his breakdown, but in ten days he had recovered completely and was released from jail without any trial.

The men I met at the military prison were of all kinds: a mixture of good guys with tough criminals. The good guys were jailed because of some minor mishap, which, due to the strict army regulations, sometimes snowballed until they reached prison. I met prisoners who could not take the stress of basic training, and deserted, or good kids who had been caught smoking grass. Sometimes I felt that the army was too strict with some kids.

There were others, however, who did not evoke my sympathy. I remember a time when I was bringing some medicine to a prisoner in his cell, and as we opened the door he fiercely attacked the policeman who accompanied me, almost killing him. This was a pretty common event. During my service there, we had at the "ward" a hunger strike, an attempt at collective suicide, an uprising—it was constant work for us.

One night I was called to deal with an emergency in a cell and found four guys with their wrists cut and bleeding. This was happening in three other cells at the same time. They were crazy. While we were trying to provide first aid, the wardens were taking out their aggression on some of the bleeding men.

Another night I remember was when we received a transport of Arab terrorists who had been moved out of their prisoner camp. The prisoners, with their eyes covered, were an easy target for the violence of some of the simple-minded soldiers—drivers, cooks and barbers, who had never fought the Arabs and who here could be heroes for a moment. At the same time, the officer standing next to me pointed to a boy, merely fifteen, and said: "You see this boy? He murdered the late Yekutiel Adam." I was torn between these two feelings: Here were some of our worst enemies, murderers—yet I could not stop seeing them as beaten, humiliated human beings.

To all my jobs was now added the duty of conducting a daily morning parade with the terrorists. When I entered their room, they stood in a line at the far end of the room, facing the wall, and their representative reported to the policeman accompanying me their special problems of the day. Some policemen took the opportunity of beating the Arab prisoners, but I threatened to report them and they didn't do it when I was present. A common problem of the prisoners was injuries from cruel homosexual relationships, and we had to treat them for it . . . Well, it was a good lesson in "knowing your enemy." A miserable picture of miserable people. At least the medical team gave them fair treatment.

We had some better wards, of course, in which prisoners left each day for work, and had the privilege of receiving visits and smoking cigarettes. On the other hand we had the solitary cells, in which a prisoner couldn't even lie down, and the light was on day and night. The better you behaved in jail, the better were your conditions, that's all.

We had some good guys in jail, too, as I said. I remember a soldier, a naval commando, who was caught with a gun for which he had not signed. He had failed the absolute credibility demanded of such soldiers, but I think that the system was very cruel to him. After the intense training and all the hardships of his military job, I could not see the point in such a punishment. I hear that this episode broke him down completely, and later on he left the country. We had also several "Lebanon objectors," but some of them accepted their sentence with good spirits. One of them used to imagine long adventures in space, and all the prison team got parts in his fantasy. He was nice, so his conditions were quite good, too.

Conditions at the military prison were pretty good for the staff. We had a friendly relationship among the men, and the commander took good care of us and our welfare. The month went by, and several extra weeks, and I was transferred from the place.

My next placement was at the liaison unit with *Zadal*.[4] It was the winter of 1983, and I reported to Marge Ayun, the headquarters of the liaison unit. The unit trained the soldiers of Zadal, and I was supposed to become the medic of the unit, and also to train Lebanese medics when this was necessary.

We lived in an old French fortress. The infirmary was cold, dark and neglected. Three medics, an Israeli and two Lebanese, were sitting there, clinging to an old, smoky heater, playing backgammon. I arrived full of energy and immediately started to improve the physical conditions of the place. We painted the room and organized the equipment. Gradually I understood the mood of the place. The Lebanese were totally apathetic. They received a salary from the IDF and could not care less about their jobs. We treated the soldiers for all their health problems, and also those civilians who arrived at the "Good Fence."[5] We worked in cooperation with the hospital in Marge Ayun. By the way, this was the time that Major Hadad was dying; the Israeli doctor of our unit was his doctor.

When I completed the renovation of the infirmary, I was sent to work in a Lebanese battalion in Sidon. I was in charge of the clinic, the local medics and some of the Israelis who were training them.

That's where I discovered the ugly face of the IDF. We were eight officers and four soldiers in the Israeli force. The officers were pretty corrupt and they behaved as if they lived in the Wild West. They were all driving fancy private cars, which they had confiscated from rich Lebanese for any reason they could think of. Our headquarters was in a villa, and the cars in the parking lot were beyond belief. I was supposed to go around the area and supervise the Lebanese medics. But since we were only four soldiers living in the villa, most of the time we were busy cleaning, cooking and guarding the spot.

Our security was a big joke. A Lebanese unit was situated in the building next to the villa, supposedly to guard us. They took turns on guard duty around the villa, while we took turns guarding from inside, and making sure that the Lebanese were performing their duty. Whenever I searched outside the building, I could never spot any Lebanese guards. Furthermore, when we complained that the guard duty was too heavy for the four of us, the officers decided that indeed we could do without guards from the inside, and it was enough if one of us slept next to the telephone. We were actually abandoned to our fate.

The whole atmosphere was like in a no-man's land. The local people were ready to be fighters for whoever offered to pay them more. When recruitment to Zadal was taking place, kids of 14, old men of 60, even invalids, were all accepted for service. One of the Israeli soldiers, who spoke Arabic fluently, told me that some of these recruited men had been in the PLO before, and they were supposed to guard our security in the area.

Gradually I understood our position. I started to lock the villa as well as I could for the night, I prepared some escape routes from the back, and I used to go to bed every night with my rifle loaded and ready to fire. I used to wake up with every sound, constantly on the alert.

The cultural level of the officers was demonstrated by the x-rated and violent films they used to watch day in and day out on the video. I cannot start to tell you how they related to the local population, they were so corrupt.

When I asked the commander for a permit to go to the base to bring instruction materials so that I could organize a course for the medics, he did not give me a pass. When I wanted to take a car to go to the different units and see what their medical teams were doing, he put all kinds of obstacles in my way. In general, I was paralyzed by the conditions, and all I could do was attend to the infrequent treatment of medical problems which had occurred right there, and, more than anything, chores around the villa. Actually, almost all my cases were local soldiers who for various reasons had shot themselves either intentionally or unintentionally. I felt that as a medic I was at the very bottom of the unit in which I served.

My immediate superior was actually the doctor, but he stayed in Marge Ayun. One day I wrote a detailed letter to him, with all my complaints, and he revealed its content to the officers who lived in the villa with me. The battalion commander, who knew that every word in this letter was true, threatened to sentence me for disobedience. I did not open my mouth anymore.

You see, my dream of becoming a medic at the front had really materialized. I even had one chance of treating Israeli paratroopers immediately after a skirmish. But I was unable to accept the norms of the unit, and my constant discontent and criticism created very tense relationships between me and all the others.

Gradually I grew indifferent to my situation. I did whatever was required of me, and tried to fill my free time by reading. I used to sit on the commander's jeep in front of the villa, in the sun, and read. It was a quiet protest: "Look what you have done to me, and how I ignore you." Reading was the only way to preserve my sanity.

I served in these conditions for five months, almost until my release. I was very rarely home, since I was often grounded by my commander. I felt like a "piece of nothing," a zero. I knew that this wasn't a picture of the IDF in general, but here I was, longing for my days as a youth leader.

I was relieved from this position only by accident. One Saturday I was called on an emergency to treat three Lebanese soldiers who had been wounded by a runaway bullet. I gave them first aid and waited for the ambulance to take them to the hospital. As I was sitting there, I met a Mental Health Officer who had been serving with an Israeli battalion in the area. I started to talk to him, and told him my story. I said that it was unbearable, that I wasn't able to carry on like this. Not only was my relationship with my superiors wrecked, but I also felt physically insecure, abandoned. Actually, at that time, most of the IDF forces had already withdrawn from Lebanon, and we were at the mercy of the local soldiers and guards.

This Mental Health officer wrote a letter to the Northern Command, describing my state and recommending my transfer. This letter did not go through the regular channels, and, indeed, in two weeks I received my order of transfer to Marge Ayun. It was very strange; when my commander received my order of transfer, he shook my hand warmly and said: "Naturally it is your right to ask to leave this spot, but thank you anyway, because any IDF soldier who serves here with Zadal is doing an extremely important job." It was strange, after all these months of silence and abuse. But I did not reply.

The base in Marge Ayun was not so different yet a little more sane. It was larger and provided me with more professional work. I disregarded the people I could not get along with, and I concentrated on my work. I was highly motivated. Again I renovated the infirmary and its equipment. With the help of the sports leader we cleared an area for volleyball and started some games. I opened an advanced course for the local medics. I enjoyed working in the hospital with the doctors who came there for their reserve duties, and I learned a lot.

There I was given, again, regular leaves to go home. Often I left on Thursday and returned only late on Sunday. However, at this stage of my service I didn't feel so keen about going home. I had grown out of my friendships at my home village, but the sense of freedom in going out of the fortress was very important.

Even there I didn't have enough work as a medic and I longed for my full days as a youth leader. At that stage I planned the integration of the two military jobs. Since a medic doesn't have enough work in peacetime, I proposed a project that would train people like me to be youth leaders during peacetime, and medics in times of an emergency. I sat and wrote the project down, including a plan for turning the Gadna bases into field hospitals during war. Naturally, nobody used my plans.

Even the end of my service was unpleasant. A few weeks before my release was due, I asked for leave to help my father in harvesting our apples. Suddenly I was highly needed. Some new medical equipment was to arrive from the USA, they wanted me to reorganize the infirmary. There was nobody to replace me—I felt as if it was all out of spite.

I remember the last time I passed the Lebanon border in the Safari truck, released from service. The truck was full of young paratroopers, who were wild with happiness to get out of Lebanon, although it was just for a period of training in the South of Israel. For me, however—this was really the last I would see of Lebanon! I was exhilarated.

We had this ritual on our way out of Lebanon. Once you crossed all the inspections and you were within Israel, you used to inspect your rifle, and take the ammunition out—we all did this together, and it made this rattling noise. To this very day this noise makes me happy with relief.

During the first days after my release I felt as if I missed a part of my body: I wasn't carrying a gun. This was like a physical habit, so deep. At first I felt exposed, defenseless, without my gun. It was some time before this feeling vanished completely.

Notes

1. Literally—youth battalion. This is an educational unit of the IDF, dedicated to the education of youth and their preparation for military service.

2. Literally—knowledge of the land. It refers to instruction in the geography and history of the land of Israel.

3. Nickname for Israeli-born.

4. The military organization of the South of Lebanon, which cooperated with the IDF.

5. An area in the Northern border in which Arabs could receive medical help from Israeli medical teams.

4

GAD

My father is an Israeli diplomat, and for the last two years of high school I lived in New York City. It was a wonderful period. I traveled a lot, and had many friends. I felt that I owed the State of Israel something for the good time I had before my military service.

In New York I studied at a Jewish high school. There was an incident that I'll never forget. One morning five Nazi kids appeared in our school yard. They wore black jackets and swastikas, and they started to paint Nazi slogans on the school building. All the students were crowded in the class-rooms, watching through the windows. I was the only one to go down and start to hit these guys. I am hot-blooded—I flare up easily. I still remember my excitement. There were five boys, and I was alone, but I wasn't afraid. I had hoped that other children would join me or that the principal would come down. As it happened, I received many blows that morning but in the end was rescued. For some reason this remains a highly significant episode in my life. From then on I knew I was a Jew. I knew also that I'd return to Israel for my military service, in spite of all the American temptations.

The truth is I had never doubted my obligation to serve in the IDF. My whole family had done so, and they were all officers. I knew I would follow their example.

After graduation I took a long cross-country trip. My parents had another year to stay abroad, and I returned to Israel alone to start my ser-vice on time. My home when on leave was to be with close friends of my parents. They came to pick me up from the airport and convinced me not to volunteer for the Infantry but for the Artillery, which they said was inter-esting and where advancement in rank was rapid.

From the airport I went directly to the absorption base, and from there to the artillery basic training camp. The first stage is basic training as

41

in the Infantry; we didn't see any cannon yet. I remember on the second day, as I was standing on parade, a sergeant came running into the square—he was almost a god in our eyes at this stage—and called me to follow him to the commander of the base. I didn't know what to expect. It so happened that one of my father's colleagues had called the commander of the base and told him that so-and-so's son was a new trainee at his camp. He introduced himself to me and said he knew that I had returned to Israel all by myself, that my parents were sending their regards to me, and finally, that if I needed anything I should come directly to him. It was nice to feel that the commanders knew who I was, but it made absolutely no difference in the way I was treated.

I was in a bad unit. Of the forty of us, only two became officers in the end, the others became simple gunners. I was the distinguished trainee. What I hated most about basic training was the kitchen duty—when work starts at 4 a.m. and is not over until 1 a.m. Furthermore, after you see how the food is prepared, you lose your appetite for the week. But other than that, my basic training was uneventful.

When this stage was over, I was given a computer job. It was quite clear that in my unit most of the men had no background or brains for such work. I took a course where most instructors were women, and I had a good time. Afterwards I was attached to an artillery battalion in the Jordan Valley.

We were five new soldiers in this battalion and among ourselves were responsible for all the guard duty. On a night when I was not on guard, I would take my turn in the kitchen. But I got a lot of satisfaction from my peformance of professional tasks. I used to work with the officers, without any 'distance' between us. The battalion was training in the field. The cannon moved around all the time, and I used to follow in a jeep or the APC[1] where a computer was installed. I was my own boss, and my hands were always clean. This made me very different from the rest of the soldiers. Since I was without family in Israel, I was allowed more leaves, and left the base earlier on Fridays to do my various errands in the city. Generally I felt good.

After about five months of this routine, an emergency condition developed in the north, and our battalion participated in action, crossing the border to Lebanon. This was frightening. For the first time I saw what war was like. Once I went to have lunch in Kiryat Shmone and a bomb exploded right there next to me. I felt so helpless. I can still see Kiryat Shmone as a deserted town without traffic, all its stores locked up. (After this experience I felt that Israel's participation in the Lebanon War was justified.) I wasn't always proud of our soldiers in battle. I remember soldiers entering Lebanese villages and misbehaving, going into a store and trying to take merchandise for free. Great heroes. Or soldiers running away when a fire started to spread in a field near an ammunition store, instead of trying to extinguish it.

After three weeks in Lebanon I was called for an advanced professional course followed by the officers' course. At that stage I wasn't only an expert on computers, but I had already learned all the different aspects and functions of the cannon.

It was a time of study, mostly, but I remember several episodes. When I was at the preparatory stage for the officers' course, a year after my recruitment, my parents returned to Israel. The course started on a Sunday, and my parents were due to arrive on the Thursday of that first week. Right away I asked for leave for Thursday, so that I could go and meet my parents at the airport—it was a very long drive from our base. The commander told me he would see later on. Every day I repeated my request and got no answer. Finally I was told that on Thursday night we would have a hike, so I wouldn't be discharged until Friday. (By the way, this was the hardest hike I ever had, with the heaviest man on the stretcher.) I was told I would be discharged after the hike, which lasted all night. But in the morning I had to stay on parade, and so on and so on—until I was mad with anger. Finally, one of the junior commanders sneaked me out against the order of the higher commander, who, for some reason, decided to be harsh. I saw my parents only on Friday afternoon.

The officers' course itself started in the winter. As soon as I arrived I saw a mountain of a man from the Armored Corps, weighing perhaps 200 kilos (450 pounds), and I felt he was a good man. We hit it off from the start, so I already had a friend. On the first evening, I volunteered to organize the trainees' guard duty, which they manage themselves during the course. I did it for the duration of the course, and our platoon was the best organized. I was in excellent physical shape then, winning second place in running of all the cadets. As a result, I had always the heaviest load to carry on the hikes. It was a good course, and I was sad when it ended.

The next stage was the special course for Artillery officers. This was another matter. The course was very demanding, including high level studies in mathematics and computers. Our commanders were very strict. We were tested all the time, and those who did not make it were kicked out. About half of the men didn't finish. The constant disciplinary pressure, the examinations and the selection made us all very nervous. We fought each other over every trivial thing. There was absolutely no solidarity among the men. I was a good trainee, yet toward the end of this half-year course, I hated everybody and was hated by the others in return. I don't know why.

The most important week of this course was, in my opinion, the week we spent on security duty in Gaza. Earlier that week a soldier from another unit had been killed by a mob in the street, the situation was tense, and all the cadets were mobilized to help. Our duty was to guard two refugee camps near the town. We had to maintain the curfew in the camps because the inhabitants were rioting. My unit included four officers: a pair stood guard at each entrance to the camp. We were on duty for 12 hours, and then had a rest period of 12 hours, and so on for the rest of the week. It was very difficult and tiring, but more than this, for me, it was frightening. The first morning we saw the Arabs gathering inside the camp. They started to throw stones at us. I didn't mind, as long as the rocks didn't reach us. I admit that I was afraid to intervene, but the officer with me said that we had to stop this. We called the Border Patrol in the radio, they arrived right away and started firing in the air. When they caught somebody, they hit him. At first I despised them for their behavior, but within a day I acted like them.

We were ordered to get people to stay inside their homes. So we were patrolling in those narrow streets, like policemen, while the children jumped at us from all the little alleys, throwing stones, running away, laughing. I found a solution. If I caught one of these boys, I took him home to his father. His father would hit him so cruelly that we had to hospitalize him. I wondered who was more humane, the father or the Border Patrolman.

My standards changed quite a bit when one of my friends was hit on the head by a rock. Until then, I was a "vegetarian," I said we shouldn't hit. But from then on, we all became violent; we behaved like animals. We shot all the water containers of the inhabitants for no reason at all. When we saw a gathering of people, we pretended to take aim at them while one of us shot in the air—all the methods we had learned from the Border Patrol. One day we caught four boys who were throwing rocks. We tied their hands behind their backs, covered their eyes, and said that we were going to kill them. We talked in Hebrew about how and where to kill them, giving them a good fright. They were hysterical: "Don't kill us, we will never do it again." They cried and screamed while we shot in the air, until one of the boys fainted. So what was this, sick sadism perhaps?

One day the people in the camp put nails and metal scraps on all the roads, and all our trucks and jeeps got flat tires. I found a man who fixed tires and forced him to open his workshop and do all the repairs. I was bothered, however—who would pay the man for his work? I felt bad. Now I remember that it was Passover and by way of repaying him I gave him a package of matzos and allowed him to fill the tank of his truck from the military gas tanker—to quiet my conscience.

Within a week I got to know all the people who lived in the camp. I knew their habits and work places. I knew which were the areas where one should take care. But the main process I noted was the change in me. When you used your gun freely in a crowded civilian area, people would be hit, intentionally or not. Everybody fired freely, as if in Texas. Until a man was killed and we were sobered.

I don't know if it's possible to behave otherwise in such a situation. We were influenced by the stress and the conditions, and we were swept along by the example of the most aggressive men among us. Some people say that in the army we have men who hate Arabs, and they cause the atmosphere to flare up. But in my course we were all kinds of people: Orthodox and non-Orthodox, leftists and rightists—and we all behaved like animals. Only two didn't participate—they stayed at the entrance to the camp, never went in, and watched us from afar. I remember that when we drove out of Gaza, back to the base, we were all depressed. We sat and asked: "How did we do it, how could we behave like this?" What I asked myself was how would I behave if I were to face a similar situation again.

As I said, for me it was the most important week of my training. I learned that everybody can be swept into violence, and that I, in particular, have "hot blood". It was a meaningful experience which had, somehow, prepared me for the coming war.

The Lebanon War was declared during the final week of the course. For two weeks we remained on the base, and completed the course. Then we were sent to the battalions as artillery officers. I was attached to a battalion which slowly crept toward Behamdoon. These were the first real battles in which I participated. At this stage it was a nondeclared war— airplanes didn't take part in it, yet we advanced a bit, fired our cannon, and took another step forwards. I was a Katak, namely a front observation officer who directs the aim of the artillery.

When Behamdoon was captured, we had two weeks of comparative rest, and I took several trips within Lebanon. I was overwhelmed by the landscape of this land. We felt completely secure, travelling without any precautions. I made some of the trips in a jeep with a much higher-ranking officer, and it pleased me to become his friend.

Later on I participated in the battle of Beirut. I was an officer in the artillery battery which was situated in the Hippodrome. I remember seeing the high-rise buildings of Beirut for the first time, such a lovely city! But there, in the streets between these buildings, we'd conduct our battles. We were placed in a building facing another which had been taken by the PLO. We had to run as we crossed the street, and had to avoid passing by certain windows. At night, the ordinary soldiers took turns guarding downstairs, while we, the officers, were invited to the flat of a Lebanese colonel to watch movies on the video. I became close to many other officers. It was like a fantasy life—shots were fired at us from windows while we had a party. Very strange. A few days later we were joined in the building by the

IDF snipers' unit, a very weird group. They used to count the number of terrorists that they had shot—like in a hunt of some sort.

One morning, as we worked with our guns, a shell fell right near us, and four of my men were wounded. They weren't hurt badly but were taken to the hospital, and the battery had to be operated with four men less. I was afraid for my life, but only for a moment, no more.

In Beirut, we conducted some kind of war of attrition. It didn't seem as if there was any general plan of operation. In the morning, an officer would walk in, say: "Why don't we give them some fire in that direction?", so we entered the motorized gun, went a little forwards, fired all our shells, then drove back. Usually we aimed at buildings which were the headquarters of the PLO, or from which snipers had previously bothered us. We knew all the buildings in our observation area, and we named them. In a cannon assault, we often took off about two-three floors from their height.

This situation went on for about two weeks. They sniped at us, and we shot our guns. It was like in a game with a wild atmosphere of some kind. I enjoyed myself so much that I didn't realize that I had not been on a leave for more than a month. I recall that I thought these were days I'd want to remember. Many high commanders arrived, and I sat in on meetings with them, feeling like a big shot. It was an adventure. Only momentarily, when someone was hit, would we say: "How fearful," but the wounded were immediately evacuated, and our fear would go away too.

One night, when the snipers' unit stayed at our building, their commander took me to a window, showed me through his binoculars a man in a far room, and said: "Man, you see, there is Arafat in person." I can't tell you that I identified him for sure, but there were many intelligence people in our building and they confirmed it. I am sure we could have killed Arafat easily that night, but for some reason it was decided to let him go.

After about a month, my whole battery team went on leave, and I stayed on as the only officer at the post. On Saturday morning, suddenly I was approached by a commander who said that I would get two motorized cannon and ten tanks under my command plus a platoon of infantry soldiers, and I was given a job in the battle of Beirut. Don't ask me how a beginning officer like me can get into such a position, the battalion leader must have been elsewhere.

All day long we advanced and fired, with me in command. We took fine aim, with a good pace of four shells per minute. I stood at the tower of the cannon all day, and the enemy shells fell all around me. At one point the window of the cannon was shattered by a shell, and my driver couldn't see where he was going, so I had to direct him in addition to aiming our shots. We had a good hit rate, and I was pleased. I heard on the radio that one of the cannon was out of order, so I ran out of my cannon and brought a tank over to haul it to a safer spot and ordered three soldiers to repair the damage. We were under heavy fire all the time, and out of eye contact with any other force. The whole battle took place in the streets of the city. Suddenly I saw burning tires being rolled down the street where we were advancing. Our ammunition truck was standing in the middle of the road, at risk of a huge explosion. I had to make up my mind right away if I was ready for a really brave act. I didn't think much, I ran into the truck, and drove it into an alley, so that the tires wouldn't reach it. On the radio I heard that one of our soldiers was killed, and others wounded. That was how the day passed.

In the afternoon I was told that a ceasefire would take place at five o'clock. I wanted to complete some tasks before it would be too late. Five minutes before ceasefire I went out of the cannon to aim the firing of a phosphorus shell for the finale, and a shell which was aimed at me exploded nearby; a splinter hit me above the eye. At first I didn't even feel that I was hit. I had no pain and I continued to order the guns and my men. I even managed to watch the phosphorus shell exploding—a beautiful sight. Then the bleeding frightened my men. One of the soldiers, a new immigrant who could hardly speak Hebrew and was usually a soldier who gave me lots of trouble, got his personal bandage, took off my helmet and gave me first aid. Then he took the helmet, which had a radio installed in it, and informed the other commanders that I was hit and needed to be taken to the hospital—doing it in the most appropriate manner by talking on the radio. I remember how amazed I was at his performance. The driver heard the message; he started to drive back, doing it carefully since he had almost no vision through his broken window. A few moments later the medics arrived, took me out of the cabin and treated me.

In the field hospital I was told I was the last wounded since an agreement had been signed, and Arafat gave his consent to leave Beirut. The doctors wanted to send me to a hospital in Haifa, but I objected because I wanted to join my unit as soon as possible. The next days were calm. I stayed in the field hospital for three days, and then rejoined my battalion in Behamdoon.

Amia: *Can you reconstruct your feelings then—why did you want to rejoin the battalion?*

Well, I knew that I saw and did things that would never be repeated. I didn't want to miss the experience. Here I was, a young officer, just six weeks after graduation from the course, and already I had the opportunity to command a battery all by myself and to work closely with very high-ranking officers. Much later, when I was a company leader, I had a lot of authority, but I didn't do even a quarter of what I had done then in Beirut. Beside that, I felt responsibility for my men. My wound wasn't serious, and my men knew it, so what would they have said: "The commander took advantage of his slight wound and took off to safety?!"

Three days after my release from the hospital, I was given leave to go to my brother's wedding in Tel Aviv. They hadn't known about my wound. I came to the party with a big bandage on my head—a hero.

After several weeks of quiet time in Behamdoon, Bashir Gemayel was assassinated. Everybody was in a deep mourning around us, people wept for him. It was so sad. At night we were ordered to return with all our equipment to Beirut, not far from the first spot we had been previously. We joined the forces that were about to penetrate Western Beirut from the Hippodrome.

We were under heavy fire constantly, and we shot our guns in return. At that time we were already in disagreement about this war, but whatever our political views, none of us wanted to enter Beirut. One man in my team was crying: "Why do I have to kill, I don't want to fight." But I, when I'm under attack, I fight back as hard as I can. I know that civilians were hit too, it was hell for them, but I couldn't help it. One of my men, who was sitting on the fourth floor of a building, took off his helmet for a second, and right then he was shot and fell down in front of us at the battery downstairs. This picture charged my hatred for a couple of days. That's about the only picture I clearly remember. The battle lasted for three days, from Thursday to Saturday. It was a confusing battle, and I don't remember it very well.

The massacre of Sabra and Shatila[2] took place on Saturday night. We saw many lights in the camps, but didn't realize what was happening. We didn't know that the Phalangists[3] had entered the camps. In the morning we saw people escaping—terrible sights. Later, we heard the news on the radio.

We were moved into an area of fancy hotels in Beirut. Throughout our stay in Lebanon I issued very strict orders about behavior toward the civilians. My soldiers didn't take a thing from Lebanon, even when things were abandoned. The day after the occupation of Beirut, I saw Israeli soldiers entering hotels and behaving as if they owned the place. I told my men that we would sleep in the street rather than take advantage of the situation. Later, I asked a woman who had owned a car store to allow us to camp in her empty lot. We parked our vehicles carefully and stayed there for two days. Of all the luxury around us, I permitted my men to take a swim in the swimming pool of one of the hotels, while I stayed near the radio, waiting for orders.

I don't recall having thought during these two days about Sabra and Shatila or about the reasons for the occupation of Western Beirut. I think that I started to ask questions about a week later, when I read that a huge political protest demonstration took place in Tel Aviv. In the meantime I was responsible for my men. I had to pay attention so they would not misbehave, would not conduct themselves as an occupying force, would not loot, nor shame the image of the IDF.

After two days there we were ordered to return to Behamdoon. Before we mounted the vehicles, I had all my soldiers take out all their belongings and I checked everything carefully for loot. I found a radio, some cameras, many cigarettes, hotel towels. I returned the towels, and I took a big hammer and smashed all the objects to pieces. I know that not all units enforced the same standards, but this was my personal "weakness," and my men had to obey me.

Our stay in Behamdoon lasted for six months. We developed a daily routine of guarding the roadblocks, patrolling and maintaining our battery. Our post was right near the Syrian border. We stayed in Lebanon all the winter of 1982–83, until after Passover. At first, many high-ranking officers came to visit us. They explained to us what had happened in Sabra and Shatila, and gave the men an opportunity to talk and ask questions. They all promised us that before the winter we would be transferred back into Israel . . . These visits gave me a lot of work—for every one of them I had to clean up and to show my men and equipment in the best condition. I myself tried to talk to my Christian friends several times and ask them about the massacre, but they maintained their silence. They were afraid to talk, or maybe they were ashamed.

As the winter started, we built two posts facing the border and equipped them with kerosene heaters. When not on duty, we lived in an abandoned villa which had been the summer resort of a rich man. We worked hard. At first it was exciting to do the patrols in this mountain area, but as it became colder it wasn't fun anymore. There were only two officers at our post, one of us commanded the morning patrol and the other—the evening one. We were terribly tired.

One Sunday I was returning to Lebanon from my home in Tel Aviv, from a military bus station where all the soldiers returning from weekends at home were gathering. It was getting late, and I was trying to get a bus for my men and myself. A major was arguing with me, demanding that his men should go first, and the sergeant-major who ran this transportation business ruled in his favor. I was mad, but I had to wait. As we drove up north we heard on the radio that the bus before us had been attacked by terrorists, and seven Israeli soldiers were killed, including that major. It was the first terrorist attack on military vehicles going into occupied Lebanon. You see, we were saved by this chance occurrence. Two weeks later I was again at the same transportation depot, and the sergeant-major saw me and said: "You see, that delay was your luck."

The winter of 1982 was a cruel one. It hailed and snowed all the time. We had to work outdoors in the bitter cold. Our spot was far from the battalion headquarters and it was difficult to get our supplies. Our guns were often buried under the snow, and we had to dig ditches to get them. The soldiers used to run in those ditches back and forth among the different posts. We were never trained for survival in such climates. But we received warm jackets and good boots, we had enough heaters, we received the first video machine to entertain us—it was bearable.

Every night we had at least one sudden alert. Often, we had three or four alerts during a night. As the weather grew colder, we had more alerts because the dark hours were so long, and my unit provided light bombs for the different actions in the area. We used to fire light bombs as directed, and go back to bed.

I was exhausted after those nights. The transition from the heated interiors to the cold outside was also very hard. Gradually our sense of security in the area deteriorated. The Druze were fighting the Christians around us, and it was our mission to go between the enemies and calm them down. We were attacked several times by the Druze, because they believed that we were sheltering Christians. As the tension mounted, it became quite dangerous.

Now soldiers became afraid to go out of the villa and were also frightened to stay on guard duty inside it. Our patrol went out in two trucks, and almost all the men had to participate in it. Only two remained to guard the villa. Moreover, it was freezing cold. When we patrolled during a snowstorm, I had two men walk in front of the armored truck to show me the track. I myself drove the first vehicle because I didn't trust any other driver. It was frightening to go on these patrols. I knew the odds. I was afraid, too, of a sudden attack or of falling into the depths. We went on a fixed route at a fixed time every day, we were very easy targets for an attack, like in a video game. To help my men control their panic, I used to order them to fire their personal guns all the time while we were patrolling the road. This gave them some rifle practice, but mostly it helped disperse their fears.

While the Infantry soldiers had a schedule of three months in Lebanon and three months training in Israel, we stayed in Lebanon on and on. Throughout this time I was on leave at home once every two weeks, and NCOs in my unit once every three weeks. The conditions of the privates, who went home only once a month, were the most difficult. I don't know how they managed. (laughs) Indeed, they started to give me problems. Every time they went home, they would vanish for two weeks, and thus make their friends pay for it. We desperately needed every single soldier, so that six months in jail for going AWOL[4] was totally impractical. The Battery Commander and I used to go and look for our men in the farthest towns of Israel, where they lived, and bring them back to Lebanon. Often we had fights with their families about the service. This is how I spent my weekends—seeing my parents briefly on Friday night, one night of peaceful sleep at home, and off to look for our soldiers . . . I think these were the most difficult eight months of my life.

As Passover approached, the weather improved, the snow thawed and flowers started to bloom. Spring was beautiful. The Seder[5] I organized in Lebanon in 1983 was the best I have ever had in my entire life. Since the war started I had not attended any festival at home with my family. For Passover I had orders to let most of my men go on leave, and I was left with the worst "criminals" of the unit, those who used to go AWOL all the time. An Orthodox soldier, a new immigrant from Italy, volunteered to stay with me and to lead the prayers. All the men contributed their best in cleaning and cooking, each of us using recipes from home. We set a beautiful table, even nicer than at weddings—and we started early so that the nightly alerts would not interrupt us. Indeed we had almost completed the Haggada[6] and the meal before the first alert came. Later on we had a rough night, with a man killed, some wounded, helicopters landing—the lot. This was our Passover in Lebanon.

A week later I was finally out of Lebanon. My last day was a sad one. I went to Damur, to our airport, to fly back to Israel. I saw some paratroopers from a battalion in which one of my best friends was serving, but I didn't see him. I asked about him and sent him my regards through his buddies. At first, I wasn't told, but then I found out that he had been severely wounded by the rifle shot of another Israeli soldier, a primitive man. Instead of going home happily, I went immediately to the hospital in Haifa. He was terribly wounded and is paralyzed to this very day.

When I finished my stay in Lebanon, I felt as if my military service was over. I knew I would get a job at headquarters, I wanted to have an easy life until my release. Only some time after I had left Lebanon I realized how demanding those eight months had been for me and how much I had been afraid there. As long as I was there, I was basically quite content. Today I can't explain this. We were happy to serve in Lebanon. We were the heroes. As we went home on leave, we felt very special, sharing our experiences. Today I can't return to this mood—perhaps because the consensus about this war disappeared soon afterwards.

My first job was that of an instruction officer to the reserve battalions of the Artillery. My hopes for a quiet job didn't materialize. For three months, I was with a group of officers who went around in Lebanon retraining our reserve forces.

By that time my mandatory service was already over, and I started my fourth year in the standing army. I returned to the Artillery base in the south. The transition to normal base life was difficult. Suddenly I lost the autonomy that I had had in my long service in Lebanon. I was surrounded by higher-ranking officers and was regarded as a kid whose room has to be inspected for its orderliness. I felt that junior officers were not treated as well as ordinary privates. While junior officers took care of their men in the units, higher-ranking officers didn't care about the junior officers under their command. Perhaps this is the difference between combat service in the front and life on a well-organized base in the rear.

I was given an extremely demanding job—the commander in charge of the allocation of all the resources on the base. All the other men of my rank managed to run away from this job. I was supposed to go abroad right then to study a new cannon we were purchasing, but the commander of the base ordered me to take that job and my trip was canceled. Actually, he threatened that I'd be imprisoned if I refused. So that was it.

It was a terrible job. To be performed well, it required two officers, but I did it all by myself, sacrificing sleep and all my free time. I was constantly under pressure. By the time I had solved one problem, there were two new ones to be solved. It was a thankless job. I had to make decisions which, though they helped some people, always aggravated others. I acquired many enemies: It was inevitable. People said I performed the job well, but I don't know if I did. I was angry all the time.

After six months, I was replaced, and was permitted to go on leave for a whole month. Recovery time. The jobs I got later on were not as important or as stressful. I also wrote a theoretical booklet for artillery men. I was withdrawing from the service gradually, you may say. The truth is that during this last phase I reviewed what had happened to me during my service, and often asked myself where I went wrong. (He is silent for a long time.)

Amia: *What do you mean by that?*

Look, I felt a certain disappointment, and I was very tired. I had thought that I'd finish my service in a different manner, and I tried to understand what went wrong in my progress. I came to the conclusion that perhaps a young officer is not rewarded in the army. It was difficult to arrive at this conclusion and stay in the service, as I had planned before. I felt that I had given a lot to the army, I contributed a lot both in Lebanon and in the function I held later on the artillery base. But I didn't feel appreciated for it. Rather, I felt taken advantage of. I didn't sign on for an extra period because I was tired of serving as a battery commander in Lebanon under those conditions. Once my superiors found out that I wouldn't sign for another year, they behaved very unfairly toward me—strictly, according to the rules and with no personal concern. This was what disappointed me. If the war hadn't occurred just at that time, I am sure I would have had a military career. Getting up in rank, I would have felt proud to be a senior commander, with a good salary, a car, the trips—it could have been a good life for me. But it didn't turn out that way.

Notes

1. Armored Personnel Carrier.

2. Palestinian refugee camps, known as headquarters of the PLO, south of Beirut. A massacre of the Moslem inhabitants by the Christian Lebanese took place several days after the murder of President Bashir Gemayel.

3. Christian-Maronite Lebanese para-military units which cooperated with Israel in the invasion of Lebanon in 1982.

4. Absent Without Official Leave.

5. The Hebrew name for the religious ritual taking place on the first evening of Passover.

6. The Hebrew name for the prayer book read at the Seder.

5

EITAN

I was born on an Orthodox kibbutz, and grew up there until my military service. I had lots of contacts with the army because soldiers were training nearby. The kibbutz always hosted soldiers for Shabbat, we saw them in the common showers, they passed our grounds on their hikes—so I grew up with these sights, of soldiers in training or on leave.

I was ready for my own service. My friends told me about their service and so did my brothers, and physical fitness was not a problem for me. I had very special plans—I wanted to serve in an antitank unit of the paratroopers, called the *"tau."* That's where my brother had served before. It is a select unit in which soldiers are trained to work with antitank missiles. The tasks of this unit are interesting, and the people are of very good quality. You serve in a small team of very good soldiers who stay together all the time, and that's mainly what had attracted me. Furthermore, I knew I'd become an officer, and serve four years—not just the mandatory three. It was a tradition in my family.

I arrived at the absorption base and don't remember anything special about it. I was accepted to the paratroopers and said that I wanted to serve in the tau. I had very little understanding about procedures and different courses, so that when a man said to me: "You want to get to the tau? Okay, I'll help you, just write as your second choice 'communication' "—I did. I then discovered that the priority of communication in the paratroopers was so high that anybody who had mentioned it in the form was immediately allocated to the communication unit and not to his first choice.

I was terribly upset. I had heard all kinds of bad rumors about the communication unit. If I couldn't get into tau, I preferred to be a regular parachutist in a battalion. But the decision was final.

During the long basic training period, which is common to all the paratrooper units, I continued to struggle to get into the tau. I felt that I had been duped in the way I was made to volunteer for communication. But nothing seemed to help until I met a friend of my brother's, himself a member of a senior tau team, who arranged the transfer for me.

The physical demands of basic training were not particularly high for me. My difficulty was more psychological. I was frustrated because of my placement. I had this dilemma: Why make an effort if you have no chance of being transferred to the unit you wanted? On the other hand, if you don't make an effort, how would they know you are really good? So this was my problem.

The other trainees were good people. But you have no friends in basic training. You do everything in the unit together, you are punished together. The individual does not stand out and you don't form any special friendships. During basic training you may find, at most, relationships based on reciprocal help, but it isn't love.

We had good squad leaders but a very cruel sergeant and sergeant-major. The discipline and punishment were out of all proportion to the offense. I remember one time that I was made to cry, but I don't recall the details of the episode. It was something like having to run with a water container, dig a ditch with no end, and when you complete it—you're told that you weren't fast enough (which is, of course, a lie), go fetch another water container, dig another ditch, etc., etc. It was horrible.

We got along somehow with the squad leaders. It was clear that they playacted: one had the role of the bad guy, hitting us, and the second was the good guy, coming to comfort us.

After basic training we had the parachuting course, which was nice. There were frightening moments in it, but in general I liked it. After this my good time in the army started—namely the course of the tau.

As I told you, the tau consists of several teams, and we were, naturally, the junior team. Every team gradually becomes a very cohesive group of people. My team was mostly kibbutz members. We became such close friends that it was a pleasure to return to the army on Sunday after our leave at home. Our training and tasks were interesting, but the main attraction was the friendship among us and the good time we were having together in the field, like singing around the fire at night. During navigation studies, for example, we used to go to one of the kibbutzim where one of us was a member, and study the topographical maps alongside the swimming pool. At night we went out on our individual missions.

Throughout this period, people were thrown out of the team, until we became a really small unit. The main basis for the selection was our own group's evaluation of each other, the famous "sociometry." I believe this is a just procedure. You have to be able to trust the members of your team completely.

I was nearly thrown out, too. Right at the beginning of the tau course I had an appendectomy, and I was limited in the physical efforts I could exert. Usually I did not follow the doctors' advice not to exert myself, and I suffered terrible pains all the time. It was a tough period. I was in agony, but I knew that if I didn't improve my fitness, I'd be kicked out of the unit. Once when we had to run carrying a stretcher, I couldn't take it, fell down, and was put on a stretcher myself. This was even worse, I wanted to scream with pain, but I shut up. Anyway, it was a slow process of decline. The commanders saw that I couldn't participate fully in training, so they often sent me to the kitchen. In the kitchen, I was yelled at by the sergeant, I fought with the cook, and a complaint about me was issued to my commander. He grounded me for the weekend, I got even more moody and didn't feel like trying anymore. This period lasted for about a month. It ended when the commander called me in for a talk and explained that he was going to kick me out if I didn't improve my performance. This gave me a shock and somehow I pulled myself out of the crisis. From then on, I was one of the best soldiers in the unit.

Gradually, we became a senior team of the tau. This was the time I enjoyed most in the army. Our work was really interesting. We were all sergeants already. When it was proposed that I go to the officers' course, I declined, since I felt so good among my friends. At this stage you become very close to others in the unit. You have more time to sit and chat. You know them better and you love them more. This is the famous love among soldiers, which is as much a mystery as love of women. We met each other on the weekends, too, always visiting each other on the different kibbutzim. Our girlfriends also became part of the team; they joined us in the base when we stayed on Saturday and sometimes accompanied us on hikes or navigations.

After four good months in the sergeant's team, it was made clear to me that I couldn't go on like this, I would have to go to the officers' course or else get a commanding role in another team. I preferred to be a commander and get some experience before the officers' course, but it didn't work out like that. So I started the officers' training—it was a year and nine months after the beginning of my service.

The officers' course was nothing. I didn't like the content or the form. I didn't like the staff either. I couldn't stand being graded all the time. I didn't like the idea of becoming an officer, responsible for others. I looked for a way to get myself kicked out.

My decision became stronger after about three months, half way through the course. I think that it was on a Wednesday morning. I received the news that one of my tau team had been killed in a training accident. He was a good friend of mine. I went to my commander to ask permission to attend the funeral although I didn't yet know exactly when it would take place. Well, first I went to my tau unit, where I found out that the funeral would take place the next day. So I went to visit his parents and sat with them all day. I knew their son very well. On Thursday I attended the funeral and again visited with the parents. In the meantime, it was Friday. I knew that all the cadets were getting leave for the weekend, so I spent the remaining time with the bereaved family and returned to the officers' school Sunday with all the rest of the cadets.

I remember that it was very difficult for me to return to the course after the tragedy. As soon as I came in, my commander asked me where I had been. I told him, and he said: "You acted like a pinhead, which is unacceptable here." Later on, in the evening parade he made an announcement: "Cadet Eitan took advantage of the furlough he had received for a funeral and returned only today." As a punishment, I was grounded for the next weekend.

I was overwhelmed. I was sure that I couldn't continue the course as long as this man was my commander. I went to the course commander and asked to be dismissed from the course. I also asked for my commander to apologize to me. Both my requests were rejected. Somehow I completed the course, with hard feelings, very hard.

At that time there was no tau team that needed an officer, and I was assigned the job of training our reserve units. I managed to be in this position for two weeks when the Lebanon War broke out. I was at home that weekend and received a phone call summoning me back to base immediately.

When I returned to the base I found a pastoral atmosphere: Everyone was sitting and waiting. I walked around like a madman: My friends are at war, they need me, and here I am doing nothing. The gates of the base were locked, otherwise I would have run away. After three days we were transferred to Lebanon, but we were given some marginal task, and actually didn't fight. I felt that my skills were wasted. When I had leave, I joined my old team, in Beirut. They fought in the hardest situations, and my former team commander was killed in one of the battles. I used to sit with them and interrogate them about all the details of their action, until I felt as if I, too, had participated.

After three weeks like this I couldn't stand it anymore. I went AWOL from the reserve unit to my former team and remained with them to the end of the war. Nobody punished me for that.

After the Lebanon War I was appointed commander of a senior tau team. It was a team of soldiers who had already served in the army more than a year, and it was highly problematic. Their former commander was very talented as a soldier, but he was unreasonably strict with his team. He constantly harassed them, even during the war, when the team suffered casualties. As a result of this, punishments no longer had any significance for them. When I became their leader, I felt that there was absolutely no means of discipline that I could use. They didn't mind my orders or the rules of the army. Their attitude was completely negative. My encounter with them was deeply disappointing. As a last resort I thought of working individually with each member of the team, using the personal approach, without threats or punishments. My commander, however, didn't agree with this. I felt I had failed on the job.

I was with this team for two months, until they went to the squad leaders' course. At that stage I asked to take my officer's rank down, temporarily, and become a sergeant with another officer, my best friend, who had been given the command of the new tau team. My request, although unusual, was granted. For me, it was an opportunity to learn how to lead people under less stressful conditions, where I didn't carry the complete responsibility. It was a wonderful period for me, but it didn't help me to get along with my senior team three months later when they returned from their course. On the contrary, they were even worse than I had remembered. They said: "Now we are sergeants, leave us alone, we want to rest."

In that state we were sent to Lebanon to man a post on the border. We were on guard duty most of the day and hardly had any time for further training. The soldiers' discipline continued to deteriorate. We were getting many visits from higher commanders and I was constantly in conflict with my men. I had to discipline them and control their appearance, especially for the visitors' sake. They objected to obeying, and I was blamed for the poor situation and criticized from both sides.

When we moved out of Lebanon, I decided to quit my job as the team's commander. I felt that I had tried my best and failed.

In the last half year of my service I finally got a position which suited me and in which I felt I could contribute as an officer. I was appointed as operation officer in a paratroopers' battalion. The operation officer is the right hand of the battalion commander, his second in command. I was responsible for planning and carrying out the training program for the battalion. This involved many complicated problems of logistics and the coordination of many units. It was a difficult role. I slept a little and drove around a lot. But I enjoyed tremendously my work with my superior. He was a good and serious man, a model commander. He would find time to listen to each of the youngest soldiers, to try and understand each individual and his problems, sitting in his office to the small hours every night. At the same time, he was an outstanding professional soldier. I learned a lot from him.

We went together with our battalion for security duty in Lebanon. It was a difficult time by then, with daily skirmishes and terrorist attacks. We, too, suffered casualties there. But, in general, we felt that we were winning the war. We caught many terrorist groups and found their arm caches. We prevented many hostile acts. But for me what was most important was the work with this commander. It was especially exciting when he, with all his experience, consulted me about our moves. It gave me a feeling of worth. Once every two weeks I would act as the superior officer in the battalion, responsible for everything. I loved it. I felt like a grown-up, with all that responsibility on my hands.

6

DANNY

I was a very active and ambitious student in my high school in the city. I was head of the students' council and head of our softball team. At 16 I had already been sent abroad with the adult team for international softball games. In addition to all this, I was a good student.

In my senior year of high school, I was invited to various meetings for tests and screening for high quality courses in the army. I expected such placements, they fit with my self image. We had a quiet competition among my friends to see who would become a military pilot. I believed it would be me.

In my sports team I acquired many friends who had already served in the army. I talked to them a lot and tried to get as much information as possible about the different units and courses from them. I was interested only in combat units and argued about it with my parents, who preferred that I get a less risky job. I told my parents that combat service was the most important and that every young man had to contribute his utmost to the security effort. I didn't mind interrupting my sports career for the sake of full military service. But this was the prevailing atmosphere among all my friends—we wanted to give the maximum. This was before the Lebanon War, remember. None of us had any thoughts about being killed.

I think that girls also had a role in building these aspirations. Many of the girls in my class had boyfriends in the army. Those girls who had boyfriends who used to arrive for leave once in two weeks all dirty and exhausted, had "men" as friends, not "babies" like us. Only later did I understand that girls really preferred boyfriends who came home every evening, "jobnick"s[1] who could take them out regularly. But in high school, the girls certainly pretended that they preferred "fighters."

Politically I was inclined to the left and even talked about pacifism. I didn't see any connection between my political views and my military service. It was clear to me that everyone had to do his best in the army for three years, regardless of his political attitudes. It was taboo to mention any objection to the military service. We were at an age of black-and-white views about everything, with no shades in between. This polarization was encouraged in my environment; only my parents were somewhat exceptional. They said that all men had good legs to run, but I had a good head too, so I should contribute to the army with my brain. They thought that I was fit for intelligence work. Anyway, nobody dreamt that I would become what I did.

I think I was well prepared for the army. Physically I was very fit, and mentally I was ready because of all the tests that I had taken for the army. As my screening progressed from one stage to the next, I became quite certain that I would be a pilot, and a good one at that. Now I know that I was prepared for this possibility but for none of the alternatives, and certainly not for what eventually happened in reality.

I went on a trip to Europe after my graduation, and waited for the date of my recruitment. I was due to start the gibbush[2] for the aviation course. I knew that it was a highly selective process, and, naturally, I had my doubts about the outcome. But I was sure that if I failed, I would have another choice of an elite combat unit. I didn't believe I would fail. You see, I had never failed before.

Indeed, after a short absorption process I went to the gibbush, which was supposed to last about two weeks. From the first moment they started to treat us very strictly. They ordered us to run, using various forms of harassment and humiliation. Maybe I shouldn't call it humiliation, because I could see the purpose to all this. They used very rough language, I remember. When a soldier answered a question, the commander would say something like: "Don't throw up in my ear." But I knew beforehand that would happen, and I was prepared to accept it. In fact, the techniques used at the gibbush turned us quickly into soldiers: We learned to be fast and on time, to stand up straight, to keep quiet, and to do exactly what we were told. They did create some situations in which whatever you did you would fail and be punished—but even that was understood during a gibbush. I knew it wasn't the army, just the gibbush. One of the commands was never to part, not even for a moment, from your rifle, which was given to us without a strap. I remember how cold the metal was. But that wasn't the hardest part. The hardest tasks were the hikes with stretchers, where even I was not prepared physically for the efforts demanded of us.

I think that the kind of hikes we were ordered to go on are required of the Infantry only after two months of gradual training. Toward the end of the first week of the gibbush, I was injured on one of these hikes. I was carrying a stretcher with a man on it, and as I walked I stumbled on a rock and twisted my ankle. I didn't say a word and kept walking with the stretcher so that the others would not have to take my turn. Then it happened again, and I fell. I didn't want to be carried on the stretcher myself because many men were in bad shape that night, and there were too many already on stretchers. Somehow I kept marching, helped by others, and I made it to the end. Then I went to see the doctor. He said that I had torn the ligaments of my ankle, that I would have to rest in bed for four days, and that I must refrain from further effort for two weeks.

I didn't know what to do. At first, because of the pain, I did lie down for two days. But then I heard that if you missed three days of the gibbush, you were automatically out. So I joined the gibbush again, although I couldn't perform most of the required tasks. In the end I failed. I prefer to think that it was because of the accident, but one can never know.

I felt bad. I was deeply insulted. I was afraid of meeting my friends back home. Yes, I know that about half of the candidates fail in the gibbush, but not me. I take failure too seriously, and I had no preparation to deal with this one.

As my leg took a long time to recover, my health profile was reevaluated. It was so low that I was unfit for any combat unit. I was disappointed, but I still hoped that the army would find a way to make use of my potential.

My recovery, and the bureaucracy involved in reassigning me, took about four months. For a long time I hung around the absorption base, and this was a very bad place to stay. It was depressing. I met people that I had never seen before. I did not understand their language or the way they behaved, and I found it almost impossible to relate to them. I tried to avoid them, consoling myself that in a little while I would be sent away to a high quality course and never see such types again.

While waiting for my assignment, I was sensitive to all kinds of rumors. It was important for me to find out what I could about good courses and the various possibilities open to me. At one stage I was called to the selection officer, who explained to me that with my abilities and motivation I would be accepted for any course. I selected two high quality courses, one in the Air Force and one in the Navy, and I started to feel a little better.

The next stage was basic training for people with limitations—some had physical and others had mental problems. Being there was an insult to an intelligent man. The commanders were used to people without motivation, and they thought that the only way to instruct was by yelling and through humiliation. But there were a few people like me there, and we tried to keep together and isolate ourselves from the rest. Again I was telling myself that all this was temporary, and would soon be over.

My leg was still giving me trouble, and again I was doing things I shouldn't have done because I didn't want to have it easier than the others. In spite of my leg, I was the best trainee in the course.

On the last day of basic training buses came over and took people to the Navy or to the Air Force—but my name wasn't called. Instead, I was ordered to go back to the absorption base. After some hours of tense waiting, without any explanation, a group of us was taken by bus to an unknown destination. We were very upset; it was fear of the unknown. Actually, we all expected to get leave after basic training, and we didn't even have clean clothes to take with us.

Finally we arrived at a huge base in Sinai. It was during the preparation for the evacuation of Sinai, following the Camp David agreement. A commander told us that for the time being we would work at liquidating the base and different military installations in the area. Nobody told us for how long. The base was almost empty, and all thirty of us were housed together in a large hall.

In the following days most of the men went out every morning for work in the desert around the base, while I remained on guard duty at the base. It was depressing, especially the uncertainty. We were all worried about our future, and every night we talked. It was like a long group therapy session. I managed to maintain my hope that this was temporary—until about a week later, when I received my orders to join the Maintenance Corps.

I went home in a state of shock. It was Saturday, and there was no one in the army to talk to. The more I heard about Maintenance, the worse I felt. I found out that I would have an unsophisticated job, in the company of low-quality people, in a low-prestige unit, with lousy commanders. All the worst fantasies that I could have had about the army seemed to come true. After my high expectations I simply couldn't accept it.

When I arrived at the base on the following Sunday, I found four others rejected from the aviation course. We were all sure that it was a big mistake, that if we went and told them that we were from the aviation course, they would immediately correct the mistake. However, very soon we discovered that there was no mistake. We had no alternative.

When I talked to the commander of the course, I told him that in all modesty I could contribute far more to the army in a more sophisticated role. He said that I was immodest and that they needed good men in Maintenance to become officers and improve the image of the corps. This was what I heard from all the other commanders I asked to intervene in my case. So this was to be my place in the IDF.

The course itself was like a class for the mentally retarded. Some of the trainees had completed only four years of elementary school. We sat in class all day, everything was explained ten times, and still they didn't understand. I was nervous and depressed. I did the minimum required and at the end of the course I was asked to stay on as an instructor . . . All the time they tried to raise my morale, but to no avail. I felt as if I were facing a wall that could not be moved by any rational means.

I refused to stay on as an instructor in the course. The level of the soldiers there was so low, and the material to teach so boring, I simply couldn't take it. At that stage I thought that if I had to stay in Maintenance, I should try to work at the store of a base not far from my hometown, return home every evening, and try to resume my career in sports. I succeeded in getting such a position.

Don't think, however, that my mood improved. I can't describe how low I felt for many many months. I was depressed. I think that it had all resulted from the disappointment of my expectations. I was disappointed in myself. I also felt that I had to apologize to society—how it was that I became a "jobnick," and in such a low place. Again and again I repeated the story about my accident during the gibbush, and still I felt very bad about it all.

The base I joined was horrible. Most of the soldiers there were criminals, drug addicts, or just mental cases. My job was boring. I was in charge of the lists at the store, a petty clerk. One day I met an officer who had been interested in softball. He heard my story and promised to help. I still hoped for a change.

After a while I was called to the commander of the base, and found many officers in the room with him, all asking me various questions and examining me. In the end they offered me the job of the cashier of the base. Right away I felt even worse—this time I realized that my assignment to this base was final, and I would never get out of there. For two days I inquired about the position of cashier and finally made up my mind to accept it.

An old sergeant, who was among the oldtimers at the base, explained to me that the job of the cashier can be defined and created by the soldier who performs it. He said that it was a complicated job with a lot of responsibility, especially at a base with the kind of people such as at ours. He said that if well performed, it can be satisfying. So I decided to take it.

The woman who had held the job before me was about to be released from service. We worked together for one and a half days. In fact, I didn't learn anything from her. I talked a little to a cashier from another base, and I started to function by myself, without any training you might say.

The cashier's job was to deal with all the financial matters of the soldiers. Among other things it involved supplying the soldiers with bus tickets and paying travel expenses to all the reserve soldiers. It also included the responsibility for those funds available to the different units for their small expenses. It was not a complicated job, but when you deal with money and with people like ours, they try to get special "favors" from you. The former cashier had allowed all kinds of deviation from the regulations. She wasn't well organized at all and the men took advantage of her.

From the moment I got the job, I decided to carry it out in the best way possible. I learned the basic requirements and I started to make my own rules and decisions. I told my superior that I would not be willing to be ordered about on my job without prior explanation. I told the soldiers that from then on we would work according to fair rules. Soon the soldiers found out that I didn't discriminate among the men, and everybody got what he deserved. It took some time, but the men discovered that it was of no advantage to them if they did any favor for me. It was even more difficult to train my superiors to rely on my work without unnecessary interference. There was one major in particular who believed that yelling would solve every problem. I used to read the orders to him, and he saw that I was always right. After several months, when the first inspection took place in my office and they found all my procedures in perfect order, my superiors finally got off my back.

Now I had a responsible job, but I still felt depressed. I was constantly angry at the system which had made me become a clerk. In addition, I suffered from the burden of guard duty, because only very few men in this base took turns at guarding. I did guard duty two nights per week and every other Saturday, while all the drivers, cooks and generally "disturbed" soldiers were exempt from this duty.

Another absurdity—while all the difficult men were never disciplined, the few of us so-called normal soldiers were punished right and left for every tiny offense: for a heating stove left on, for a door left unlocked, for something missing in our uniform—any excuse was used as a reason to sentence us. The majority of the men were left alone. From time to time they were imprisoned for a couple of weeks, and then they returned and continued in the same way. At the same time, good soldiers were constantly under the discipline and control of their superiors.

I made the utmost effort to behave correctly, yet I too was sentenced three times. Even after six months at the base, when my standing was somewhat established and I wasn't harassed that much, I wanted desperately to get out of there. I remember one day when I was so upset that I sat with my head on the desk all day and couldn't do a thing. I almost cried. I felt so bad, but nobody tried to help me get a transfer.

For a while I thought that if I went to the officers' course, I would have a way out. Perhaps I could get a transfer to Intelligence. When I was called to the course, however, my commanders started to tell me how good I was at my job and how much they all liked me. They wanted to convince me to stay. At that time I felt that having to sign for another year of service, which I might very well spend in Maintenance, was too high a price to pay for the possible transfer. Furthermore, I was afraid of hurting my leg again. All in all, I was tired of the army and wanted to get out as soon as possible.

I think that my growing acquaintance with the military system killed the rest of my motivation. I found the system to be stagnant and corrupt. I served with criminals, and I managed to witness rape, suicide, drug abuse, stealing—what have you. I had to isolate myself from the other men. Sometimes I was so lonely, there wasn't even one person on the base with whom I could talk. In fact, only the women soldiers on the base were of some quality. I felt that I was losing my brain from lack of use. The only benefit from my service there was that I learned how to speak and relate to the kind of people I had never met before.

My superiors were happy that I had decided not to go to the officers' course since they knew it would be very hard to replace me. For some reason, my order to attend the officers' course was not repeated. Another bureaucratic error, I guess.

Pretty soon afterwards the Lebanon War broke out. As strange as it may sound, the war had positive effects on the base. You see, our base was like a huge factory where all workers left to go home at four o'clock. Almost nobody stayed overnight, and there was little chance of meeting people who worked in different positions. There was almost no social interaction. When the war broke out, the base was on alert and we were all ordered to stay. We had plenty of work and everybody wanted to contribute. Even on our base the men's morale was high and we developed a feeling of togetherness. As we stayed overnight we got to know each other. There is nothing like stress to make good people stand out. So, suddenly, I found people who could be my friends, people whom I didn't know before. I discovered about ten men on base, whose situations were similar to mine. Together with some of the female soldiers, we formed a circle of friends, and we shared our problems and complaints. During that time, I also found a girlfriend on the base.

On the other hand, the war made me feel guilty. I was thinking: What am I doing here when my friends are being killed on the front? I asked to go out to the front with the maintenance people, but my commanders said that I was needed on base. Only my parents were happy with my lot. They

said, "Thank God that you are going to spend the war right where you
are." As the war continued, however, and I understood it better, my attitudes also changed. Politically I didn't support what was happening in Lebanon and I didn't regret the fact that I 'missed' the war. Still it was difficult
to be a young man on the homefront. I was embarrassed by all the attention
that civilians gave me: the sandwiches at the roadside, the hitchhikes home,
as if I were a combat soldier. I felt that I didn't deserve this kind of warm
attention.

    Luckily, none of my friends was killed or wounded in the war. I was
happy for my friends, of course, but also for me. Had any of my friends
been hit, I'd have felt even worse about not contributing my maximum
effort.

    In the summer after the war my mood improved a great deal. I had a
great deal of work to do, due to the war effort; I was given total freedom in
my office, and rewarded by the full support of my superiors. I was promoted and relieved of guard duty. Instead, I took upon myself some extra
duties in the office. Back home in the evenings, I was active on the softball
team, I took some courses at the university and I had a good time. My only
regret was that most of my friends didn't come to the city very often, and
the original group of my high school friends gradually disappeared.

    My leg kept bothering me. I went to see the doctors and they said
that the first treatment I had received after my accident was not good
enough and that the healing process was never complete. After several
treatments did not show any improvement, they decided to operate.

    I knew that I'd be out of the base for a long time. I found out that a
soldier who missed 60 days of service was returned to the absorption base
for reassignment. All my hopes of service elsewhere were reawakened by
this information. At the same time, a new commander arrived at the base,
a man who didn't know me and was convinced that the planned operation
was nothing but a trick to keep me away from my duty. We had some
unpleasant confrontations and I came out feeling very bad. Still I insisted
upon having the operation and asked for a replacement for my job. For a
long time it was delayed, and then several unstable soldiers were sent for
me to train as cashiers—people I knew would ruin all that I had achieved
in building the office. Finally they found a man who had been transferred
after failure in the aviation course. He learned the job and I was able to
get out.

    The operation went well. I was at the hospital for a week and then
home for three weeks. After this, I was given a walking cast and sent back
to the army. So I didn't miss the 60 days required for a transfer. I remember
the first days after the operation, coming daily by bus to the base, on
crutches; it was painful and useless. I didn't do any kind of work anyway.

Later on I was sent to a convalescent home for another month. I remember how angry I was at my commanders who showed little interest in my condition and very rarely visited me.

My leg was finally better. To this very day I still think about what would have happened to me if this accident had not occurred. (Here Danny was quiet for a long time.)

Returning to the base when my treatment was over became even more difficult. Again, I was shocked by the low level of the people there, the regular soldiers as well as the officers. There was nothing substantial for me to do, yet when the academic school year was about to start, and I asked for an early discharge (which is usually granted to soldiers who are accepted to the universities) my request was rejected. But finally I did convince whoever had the authority to reverse this decision. Consequently, I received an early release, two months before the three years were over, and I came to the university. The bad times were over.

Notes

1. A term used in Hebrew to describe soldiers who have a desk job in an office during their military service.

2. A selection process for the elite units of the IDF. The gibbush usually lasts for several days and includes various difficult tasks, whereby the recruits are evaluated.

7

IDO

I see myself as an ordinary guy. I come from a city, from a very stable background. All my life we lived in the same apartment, and I spent from kindergarten to the end of the 12th grade in the same school. I have a very close relationship with my parents. I was what you might call "a good boy."

I started to think about my service when I was about 17. I knew I wanted to serve in an elite Infantry unit. I had many reasons for this. First of all, I liked to walk and hike, and thought that that would be a good place for me. I wanted to serve with high quality people and to have an interesting service. Also, as much as it's hard to admit, to serve in an elite unit is prestigious. And, last but not least, there was also some Zionism involved—I wanted to contribute. I had no doubts about the military then. My only worries were about what I would do if I were rejected.

Amia: *When you volunteered for the reconnaissance unit, did you consider the risk and danger involved?*

Look, at the beginning we didn't know anything about the dangers. But even later on, when we knew our business, we never thought about the personal risk involved. You compute probabilities of casualties, but it's strictly theoretical. And rightly so. What's the use of paying too much attention to danger?

I knew that my service would be difficult, physically and mentally, but I really didn't know how difficult. I could never have guessed how immense the physical and psychological efforts we would be required to make would be. Naturally, I'm much wiser today. I prepared myself as best as I could. I jogged, I worked out, I walked long distances. I got advice and

71

some helpful tips from friends. Small things, but they probably helped my chances of passing the screening.

Although I had passed an initial screening before my induction, I was completely unclear about the next stage. I was drafted in August, after my matriculation exams. Waiting for things to clear up, I had to spend two weeks in the induction base, which is undoubtedly the most disgusting place in the whole army. There were all these silly parades and inspections, mess duty, cleaning. But I didn't take it seriously, knowing that this was only temporary. There is no use in adjusting to the induction base, anyway. It's just a brief encounter with the ugly face of the military.

Finally I was sent to the reconnaissance unit. What am I allowed to tell you about it? That it was really hard. (laughs warmly) Long and hard. You never know how long it will be, because part of the training is dealing with uncertainty. You have just finished a forced march with stretchers, you put the stretcher down, expecting a period of rest—and immediately you are ordered to be ready to leave in two minutes.

The best test of the selection process is the stretcher-hike. After an hour of that, you know a lot about a person. You simply see who breaks down and who doesn't. It's not enough to survive. No matter how hard it is for you, you have to help the others. That is the kind of person they were looking for. In addition to that, they give you all kinds of absurd orders, they test your technical skills, your initiative and leadership. But all those are secondary.

What I'm telling you now is the wisdom of hindsight. At that time it was simply hard. Hardest of all was perhaps the lack of any feedback. Nobody talks to you during the selection period. It's as if you ceased to exist as a person. Right up to the last moment of the week I had no idea if I was going to pass or not.

On the eighth day we were gathered together, and they read out the names of those who were accepted. It was a very short list. The majority of us were kicked out. Well, I was not on the list and I was terribly disappointed. I received a furlough for the weekend, and instead of going home I went around looking for a way in. There was another unit whose selection was scheduled for the next week. I didn't know the difference between the two anyway, so I asked to join them. I was allowed to try my luck once more and this time I passed. I'll call the unit which accepted me "the Unit." I didn't know the first thing about it anyway.

For the next two weeks we were given time to recuperate and train in a sports center. We started to get to know each other a little. Although we had difficult daily workouts, this was not a military base, and we certainly felt privileged to be there. But to make the experience a little more military, at the end of the period we had to march to the basic training base with stretchers . . . That's how my basic training started.

We did our basic training with the paratroopers, and were dispersed among their units. Basic training is a period when you gradually build physical and mental strength. The men from my unit were the best soldiers there, and were outstanding in their performance.

After basic training we did a short parachuting course. The course was easy, but jumping was the most frightening experience I had had up to then. But one gets over fears like that easily. So many people have jumped, even women! Later, in my service, I did much more frightening things.

The next stage was the "Unit's basic training," which went on for several weeks without any vacation, and with almost no sleep at all. For the first week we had no sleep from Sunday to Thursday. Then we slept the whole weekend. Next week, we were given 90 minutes of sleep per night. The policy was that those who were good soldiers could complete all their duties and find time to sleep. In practice, however, there was so much to do, so many details to follow through, such a level of emergency all the time, that we were constantly working and constantly punished with repeated inspections for not doing it all perfectly.

Frankly, I hardly remember anything from that time—I was in a haze. Sleep deprivation is the most difficult thing. You fall asleep while you walk—you fall down and don't know it. Later on you learn to sleep with your eyes open. You see things, but you're not there.

Another tough aspect was the commanders' attitude toward us. We felt degraded. The most popular punishment was having to carry another soldier on your back in a 'fireman's hold,' which we called "one-on-one." Traditionally this is the method used for carrying wounded soldiers out of a combat area. Personally I think that turning this into a punishment is very uneducational. For a great part of the day, we used to stand in the "one-on-one" position. We never knew how long this might last. The ones on top often fell asleep. The ones underneath were moaning and crying. And our squad leaders just stood there and watched. Imagine all this in the context of our expectations from the reconnaissance unit! We, the volunteers, the elite!

Every one of us broke down at this stage, each in his own way. Some cried a lot, some started to act funny. We were constantly reminded that we were free to leave, and there were three or four men who actually did.

One of the basic values they were trying to instill in us was absolute credibility. You have to report on everything, and to tell the complete truth. We were told: "It's bad if you didn't do something, but it's much worse not to report it." If you fell asleep during guard duty and reported it, you got punished. But if you didn't and were found out by others—you got kicked out of the Unit. Once I got into trouble because of this. We were supposed to load our magazines with cartridges in a certain order. Once, when shooting, it was discovered that someone had the wrong order. The commander asked who had not arranged the cartridges properly, and I didn't react because I didn't realize that it was me. So we were all put in "position," namely one-on-one, until somebody would confess. After a long time, when nobody confessed, the commander announced that it had been me. Nobody believed me that I had not known, had not been aware of my mistake.

Well, I was ordered to take two 20-litre water containers, climb a hill nearby, and sit there to wait for my next orders. I sat there for about three hours, the longest hours of my life. I even started to believe that they were right, that I had cheated. I was sure that I'd be kicked out.

Later I was called for a talk with the team's commander. He said that I was under suspicion, but he had decided to give me another chance. It was never mentioned again, but it was a trauma for me. I remember another guy who was, indeed, kicked out for something similar. We were supposed to do 50 push-ups before every meal, each one by himself. One day they accused him of doing less than 50, and he was dismissed from the Unit. But probably he had other problems and this was just a pretext.

Credibility was the central issue in our navigations as well. We did most of our navigations alone. Nobody followed you to check which were the coordinates that you had really found on the route. You came back and reported. If you said that you missed one coordinate, you were supposed to return to camp on Saturday night and repeat the route. It was up to you. But if somehow it was discovered that you had not reported accurately, you were out. I don't think it educated us to be honest, however; it just helped them select the most honest ones among us for the Unit. And this is really important.

We had many forced marches. The final one was without our leader. We had two stretchers to carry, and a route to cover, all by ourselves. This is where you get to know your team members really well. Without the leader, there is much less pretense. It is also a rare chance to express some of the pent-up anger toward those who were always on top of the stretcher.

You get to know people and you also develop the famous 'soldiers' camaraderie'. Your life depends on each other. After the whole process the team that remained was so close together that I don't know how to describe it. There is no parallel relationship in any other life circumstances. None of us thought of leaving the Unit of our free will. Not because of our earlier reasons for joining, but simply because of our brotherhood. And the challenge, too. Or inertia, perhaps. . . . None of these is a good reason, you know.

The end of this stage—and its climax—was a final hike of 120 km. Its destination was the Unit's base, where we had not been before. Actually, until then we didn't really belong to the Unit, and its function had not been revealed to us. I myself did not participate in the hike. I had severe shin splits, and the doctor forbade me to go. But don't worry, I did the same hike with the next team, several months later. Anyway, I was on the base already and waited for my team to arrive. You cannot imagine how they looked after this. I had to carry several of my buddies to bed. Later on, someone noticed that one of the men was missing from the rooms, and I found him sound asleep in the shower. But they recovered. We always did.

Afterwards we started a long period of advanced training. Its aim was to reach the highest possible level of physical stamina and infantry skills. This was the principle of professionalism. A second principle of the training was living with uncertainty. We never knew what to expect the next moment, and our expectations were broken again and again. I see this as a building of mental discipline. What you get out of this training is the sense that there is no limit to your abilities. Or, that the limit is where you stop trying, and this shouldn't happen until you actually fall and faint. This limit is very rarely reached, and if so, only if you're sick, dehydrated or something of that kind.

Obviously, we were under terrible stress all the time. People were constantly dismissed from the team, and it grew smaller and smaller. Our peer-evaluations had tremendous impact on who was to stay or to go. You could never be sure you were in for good.

Navigations were the most important thing we learned. At the beginning we did group navigations during daytime. Pretty soon, however, we started to navigate alone, and at night. Navigating alone at night is a risky matter because people may be injured or kidnapped, and in some parts of the IDF they have discontinued this practice. The weeks we spent in those navigations were really difficult. It's a mental effort that I don't know how to describe. All day you learn the route by heart—since it is strictly forbidden to take a map along—and at night you go. Each of us developed his own system for memorizing the route. Studying for it was stressful, but the navigations themselves were simply frightening. I think that those were the most frightening experiences I have ever had.

What were we afraid of? The darkness, being all alone out there. You can't use a flashlight, you mustn't walk on a road. There are those imaginary fears that come up in the dark, and others which are very real. You may fall into a pit. You may break a leg. You may be captured by terrorists. Or, you may lose the way. Once you start to stray, you lose time, and come late for the debriefing the next morning. Then, you have less time to sleep during the day, and you start your next navigation, on the next evening, with less of a chance of making it. And so it went on and on for weeks. Terrible tension. I remember the hours in the truck on the way to our individual starting points. Everybody used to be so nervous. We were usually completely silent on the way, or sometimes we would fight and yell at each other. I used to pray for a miracle—that we'd be suddenly ordered to an emergency, that the truck would break down . . . When the truck stopped for one of us to leave, its motor had a special sound. Even today, a sound like this makes me shudder.

Some of us performed better, although we were all highly motivated to succeed. Perhaps it's a matter of talent, or of character. Those who made it, remained in the team. Interestingly, we all carried on as if we had no other choice. After all, you can leave at any time, you just have to say you've had it. Nobody did. All you think about is *how* to survive. You simply feel that you have no choice.

During those weeks of navigations we felt new social pressures building up. On the surface, everyone was on his own, with his own route to memorize and his own success score. However, we lived in the field, someone had to cook for the team, to wash the dishes. The best navigators, who always arrived first, had more free time and were expected to do all the chores, as well as to help the others study, while those who never had time to help and do chores felt bad.

I was among the best. But our group of good navigators gradually grew, and toward the end of the period we were all real experts.

As the end of the advanced training period approached, we had very complex exercises, including lots of hiking, carrying loads, with frequent changes of orders to break our expectations. Some of these tasks were a week long. In one of them, for example, we suddenly received the message that our team leader had been "killed," and we had to continue on our own. Indeed he left us, and for the next two days we were a leaderless unit.

The last task before graduation was an individual forced march with a complex set of orders to carry out. Mine was a route of 150 km for the week. Every night I had a navigation and a task to perform, all by myself. This was the test of everything we had learned. You had to plan all your time by yourself, including meals and rest periods, as if you were on a mission in enemy territory. All this is based on the credibility I mentioned before, because obviously nobody can check your performance all the time.

I remember that on the third day I was at the bottom of a mountain with a rock formation on its top. I was supposed to leave my note at the top. I remember sitting there, under the mountain, so very tired, asking myself: to climb or not to climb? It was a huge temptation not to. Suddenly I saw another team-member passing by on his route. I left my gear with him at the bottom of the mountain, and ran up while he watched my things.

Well, this wasn't completely legitimate. It was a slight cutting of a corner, you might say. We all cut corners sometimes, in spite of everything.

I didn't continue along the route with this friend. Not only because it was against the rules, but because he was a tall guy who walked much faster than I did, and I didn't want to slow him down. Somehow we all finished. We were given a huge meal at the base, then we had a ceremony with our parents, and we were finally accepted as members of the Unit. That's when we met the battalion commander for the first time, and were briefed about our military functions.

On the whole, we started a new period. But essentially, it was another period of training, although somewhat more specific to our tasks. It was easier from then on, and much more interesting. You see, this kind of training never ends. It is not like in some other infantry units, where you train for eighteen months and you're done. In the Unit, usually you finish your service before you have completed your training . . . Sometimes we were in action, too, during that time. You get the chance to apply some of your training. However, the feeling that you have all the time, which people find hard to understand, is frustration. Because you practice a lot, and you never get the chance to perform even the smallest part of what you have been training for. As a civilian, and a peace-lover, I obviously understand this. But as a soldier who has put so much effort into training, even the most ardent pacifist wants to apply his skills. It's not a political matter. It is a matter of being professional. So, we were frustrated. And this was even more pronounced during the war.

We prepared for the war, it didn't come as a surprise to any of us. During the last two months before it broke out, we were constantly in a high state of alert. The state of waiting is the worst of all. You want to start action just so that you wouldn't have to wait anymore. We had plenty of free time, and we used to argue about the political value of the attack. We knew that it was going to be a large-scale operation, aiming at the Beirut-Damascus road. Nobody believed in the "forty-kilometer-line" which the government declared, or in the limited goal of destruction of the PLO. Our opinions were divided. I was one of those who violently objected to the attack. I felt that the existing situation was far better, and that there was no sense in risking our lives for this operation. On the other hand, as a soldier, I wanted to go to war. I cannot explain this contradiction, but I know that it characterized many of us at the time. I felt split. I knew that I wanted to go to war, while at the same time I considered it an unwise move on our part. However, I am convinced that this state of mind had nothing to do with our actual preparations or performance.

Our team was assigned with a very specific task. All I can tell you is that it was a technical job, something which could be called a 'clean' job.

We were all very tense, naturally. Just nervous, not afraid. We were frustrated because of the waiting. We had many arguments among us then. Some said that it would have been better to be with the regular military forces, participate in any action, rather than wait for the order to carry out what we had been trained for. Of course we had no choice but to obey and wait. One of my team-members simply ran away and joined another unit at the front, a unit to which he had belonged before. We decided not to report him. Several others said they envied him because he had an alternative, while most of us had nowhere to go. Only one guy admitted that he was happy to sit quietly in the base, rather than fight. At that time we thought it was going to be a short war, and would soon be over.

After two-and-a-half hard days of waiting, we were finally taken by helicopter on a mission behind enemy lines. It was not the original plan that we had trained for, but something else for which we were very well prepared. I remember the moment of boarding the helicopter. It felt a relief blended with fear. In no time we had left the quiet of the base to the midst of the fighting. We were under serious shelling as soon as we landed. Our task, however, was performed quickly and perfectly, without any special stress for the team. We felt anxious only when we had to interact with other IDF forces in Lebanon. They seemed to be in a huge mess. Trucks were going back and forth, tanks were stuck everywhere, as if there was no coordination. It was very frustrating to hear them on the radio, or to see from the hills how the battles were conducted.

We had a huge army, you know. But it was so clumsy! It moved only by daylight, and at night sat still, waiting to be hit. We had been educated for a completely different kind of set-up. To work at night, in small units, few against many, with sophistication rather than force. Here we saw a conquering army, big and visible, modelled after the American army perhaps. Where was David and where was Goliath, I kept asking myself. We felt like fools. There were all these elementary things we were trained to do. Work at night, infiltrate the enemy lines, hit specific targets. Trivial things. But we were not allowed to carry them out. The dominant conception was that of the "iron arm"—a big army, with tanks and planes. Let them destroy the whole village, why should we send in a commando unit and risk our soldiers' lives? I can understand this approach, but at that time I objected to it. We felt that the army didn't need us, or our special skills. If I'd range our skills on a 100-point scale, they used only about 5 points of it in Lebanon. I think that the IDF position in combat would have been better, had they used us some more.

After the war, from a more general perspective, I was able to justify the dominant view. I think there is a place for commando units like ours in the IDF even if they use us only once in a thousand years. Just for the slightest chance that we would be needed. But personally, it was tremendously frustrating. What had we trained so hard for? This experience questioned our very existence.

After our mission, we were sent back to our base. I was appointed to be the leader of a younger team. Later on we were sent into Lebanon, during the siege of Beirut. We participated with the other forces in surrounding the city, putting pressure on the PLO forces inside. We didn't have any special mission then. Just like the other forces, we surrounded the enemy inside the city, fired when ordered to, and waited. I felt like a part of a conquering army, ready to take over a city full of people. I was fully aware that the whole thing was immoral and unnecessary.

I remember one night in particular. The PLO had shelled our forces during the day from their positions in Beirut. During the night, I witnessed the retaliation of the IDF. It was something incredible. This was a night which shook me out of my senses. I simply sat at a good observation point and I saw how the city was being blown to pieces. It was a city of many innocent bystanders, not just an enemy post! That night it was bombed over and over again until daybreak. To me it seemed totally out of proportion. As if for every three shells of the PLO they got about three thousand from us. It was horrible.

The truth is that Beirut didn't look like Haifa even before that night. It had suffered several years of battle already. But just the same, that night was my night of disillusionment. My beliefs in the IDF's values, in our "purity of arms,"[1] were demolished together with the city. It was a terrible night for me.

What could I do about it? I sent a letter to my family, and then went on with my routine. I think that I haven't discussed that night with anyone since. I'm quite pleased that I have the chance to talk about it now.

Actually there were other moments when similar feelings were aroused. Once I was at an observation post on a mountain overlooking a Palestinian camp which was considered a stronghold of the PLO. With my binoculars I could follow the combat very clearly. The terrorists were defending their camp, while our tanks advanced and attacked. Tanks against men. Whoever saw this battle could not prevent the association between this event and the battle of Degania.[2] The terrorists had several rifles, a few RPG launchers. Every couple of moments they would retreat a little, while our forces advanced. (He is quiet for a long time.)

Amia: *Did your unit have had any casualties during the war?*

It's strange that I haven't told you about it so far. Well, during the first stage of our participation in the war, our team was divided in two, each doing its own mission. During action, we often asked by radio about the other half of the team, and were told not to worry, that everything was fine. That's another of the rules which I can justify today—if you don't have to, don't circulate bad news on the radio. When we returned to base, however, we saw all these sad faces around us, and that's when we found out that our team had three wounded, one of them seriously. From a group as small as ours, this is a tremendous percentage. I remember that that's when I realized that we had really been in a war. I felt kind of helpless. But they all recovered, and that's the main thing.

Let's return to Beirut. We participated in the occupation of the city, which was pretty fast, with no special events for my unit. Later on, we stayed on and worked with the Christian forces. We were helping other units searching for the vast amounts of weapons and ammunition which the PLO had stored in caches all over the place. Often we had to look in houses, face to face with the population. That's when I realized that Lebanon was actually some kind of a "Wild West." Everyone was against everybody else. Often I met Christians who said to me: "Thank God you have come. But now you must leave as soon as possible." In my conversations with the Christians I felt that they were convinced that our aim in invading Lebanon had been solely to help them out. At the same time I was trying to convince myself that we were doing something that made sense for Israel. Most of the time, I simply felt like the conqueror of a foreign land. That's what we really were. What was the sense of our being there and making a war . . .

That's the dominant feeling I have now, as I tell you about those days. A sense of not knowing why, what for, or what would be the end of all this. We were in a fog. We sensed that it might be the result of disagreement and confusion right at the top, between the government and the military, and all through the various echelons of command. People were speaking half truths, nothing was clear. It was a very complex and dangerous position to be in.

When our tasks in Beirut were completed, we returned to base, trying to resume training and routine activities. It was obvious that if they needed us in Lebanon, we would be recalled. For me, however, the war was over. My team broke up. Some of us became leaders of younger teams, three were recovering from their wounds—we were all dispersed.

I had another year of service to complete. I could go on as a leader of one of the teams, but that would have required signing up for additional time in the army, in addition to the time I had already signed up for. I didn't want that. In Beirut I experienced leadership during combat with my team, and that was enough for me.

In the meantime I had become one of the senior members of the Unit. From time to time I was in charge of the selection of younger recruits. That's when I was able to observe the process from the outside. In fact, I don't know if I would have encouraged any of these young men to continue in the path they had chosen . . . But my main job was a project having to do with the lessons of the recent war, which I cannot talk about. It was pretty interesting, but essentially I was eager to leave the army. I was extremely happy to be out of the system. Two days after my release I was already on an airplane to the farthest possible destination—the Far East.

Notes

1. This phrase refers to the central value in the education of IDF soldiers, see Gal (1986).

2. The first kibbutz in Israel, near the Sea of Galilee, which was attacked by Arab armies in the War of Independence, 1948. It is a famous example of the 'David-and-Goliath' pattern of the Israeli-Arab conflict, with a small, ill-supplied group of Israeli men repulsing the attack of a large armored Syrian force.

8

GIL

Gil often speaks about himself in plural form, especially when he is embarrassed. He also tends to use present tense when describing vivid memories of past events. These stylistic features have sometimes been preserved in the narrative.

I used to be kind of a good boy, you know. I cared about others and about the Scouts, more so than about my school work, for sure. I had many responsibilities in the Scouts. During the summer before I was drafted, I went with the kids to the Scouts' summer camp, to help the young ones. They are my friends to this very day.

At first we thought about joining the Nahal,[1] and we formed a Garin.[2] We used to visit our adopting kibbutz, especially if we could use these visits as an excuse to miss school. But eventually we felt we didn't like the people who joined this Garin. Finally we announced that we were leaving the Garin and going to the regular army.

My initial shock was to find out about my medical profile, which was very low. The truth is I was scared of the service. What frightened me most was the fact that any idiot who might happen to be my commander would have all the power in the world to make me feel miserable. We would be reduced to an I.D. number, living in a barracks somewhere. We were afraid. So I decided to try and get an easy job near my home, so I could come home every evening. I would always be able to transfer further away later on, I thought.

My parents were also worried—they had had bad experiences with my older brother during his service. They knew that people tend to take advantage of a good boy like me. They said that people use their connections to find a good place. I said, however, that I would go wherever I'm sent.

That's how I arrived at the induction base. Luckily I met an old school friend, who also had a low profile. We clung to each other from then on. What a time! The uniforms didn't fit, we were given a sack full of unfamiliar things, we were all so "green," and a dumb guy was ordering us around. On the next day, we were sent to kitchen duty. The sergeant major doesn't talk there, he only yells: "You two come over here and stand at attention in threes!" "But we are just the two of us," I said faintly. "So bring a pot as the third one, right away." What an idiot, I'll never forget him.

We laughed. We didn't let ourselves feel that we were in the army already. After two days, I finally got to see the selection officer. Waiting for my placement, I heard all these stories. "Flight controllers go abroad." "Intelligence is a really interesting job." Would I, too, be lucky? Finally I was called in. "You low-profilers," he says, "you are good for nothing. There are three jobs I can offer you, transportation, maintenance or personnel." I come out completely heartbroken. What is it, I'm a second-rate soldier?! What a shock.

The next day we were taken to basic training for low-profile soldiers. It was just a couple of weeks, I knew it would pass. But I worried about my future. Actually, basic training was not so bad. We had a woman as our sergeant, and this made things easier, I'm sure. But the male commanders were awful. Yelling, yelling all the time. How did I reach such a state, to be yelled at by an idiot?

One evening, they asked for volunteers to patrol an Arab village nearby. Good soldiers that we were, we volunteered, and worked all night. We arrived back at the base exhausted, in time for morning inspection, and had to be ready like anyone else. After all our good work! We felt like two beaten dogs. So why volunteer?

A few days later, the sergeant came in and asked: "Who has a driver's license?" I was smarter by then, and I didn't budge. Two guys jumped up. "Well, you do kitchen duty today." How happy we were that we sat still! We had learned our first lesson.

I remember how every simple soldier could harass us, the trainees. Once I was doing guard duty at the armory. A soldier passed by and said to me: "You were sleeping. Tomorrow you will be court-martialed." I hadn't slept, yet how could I prove it? I was so scared. I felt so small, helpless. But nothing happened after all.

What helped me through basic training was my buddy. At night, our bunks were one above the other, and all day we were inseparable. However, the moment basic training was over, we each went our own way and we lost track of one another.

On the last day of basic training, people were sent to their various destinations. Men came from the Air Force and called out names. All their people were given an insignia and went off on a bus. Then Navy officers came for their men. So good-looking in their white uniforms. Only we were left standing. Nobody wanted us. We felt so small, waiting. At last we were taken back to the induction base. We felt miserable.

Rumors were that nobody paid attention to our wishes or priorities. We just stood there and waited for our names to be called. Four hours later we were told—Maintenance. We went home for an overnight furlough, trying to find some channel of information—what is maintenance all about? But quartermasters are such low quality people, who knows any of them?

We were sent to our barracks—about twenty men in a long room, all depressed. Nobody wanted to be there in the first place, and as the course started, we liked it even less. They had tough discipline there. Marching us in triplets to mess and to classes, lecturing to us all day like in elementary school. Some of the trainees asked to transfer. Others knew already that there was no chance of transfering. So you might as well do your best so that you would get a good job afterwards. We were not trying too hard, but we were not among the rebels either.

On the first Saturday of the course we were given security duty, to patrol on the beach. How important we felt in our uniforms, patrolling. So we are needed, after all. We are protecting the people. But back at the base it was as bad as before.

On the first leave I got, I went to the Scouts. All the girls surrounded me: "Well, Gil, what are you doing in the army?"—"I'm in this course somewhere," I tried to bluff. "What course?" they insisted. I could not utter "maintenance," it was too low. "I'll be a noncommissioned officer, you know, dealing with accounting." I talked rapidly, cheating my closest friends. I could not admit that I had failed in the army. (Quiet for some time.) It was tough.

On our next leave, my father said that he had found an acquaintance in Maintenance, and that he had promised to get me a good job. Close to home, my father said. I didn't object. On the last day of the course, I was sent to a military fuel base not far from Tel Aviv. I guess our contacts did it, since most of the trainees were sent off far away to the north. Well, I figured that fuel is an important commodity, it's not just a store. On Friday I went to the Scouts feeling a little better. "I'm going to this place that provides fuel for all military operations," I bragged. It sounded important enough.

On Sunday I took a bus down to the base. Millions of tankers and a few long barracks in between. A secretary said to me: "Oh, you're the new soldier. Go and wait for the officer." I sat near his office from 10 to 3, and then she took me to see the commander of the base. I entered, saluted, and saw a fatherly man of about 50, smiling. For the first time I felt good in the army. He asked me all sort of questions, and ended up by telling me that I would work as a quartermaster. "But I'm trained for records handling," I said. "Just the same," he answered, "it's all the same job anyway."

Well, he saw that I was hurt and added that I'd have a nice sergeant for a boss, I would drive these tankers and have fun, and go home every evening. "In the meantime," he finished, "I am giving you a week furlough. Go home and relax."

This really made me feel better. My first real furlough so soon! I felt like an old-timer while some of my friends had not even started their service. I went to the beach, barefoot in the sand—forgetting about those military boots that I hate. A movie every day—vacation.

A week later I was back there. I remember the first time I saw the store from inside. It looked so huge. Full of uniforms, machine parts, pots and pans, and all these small items—badges, insignia. I looked gingerly, peeking into the boxes. The sergeant explained to me that I should be careful here. "There are many criminal types on the base, and they will try to bully you and get what they want. Only the girls, and men from the regular army, are okay," he explains. Slowly he showed me around and explained my duties. And at 5:00 I went home.

After a few days, I was given some rifle practice and night guard duty. That's when I started to understand that night guard duty is the burden of this base. You get your turn once or twice a week. The next day you're really tired, but you have to work just the same. The base has many soldiers, but only about 10 of us were what you'd call "normal." The others were "criminals," and nobody could tell them what to do. They did not do guard duty, they didn't cut their hair, they hardly worked. But some of them were our drivers, and in order to deal with them we had to establish relations with the transportation officer. Contacts are the key to everything.

That's how my story really begins. Coffee—especially instant coffee—was a very important commodity on the base. We created a whole "mafia" of coffee distribution. I would cheat a little in my records and give coffee to the transportation officer, so that he would help me and assign me some of the more decent drivers. Every Sunday, as I drove to the central supply post, I wheedled our supplier into giving me an extra box of instant coffee, which I packed in small packages and handed around as gifts. Coffee for contacts, and sugar, too. (smiling) Everything ran smoothly. My records were fine and no harm was done.

Eventually my boss, and even the commander of the base, realized what was happening. I was called in to explain. I told them how we had to deal with these "criminals" every day. They refuse to do guard duty. We have problems with crazy cooks, mad drivers, and our lives depend on them. So one manages, this is our defense, and no harm is done. We promised the officers that there would be no complications, we just dealt with small traffic—coffee and sugar, nothing else.

From then on we were in the open. Suddenly, drivers smiled to us, the cook baked a cake for tea and the whole atmosphere had changed. Give and take. We found our way in the system. I call it survival.

But not everything could be fixed, you know. I had my moments of panic. I was on the roads with these drivers all day long. One of them used to stop for an hour a day for a private lesson in bus driving, while I sat there and waited for him in the truck. These were moments of tremendous conflict. You are not supposed to squeal, because that would be the end of any working relationship you had built with these people. If you were caught, however, you would pay the price. Sometimes I had to cheat my superiors in order to cover for such men. I hated it. It was scary. But you live by the second, not even by the minute. Once the incident is safely over, we forgot all about it and went on to the next.

After half a year on the fuel base I was sent to go for screening tests for officers' training. Going to officers' training course would have meant signing up for another year in the army. That seemed a very unlikely thing for me to do then. But going to the tests gave me a day of leave, so I went. And I told everybody that whatever the results, I wouldn't be going to the course anyway.

In the meantime it was spring, and the Syrians started their threats from the north, like every year. Tension built up and none of my buddies from the combat units came home on leave, while I used to come home almost every evening. Friday at the Scouts, it was only me and the girls. I started to feel bad. I had found an easy job in the army, but I know I could do more. Keeping store with mad drivers, a small coffee business, sleeping every night at home—is this what I would do for two more years? On the other hand, I had received my orders for the officers' training course. Maybe I should go. Would that be a way to change direction?

The first time I mentioned it at the Scouts, all the girls started screaming around me: "Go, go, how wonderful for you!" I couldn't retreat any more. I was the first of all our group of friends to be summoned for officers' training. I felt how the social pressure built up. You are the first and you have to make it.

Down at the fuel base, they didn't want me to go. I was doing a good job there, you know. My parents—this was funny. My father said: "Why don't you try?" But I knew he didn't believe I could pass. My mother was hysterical: "Don't go. Why do you want to serve an extra year in the army? We'll buy you a car to drive to your base every day, just stay there."

Maintenance Corps organized a prep course for us. Physically I was in awful shape, and it was very hard for me. Night navigations—really, that's not for me. But nobody was going to flunk me from the prep course. And what would I tell my friends at the Scouts if I dropped out? This became my motto for the next few months of hard work.

We started in the middle of the summer. Right at the beginning I was separated from my buddies from the prep course. It was hard. For the first time I felt like a real soldier, not a "chocolate" one. We had to prepare emergency gear, wear a helmet—all this was completely new for me. We had two forced marches during the first week, and lessons about different firearms. I put my mind to it, as I never did before. I studied at night and prepared my gear. The secretary from Maintenance came for a visit with goodies. "Just work hard and don't fail," she said.

We were in the field all the next week, running in circles around the only tree in this desert. I had never lived outdoors like this before. Sleeping in a tiny tent, a storm blowing dust and sand all day long. We constantly had to clean our rifles. No showers. No going home Saturday. It was hard.

We were treated fairly, though, and I met many good guys, and this helped. And the joy of a parcel from your mother, in the midst of it all!

The hikes were really difficult for me, but I struggled and completed each one. I remember the happiness at the end of a march, when the lights of the base could finally be seen in the distance. It was as if you had surpassed yourself. The motto was to work. Not to flunk. Failing would be such shame.

I wasn't used to staying in the army over the weekend, as "normal" soldiers often do. The first time I did, in the course, it was a crisis. "Friday night, everybody is in the Scouts, and I am in the middle of nowhere." I called my friends on the phone, and it helped. "Take care," they said. "Next weekend we'll come down and visit you." Like a breath of fresh air, energy for another week. So, I made it without a leave for the first three long weeks.

We had difficulties with our girlfriends in town, who were used to us coming home every night. And now, for more than six months we saw them only once every couple of weeks. Gradually, it broke up our relationships. Toward the end of the period, none of the cadets in my unit had a girlfriend in town. But for me, my original group of friends from the Scouts proved to be a source of unending support. They sent me letters and packages, they prepared tickets for shows for me during my furloughs, they gave me a wonderful feeling all along. On my worst days when I wanted to quit I used to imagine their package returning to them with a note: "This cadet has been removed from the course." No, this would not happen to me.

Today I often wonder how I did it. Digging trenches all night without complaint. Working hard with almost no sleep. Learning to be precise and accurate in my reports. Never cheating, never taking a shortcut. I think that I made it due to the trust of my buddies in town.

I remember the week in which I was the cadet-on-duty. All week long I felt under scrutiny by my superiors, and I made tremendous efforts. This week demonstrated for me what it means to be an officer in the IDF. Everybody looks up to you and you have to be the best soldier in the unit in all respects. You mustn't fail or make a mistake. You mustn't discriminate among your men. You have to be trustworthy to the end.

It was both discipline and self-discipline, you see. You do as you're ordered to do, because those are the orders, even if they seem completely wrong at the moment. At the same time there was a tremendous amount of self-discipline involved. We used to check each other's rifles. Total credibility was what we were taught. For me, it was simply an education.

The lesson of the course remained with me all through my service. It really changed me. A year later, for instance, I served as an officer during an extremely difficult winter. I was freezing, but I was the last one to take a snowsuit or a heater for my room. It was important for me to set an example for the soldiers, you see. I would be the last one to go home on Friday, and the earliest to return on Sunday. My uniform and haircut were always perfect. It was a matter of responsibility and self-discipline, that's all.

Anyway, we passed the course. At the graduation ceremony my parents attended, and so did my friends. We received our officers' insignia and were proud to wear them. My only regret was that my girlfriend had left me towards the end. For my first job as an officer, I was sent to the Nahal and was pleased with that, of course.

On Sunday I arrived at the Nahal Command for my orders. It was winter already, very cold. Somebody yells: "Here comes the new officer." I blushed. I am "green" again. The Nahal Chief Officer of Maintenance explained that I would be sent to a new battalion that had just been formed, a string of outposts in the Judean mountains. They didn't have their complete staff yet, and he advised me to join them right away. I was supposed to receive a week-long furlough, but I was willing to start whenever I was needed. That meant immediately.

I met the Services Company Commander, a redhead who was my immediate superior. He told me to take his car and driver, go home, and bring all my things. We would be leaving for the battalion headquarters in the evening. I remember that moment: For the first time I receive a private military car as an officer. The driver looked up at me, and asked me to sign his work-chart. I'm a big boy now. I signed, as if I were used to it.

At home I quickly packed all my winter gear, gloves, warm underpants, whatever. My mother fussed around me: "Why aren't you getting your leave? Where will you be posted? Oh, it's too far. When will you come home? Do you have a phone there?" She was in panic, in tears.

At night we drove out of the city, passing Jerusalem and starting our climb up into the dark mountains. At the new headquarters, I stepped out from the car right into a mud puddle, but inside I was greeted by the smiling face of our (female) secretary, and a kindly sergeant. We sat drinking coffee, and I let them tell me all about this new battalion till 2 a.m. I suddenly realized that I don't understand anything about my new job. With all my studies and courses, their talk was Chinese to me. What did I know about the Nahal!? Only that I once dreamed of serving there. All my memories came back.

I spent the first night in a sleeping bag on the concrete floor. It was freezing and I couldn't sleep. All that excitement.

For three days I watched and learned. How to order food, fuel, and equipment. How to send mail to our various settlements. Who works for whom. Where the stores are. They were very full days, and at night we drove to visit the outposts. I remember those drives on the muddy mountain roads. Most of the time I dozed off. Suddenly I woke up to see a few lights, a sleepy soldier at the gate. "How are you doing? Do you need any supplies?" "No, we're fine, but it's just too cold." I went to bed at 4 a.m. every night. Three hours later, my day started all over again. It took some time to adjust. For the first two weeks I felt completely in a haze most of the time. When the battalion commander inquired, I told him: "We're building the store for the battalion." (Laughing)

Gradually I started to understand what was going on. I was working together with my soldiers. After two weeks, when my turn came to go home, I asked to stay in the battalion. I took the jeep and went to visit all the outposts in the daytime, at my leisure. I started to recognize faces, some names, and everything began to take shape.

We were building the battalion then. We had to allocate a lot of supplies and equipment. Actually, the army has standard procedures for all these things. What should go into the kitchen of an outpost, or how to furnish a social club. But a lot was up to me. Some outposts were functioning well, and had well-organized stores, so I gave them more things. I gave out games for the clubs, and stoves for the kitchens, and I had my demands as well—to take care of the equipment and maintain proper records. I know that in the Nahal they have frequent inspections of the stores, and I am in charge, after all.

One of the outstanding things in those first weeks was to be working with so many women, both in the outposts and at headquarters. It's impossible to work around women without a smile, you know. The male officers knew my reaction, and would send their secretaries to me. Go bring such-and-such from the Maintenance officer.

I was sort of a "good guy" for the men, too. When I found something missing in the records of an outpost, I wouldn't run off to the commander to complain. I told the men to look for the missing winter coats, or whatever, and I'd come and check again later. We maintained good relationships, and the stores had accurate records too.

They were unable to fill all the officers' positions in the battalion, and gradually I received more and more responsibilities. I was in charge of all the drivers and cooks, and of all maintenance in our outposts. I had to solve problems from a leaking sewer to low morale among my men. But we all worked hard. The most urgent problems had to do with the rough winter we were having up in those mountains. Outposts were snowed in, they needed fuel for their heaters and the road was out, the food truck could not get through, or they had no supplies for the social event they had planned for their Friday night. Suddenly I became an expert about all of that. I was on call twenty-four hours a day, and was known to be able to solve all sorts of problems. That was my job.

As my reward, I got compliments from my commander. "That's how things should run," he said, and that's all I needed to hear. Another reward was our social life at headquarters. We formed a nice group there, and at night someone would play the guitar, we'd sing together—we had a good time.

Often I drove around on inspections, counting the stocks. Once I saw a new road being paved in the hills. I asked the Arab workers, and found out that a new outpost was planned. It was the government's decision evidently, an additional outpost for my battalion. Over the next weeks I could see how the landscape was transformed, the rocks were moved away, and lots were prepared for construction. The architects arrived: Here we'll build the dining hall, and here the women's showers. These will be the bedrooms. I had to drive all the way down south to Eilat to bring prefabricated houses for the outpost. So much responsibility! But I felt great. Driving the commander's jeep around on my own, showing the crane the proper place for the new houses—I felt that I was building a settlement in the historical land of Israel. The commander calls me to ask about our progress, and I told him: "We're making history." That's how I felt.

My "business" in the battalion was much bigger than my former "coffee business" in the fuel base. A kerosene heater fell and we had a fire in one of our outposts, and had to replace everything that had been burned. I would drive around to central supplies, begging and threatening for things—a daily struggle for survival.

After about six months on the job, two things happened at once. The Lebanon War broke out, and I had to organize a rotation of the forces. In the Nahal, you know, everybody is transferred once every six months. The men leave their kibbutzim or outposts for military duty, and vice versa.

This is a terrible headache for Maintenance. The stocks have to be counted, and all supplies, firearms, etc. have to be accounted for and prepared for the new soldiers. This is a project that requires all your energy for a couple of weeks, and all the help you can get. Especially when you go through these motions for the first time.

I was in the middle of organizing the rotation, and staying over for the weekend, when the war broke out. I was the only officer there, and we were having a festive Sabbath dinner when I was called to the field telephone, and given the news. I had to recall all the officers and men who were on leave, and start preparations for the transfer to the north. I returned to the table, told the men to continue their dinner, and asked the two secretaries to accompany me to the office. Together we started the whole process going. All the officers were brought back, buses were sent for the men, and we started to prepare the emergency supplies. By noon the next day all the men were back, and I left with the Services Commander to take care of the logistics for our move. For more than two days I was constantly on my feet.

But we were not ordered to move. After two days we were already impatient. "When will we join the battle?" we kept asking the commander. The other Nahal battalions were at the front, but we were kept waiting. The combat soldiers in the outposts, men who had trained for this war, were terribly upset. They wanted to participate. So did I. To be with everybody else. Only the Services Commander, who had fought in the battle of 1973, said to me quietly: "But you are so stupid! Don't you know what war is like? Thank God you are sitting here."

The battalion commander was often at his radio, and he would call the officers in for briefings. On the third day of combat he informed us that the squad-leader training course had been transferred to Lebanon, and had many casualties. I started to worry about my friends. I felt a restlessness that I couldn't let my men see. They shouldn't feel my anxiety. I was a very young officer, remember, and I felt that this was another test of my leadership. Inside, however, I was quite scared.

You know, at times like this everybody wants to pitch in. If we had to load a truck, they all wanted to help. At night we would crowd around the only TV and watch the news together. All my buddies from the Scouts were in Lebanon, they were all combat soldiers. So all the first week we were worried and frustrated, but we had not been ordered to move.

When the war was over, the Nahal went through some kind of reorganization and several of our officers were transferred to other positions. Our battalion received a new Services Commander—my immediate superior—a man I did not like right from the start. I wanted to ask for a transfer too, but I thought that this would ruin all our achievements in the battalion, and decided to stay for a while. My new superior, however, gave me lots of trouble. He limited my responsibilities, and maintained extremely formal relations with me. I became very tense, and I felt that I had no support from above. It was a bad period. I started to take less initiative and do only what I was directly ordered to do. Everybody knew what was going on.

Two months later, a new Chief Officer of Maintenance was appointed for the Nahal, and all the officers were invited for interviews to meet him. For some reason, we liked each other at first sight. I told him I didn't like my present situation, and he promised that he'd see what he could do. "In the meantime hold on," he said, "since you are the only man around who knows what he's doing there." I felt flattered. Two weeks later, he came to inspect my battalion and gave me a perfect evaluation. "This is one of the best organized battalions I have visited," he said in front of all the officers. It made me happy, of course.

For a while things were better. I managed to ignore my immediate commander, all the remaining staff worked well together, and the battalion was doing better all the time. I remember my second rotation. It was so much easier this time, I was prepared from the first round. This is when I started to feel that I really understood the military system. Personal problems, power struggles between officers, as well as the mentality of drivers and cooks—and their wives—it all fell into place for me. Often I thought: I'm just 19 or 20, but I see the world with the wisdom of an adult.

A few weeks later I received my own transfer orders. I was to become a Services Commander in a basic training base of the Nahal. I was shocked. Who? Me? I'm too young for that. How will I manage such responsibility? But I knew that I had the full backing of the Chief Officer. Indeed, one of his assistants sat me down and practically dictated to me my first steps in the new position. "Don't worry," said the Chief Officer. "You go there tomorrow, and the next day I'll be there to visit you."

We drove down to this new camp. All the soldiers were there to greet me. "I'm the driver." "I'm the barber." "I'm in charge of the mail." Many nice female secretaries seemed pleased to have a young officer around.

Throughout the first day I talked to people and made lists of all their needs. I found out that they were in very bad shape there. Next day, the Chief Officer of Maintenance was coming for his visit. The commander realized that it was because of me—nobody had visited the base for the last four months. We sat together, I brought in my lists, and the Chief Maintenance Officer agreed to almost all my requests. Even new cars would arrive in two months. The local commander was deeply impressed.

In a week our supplies began arriving. We had enough utensils for the mess hall, and we all ate in one shift. The offices were re-equipped, everybody felt the changes. In the meantime I started to take care of the men's personal problems, too. Gradually we rehabilitated the services. A few months later we had an inspection for which I worked like a mule, together with all my men. For the first time I conducted my own inspection of the men, we cleaned and shined the whole place, and our evaluation was 94 (out of 100)—a terrific achievement.

After some time, though, I had the feeling that people had gotten used to the good life, and my accomplishments were not appreciated as much as before. My work lost its challenge for me, it was just routine and I had too much time on my hands. Again I was ready to move on and to grow.

I asked for a transfer, and this time I received a new placement within a week. I was appointed as Services Commander in a Nahal outpost battalion near the Jordan River. Again there was the phase of entering a new network, a new system. I was happy to drive the next day and visit the outposts. This was the army I liked best, and I was familiar with it through and through.

This was a battalion whose outposts were spread out over tremendous distances. Just running the transportation there was like managing an Avis branch in a city. Cars often broke down, the officers didn't like to worry about costs and budget limitations, and I had to bring some kind of order into this chaos. In addition, I was responsible for many men, had to supply all the equipment for our military training, had to supervise the kitchens and mess halls, to solve sanitary problems in the outposts, to see to the special needs of female soldiers, to deal with the marketing of our agricultural products—such a variety of things. I cooperated with the other officers, of course, but gradually I acquired more and more responsibilities. Informally, I knew I was second to the battalion commander in my power.

My inspections in this battalion were as good as in the former ones. Once, after the inspection, I overheard the superior officers talking about me. "Where did you get this energetic young officer?" somebody asked. And the Chief Officer of Maintenance bragged: "This is a kid who grows straight up. He does not look towards his home, he is all here. You'll hear about him in the future, you'll see." Of course I was proud. When asked about my personal requests, my rewards, you might say, after the successful inspection, I asked that two of my men be sent to a military drivers' course, so that they'd have some skills when they were released from the service. I never asked anything for myself.

It was sometimes frightening to have all this responsibility, you know. One Friday night, when I remained as officer-on-duty, I received a message on the radio that one of my trucks had been involved in a traffic accident. I hurried to the spot and arrived just as the two injured soldiers were being taken to the hospital. The truck had overturned. Luckily, my men were not wounded too seriously. But I was sitting there in a daze for a while. I had sent these men. What if I had sent them in an open command-car? Suppose they had been killed in the accident? I had many nightmares about that accident.

When the end of my term approached, people started to put pressure on me to sign up for the regular army for an additional period. I said: No. The Chief Officer of Maintenance was truly disappointed. He wanted me to make a career out of it, or at least to remain for a couple more years. But I had had enough. I felt how my behavior, my language, were being influenced by the low-level people who surrounded me. My friends who were not officers had been released long before, were making progress at the university, while I spent my days talking to truck drivers. Enough is enough.

On my last Saturday, I stayed in the battalion, and so did most of the staff and all my men. They gave me a great party, cooked a special dinner, made me feel wonderful indeed. This was my reward. When you apply yourself to the maximum and cope with all the difficulties and then people appreciate you for what you've done—what more can you expect?

It was sad to depart. I had given everything to this battalion, and I had received everything in return. I had such power there! I felt how I became, abruptly, just one more young civilian in town. But this feeling vanished ten days later. I had new challenges before me.

Notes

1. Literally, Fighting Pioneer Youth. The Nahal is part of the IDF. The three year army service in the Nahal normally consists of cycles of six months in a kibbutz, and six months in active military duty. There is usually one particular kibbutz that the unit is attached to (the adopting kibbutz), and it is presumed that most members will settle there after their release from the army. One of the early six-month periods is usually spent in a military agricultural outpost in border areas.

2. Literally, kernel, this means a group of youths who plan to serve together in the Nahal, and settle in a kibbutz.

PART II

Routes and Issues
—— *of* ——
Psychological Development

9

COURSES OF MILITARY SERVICE DURING PEACETIME

At first glance, it seemed that each young man had experienced the military service in his own unique way. In spite of some objective commonalities, the pattern of changes in mood, self-esteem, attitudes and coping mechanisms seemed to vary from one case to another. These were determined by the complex interaction of a great variety of external conditions with the pre-military personality of each man and his own particular expectations regarding military service. On this level of discussion, one may do best by leaving the narrative accounts without any analysis or by dealing only with generalizations *within* a person.

When many of the individually characteristic details are ignored, however, one may reach more general conclusions, and suggest a universal pattern which outlines the course of development for the majority of our cases during military service. This will be attempted in the first section of this chapter. In the second section, the outlined processes and experiences will be discussed in the context of previous literature in the field.

The General Course of Military Service

One of the clearest impressions gained from the wealth of our material is that while all the men described their military service as a difficult time in their lives, the great majority of them summarized it as mostly positive and worthwhile. On the basis of general stress theory (Selye, 1956; Janis, 1958; Lazarus, 1966) we could expect a three-stage adaptation process. First, there would be a crisis or a shock due to the initial encounter with the new demands and the stressful situation. This would be followed by physical and mental attempts to adapt, and the beginning of a stage of relative well-being due to the massive activation of the individual's coping mechanisms. Later, however, we might expect the appearance of strain due to fatigue, exhaustion, burnout or the decline of motivation toward the end of the service. Let us examine how this general scheme was expressed in the personal accounts of the participants.

The Initial Stage

A general pattern can be seen as beginning in high school. Almost all the men who participated in the research told me that they were deeply affected by the Israeli norms of heroism and voluntarism,[1] and as a result hoped to serve in combat units during their military service. These men, who had finished high school at the beginning of the 1980s, saw it as their primary obligation—as well as their right—to defend the country by doing their best within the IDF. They had known that such service involved many difficulties, both psychological and physical, but they stated afterwards that nobody could realize the enormity of these difficulties without having experienced them. Easier military roles, the clerk or the quartermaster, were scorned and avoided by most of the participants. When I asked them directly, they all claimed that in their decision to become combat soldiers they had not taken into account the fact that by doing so they might be endangering their lives. Their decisions were generally felt by the interviewees to concur with their parents' expectations. Said one of the participants:[2] "In high school I felt this pressure building up. You have to volunteer for one of the elite units, to be a combat soldier, this is the actualization of all you have been educated for. I received the same message from my parents, although they had never said so quite so openly. Nobody discussed the risks involved, they were just taken as a natural part of volunteering. It was all so very clear then . . . "

This trend was especially pronounced within a subgroup of young men who volunteered for special elite units, and planned to become Air Force pilots or commando soldiers. Since these units are highly selective, many of these young men were rejected from them, and as a result experienced a deep sense of disappointment.

Thus, for most of the participants, disappointment and frustration characterized the first phase of military service. For some, this was because they did not receive the placement they had hoped for. Most of the participants had wanted to serve in more combatant roles than the ones to which they were finally assigned. A few, however, experienced the opposite disappointment—they had hoped to receive desk jobs near their homes, but instead were sent to the field.

But placement was not the only, or even the major, cause for discontent. Once at the induction base, or in basic training, most soldiers experienced disappointment with their commanders' attitudes toward them and with the type of assignments they received. Most of them reported a scornful, if not humiliating, attitude on the part of their leaders. They complained about cleaning and mess duties, and about collective and unjust punishments, which very soon cooled off their enthusiasm for the military service. Although the age difference between soldiers and their commanders in the IDF is likely to be no more than a year (Schild, 1973; Gal, 1986), recruits had to adjust to the fact that a new soldier was treated like a creature without intelligence, and had no rights *vis-a-vis* his superiors. Many discovered that their daily routine was highly unpredictable with uncertainty as the only constant. Finally, tremendous physical demands were made of them, for which most soldiers were unprepared. "I knew it would be hard, but I couldn't imagine how hard," was a sentence often repeated in the interviews.

Many men who had come with highly positive intentions discovered in their first days that these intentions did not guarantee any better treatment by their superiors. Volunteers to the elite units found, once they started their training, that their act of volunteering was irrelevant. A positive encounter with a helpful commander of any rank was almost entirely missing from the participants' accounts. The recruits' frustration was only slightly modified by their understanding that these are the "rules of the game" in the military, and are not personally directed against them. When Ido describes the various selections through which he passed in his attempt to be accepted to a commando unit, he still feels the pain of the dehumanizing experience, which was especially salient against the background of the recent separation from a warm family and a permissive high school. Another man succinctly describes the same feeling during his basic training: "We had this platoon rap session and I said to our leaders: 'Look, we came here highly motivated, why break us down? You could use what we have— why destroy it?' My leaders said that I was weird."

For all these reasons—and many more—the first stages of the military service, especially during induction and basic training, were described by most as periods of crisis. Tremendous efforts have to be made by the young soldiers during these stages in their attempts to adjust and cope with the new situation.

Initiation to the military service was especially difficult for the small group of young men who came to the army with a relatively negative attitude, or whose personality was highly unsuited for the military. These were the minority in our sample, and their course of service was demonstrated in the detailed story of Yochanan, presented in Part I. His story provided an example of the extreme conflicts between an individual and the establishment which, in a compulsory system, may easily develop.

Adaptation

Following the initial period of conflict, disappointment and the shattering of expectations, the next period of the general pattern may be characterized as an adjustment to the demand. This is a stage that lasts for about a year, and brings many of the soldiers to the middle of their service. For most of the men it is a stage of finding one's place and deriving some satisfaction, varying from high morale and pride in one's service to a more moderate sense of coping with hardship. This is, naturally, not constant across times and places. For a minority of the participants, this period was characterized as a continuation of the struggle and the frustration described above. The middle of the three-year service was, for most of the men, a significant date ("turning over the record" in their words) which coincided with their sense of regaining control over their lives and finally understanding the military system.

The successful adjustment made by the majority of the participants may be attributed to the fact that these comprised a relatively select group (see the description of the sample in the Introduction), to the military selection and socialization processes, and to the healthy tendency of individuals to adjust to their circumstances. Several mental mechanisms were mentioned by the interviewed men in their description of their adaptation process. These included their awareness of the national importance of their mission, the support of and identification with the role of the IDF which they had sensed in their family and friends, their knowledge that everybody serves in the IDF and that this situation is time-limited, and their gradual acceptance of the "rules of the game" as justified by military, educational, and organizational considerations.

One of the major sources of support in this process, especially for the combat soldiers, is the tight "buddy system" which develops within the units, especially in the Infantry. As has been long known by social scientists who investigate the military,[3] the army becomes worthwhile for the sake of your friends in the unit. As explained by Eitan: "At this stage you become very close to others in the unit. You have more time to sit and chat. You know them better and you love them more. This is the famous love between soldiers which is as much of a mystery as love for women." Second in their importance as sources of support are members of the family and former friends at home. It has been the policy of the IDF to allow and encourage the maintenance of a close relationships with the home during service (Schild, 1973), and lately even to engage parents in the difficult training stages of their sons (Gal, 1986). Soldiers visit their families frequently, and report that these leaves at home are tremendously helpful to their adjustment and well-being. Significant commanders can also contribute to the adaptation to the military, although they were mentioned less frequently than were friends or family.

In addition to these mental mechanisms, training during the first year gradually builds the men's physical fitness and stamina. All the men described the immense difficulties of the first forced marches, carrying a stretcher or other heavy loads, running long distances—and the sense of improved fitness as a result of training. They later looked back at their initial difficulties with amazement. It is obviously possible to train people to be faster, to sleep less, and to surpass their former levels of achievement in many areas. Tolerance of pain and hardship is acquired by repeated practice and through the personal examples of leaders and peers. Among the learned skills, however, are also social survival habits which sometimes include cheating and the evasion of responsibility, violence and intimidation, stealing and generally taking advantage of others. Although many of the participants described their reservations about using these means (*e.g.,* you don't steal from others in your unit) or expressed their disgust regarding them, they often admitted using them, "like everybody else."[4]

For several of the men, the process of adaptation included changes in their real environment, *i.e.,* they managed to transfer to a better job, or to achieve an improvement in the definition of their roles. One of the men went repeatedly for medical examinations and was given an easier job, more suitable to his physical condition. Starting from the infantry, he transfered to become an NCO of personnel, a job in which he found a great deal of satisfaction and challenge, despite its low prestige. In his account he describes his service as consisting of a bad half and a good half. In the first half he tried to adjust to the circumstances which, due to his high-school expectations, he had chosen wrongly, while in the second, he made more mature and realistic decisions which changed his lot. "In the first half," he says, "it was always the situation of 'them' against 'me.' From the middle of my service onwards this distinction was gone. I myself had become a part of the army."

Similar drastic changes in placement or role appeared as part of the adaptation process of several other soldiers too, such as Yochanan, who applied much pressure to become a combat medic, a role in which he expected to find an opportunity for contribution, challenge and prestige.

Another course of adjustment common to several of the men involves the transition from the status of a trainee to that of a leader. Most soldiers complained about their low status in the first part of their service. which implied also more turns in the mess hall, kitchen, and guard duty. As time passed, they were no longer the youngest in their units, and their standing consequently improved. They were less restricted and had more individual freedom. This process of change was gradual for some of the men, but abrupt for others. One of the interviewed paratroopers talked about his 14 months of training as "a grey period. It was always so hard to come back to camp after Saturday at home. I hated it." However, at the end of this training, when he himself became a squad leader, "everything changes. You start to love the army. You like your work and your trainees. Suddenly the hateful feeling of Sunday morning has almost disappeared." This change of attitude was typical of many others as well.

Seniority

As they moved to more senior positions in their units, many men became commanders or officers. While a few of the men entered almost naturally into the traditional role of leaders in the army, many others described their aspirations toward developing a different model of leadership in their relationship with their men. They shared a fantasy of the ideal leader, who was often unlike the real leaders they had encountered in the past. They hoped to achieve a high level of performance and discipline from their men without using the old methods of distance and punishment. Rather, they believed in a more democratic leadership, based on mutual trust and understanding. Some of them scorned the "trivial details" of cleaning or their appearance, and wanted to dedicate their attention to the "major" military tasks instead. With these dreams, they started their careers as commanders and junior officers, and often discovered that their brave new models did not work in reality. Eitan discovered that his soldiers took him seriously only when he applied punishment. Some officers were deeply insulted when they discovered that their trust in their trainees was unwarranted. Gradually they understood the shortcomings of the liberal model, and became more tough and distant from their men.

This is, for example, the lesson derived by one of the participants (who had served in the Armored Corps) after trying a more liberal style of leadership:

"I decided that I didn't want to become the strict leader, standing above the men and ordering them around. I decided to act cooperatively with them. They knew I was an expert on tanks, much more so than any of them, so I assumed that all the mannerisms of distancing or leadership games were superfluous. Furthermore, I made my priorities very clear, putting all the pressure on security and maximal functioning of the tank, and much less on cleanliness, etc. I didn't give in on any detail as long as I could explain its logical necessity for the maintenance of the perfect operation of the tank. I relied on my unit to understand this. Well, one night I did decide to surprise my team in the tank, and discovered a catastrophe. Real negligence. It seemed that my trust didn't mean a thing to the men. They worked according to a different formula—since I hadn't visited the tank for the last ten nights, why should I be doing it tonight? So, after being extremely fair toward my men, I received, in return, a slap in the face. This made me rethink the whole approach. First I punished my men severely—I never imagined previously that I'd be in that position. But I remember this episode as one of the most formative moments of my military service. I understood how a compulsory, strict system, which never stops controlling the individual soldier from the outside, actually prevents the development of a responsible individual. The ideas of trust and responsibility become meaningless in a system built on punishment, discipline and continuous external control.''

Generally, the second half of service was described by most of the men as less stormy and disturbing than was the first one. This would have been even more so, had the Lebanon War not become a major event in the second half of the service of most of the men. Since we will discuss the impact of the war in a separate chapter, we will concentrate here on several crises which appear repeatedly in the men's accounts about the latter part of their service. One of these involves friction with superiors, which may lead to immense tension and difficulty in the performance of daily tasks.

Another source of late crisis is related to overload. Many of the combat soldiers suffered some kind of injury—back and knee problems, for example—as a result of the ongoing efforts of their duties and training. For some, the overload was mental as well. This, for example, was the case for one of the soldiers, who did intelligence work under the command of a highly demanding and perfectionistic officer. For long months he did not complain about his overload. ''A person himself is often unaware of his limits, and if he is faced with a perfectionist, he may go to the end of his rope. You see, I often went out on missions, 30-40 hours without sleep, and upon our return, I'd be exhausted. This fatigue accumulated, but I never said 'no' to my commander. Until I had a breakdown—I came down with fever for weeks, and I understood it was a stress reaction, nothing else.'' As a consequence, his job was redefined and he was able to go on successfully with his work.

The social network of friends is one of the important sources of support during military service. As the years go by, several of the men described problems related to this important network. For several of them, old high-school friendships, which had supported them through the earlier phases, did not stand the strain of distance and infrequent meetings. Girlfriends, who expected to see their boyfriends more often, looked for other relationships instead. The men who were in combat units at distant camps—and probably in greatest need of support—suffered most from the breaking up of former relationships. While all the participants reported that the buddy relationship within units is tremendously important for military functions, these could not always replace the social network at home, which was most important for the soldier on leave. A few of the men from elite combat units, like Eitan, or from the Nahal, like Alon, reported that their military buddies also became their off-time friends. However, many men, during the second half of their military service, complained of social isolation at home. The few men who did maintain deep relationships outside their units—like Gil—gained tremendous support from them.

During the second half of their service, many of the men were summoned to officers' training course. While this step included the promise of a promotion, many of the men felt ambivalent about it. The course itself was considered difficult and, moreover, the requirement to sign up for an additional year of service was not welcomed by all. A wide range of reactions to this significant event in the soldiers' course of service was reported in their stories. Some were looking forward to this opportunity, which constituted a realization of their initial hopes. Most, however, agreed only after some hesitation to try the course. They were aware of the prestige of officers in the IDF and in Israeli society, they had role models to emulate, and they hoped for better conditions or the chance of a career.

For a few of the men, as for Gil, the chance to become officers came as a surprise. They had been shy boys before their service, and they did not envisage themselves as persons of authority. However, once they went through the course, they succeeded beyond their expectations, and this profoundly changed their self-image. On the other hand, several men failed in the course, and several, for different reasons, refused to participate. Ideological reasons, such as an objection to militarism or to government policy, and a strong wish to return to civilian life sooner, were the major reasons for refusing to attend the course.

Since this was an elite group, the majority of the men spent the last part of their service as officers or NCOs. For most of them this was a gratifying experience, as in the case of David, but not for all. There were a few who were disappointed in their limited authority and difficult work and, like Gad, complained that burnout in the role of commander was much greater than in the role of subordinate soldiers.

Termination

The very last phase of the service may be characterized as the burnout period. Most men described a tendency to reduce their involvement and to look for easier jobs. They felt that they had contributed their share to the army, and were entitled as old-timers to collect their dues. Since most men had acquired personal contacts with authority figures, they indeed managed, toward the end of their service, to receive better placements, often near their homes. Younger soldiers took over their responsibilities, while they described their activity as "having a good time" or as "counting the days to release." They worked less, yet they often complained that "time seems to stand still." Several of them were already involved in planning for the future after their military service. Even those soldiers who had almost no crises during their service described the last phase as difficult, expressing fatigue and satiation from the military. Only very few of them mobilized their energy during the last months, *e.g.*, to preserve their contributions by writing up reports and making recommendations to their units.

Upon their discharge, most men feel elated. However, even this much-awaited event evokes mixed feelings in many. They call the transition "the shock of civilian life." Suddenly they feel like young adults at a cross-roads, free to choose their way. Without orders and immediate superiors, many of them feel "strange." For the first time in their lives, the responsibility is solely theirs. Thus said one of the interviewed men:

> "I had thought that I wanted to be independent. Suddenly I discovered that I actually liked to live within a framework of some sort. I arrived at the student dorms in Jerusalem, and received my room a month before the beginning of school. I told myself—how wonderful. You can walk to the market, get all the groceries you like, cook a meal for yourself. I disliked the food my mother used to cook, and hated the food in the army. But I couldn't get enthusiastic about it. It was difficult to live without a system which dictated what was to be done and which took care of my needs. For days I used to lie in bed in my new room. What was I to do with my time?"

The striving for freedom finds its expression in the fact that many soldiers, directly after their release, go on long trips abroad. The participants in this research, which was limited to those who went directly from the army to institutions of higher learning, often mentioned friends who were abroad on long trips and discussed the merits of their decision.

Another aspect of the transition to civilian life is the loss of power and authority which had been gained in the army. After having the experience of being in charge of many men and of large-scale projects, the participants reported the feeling of a shrinking of their selves as young adults in town. This was the case of Alon, who had taken on the responsibility of building a pub in memory of his friend—a rare professional opportunity for a young man. Or, according to Gil: "Where in the world can you see a man of twenty in charge of forty men, with a company car and a secretary of his own? This was my standing in my last military role. When I took off the uniform, I became just another freshman at the university, struggling with 'Introduction to Economics.' Who cares what I had been before? But the feeling vanished after a couple of days,'' Gil hastens to add.

In the same manner that Yochanan found it difficult to adjust to walking around without a rifle on his shoulder, the ex-intelligence soldiers found themselves suddenly cut off from their information sources. But all the men mentioned these regrets as minor when compared with their relief at their release from the army.

We have traced the general pattern of development during military service, with its characteristic crises and transitions. This, however, is an abstract of many unique individual cases, and its accuracy regarding each single one is far from perfect. In the next section we will examine former studies and compare them with the material presented.

Psychological Aspects of Military Service in Peacetime

In the following section an attempt will be made to extract from the literature on military service in peacetime some points which are relevant for a comparison with, or to shed light on, the data presented so far. Although research was done in many countries, it was decided to concentrate only on American and Israeli armies, and on studies published mostly after 1970. In fact, there have been few serious descriptions of the lives of young enlisted soldiers in peacetime armies in the U.S. or elsewhere. The classical analyses are sociological in nature.[5] Psychological aspects of the military experience during peacetime and its effects on the individual soldier were rarely documented or investigated. In Israeli literature too, the question of personality changes during military service is entirely absent.

Basic Values and Motivation for Service

The recent psychological literature on the military in the United States includes mainly studies about attitudes toward military service, which is a subject related to the problem of manning the All-Volunteer Force of the United States. Related subjects are the evaluation of manpower quality, studies on job satisfaction, the military family, and creating incentives for service.[6] All these point to the major trend in recent developments of the American military forces, namely its transformation from an institution of service and a way of life to an occupational system, offering 'just another job' (Janowitz, 1964; Moskos, 1978). According to Moskos' conception, an institution is seen as being legitimated in terms of values, a purpose which transcends individual self-interest in favor of a presumed higher good. An occupational model, however, is legitimated in terms of the marketplace and implies priority of self-interest. This transformation has many psychological implications, far beyond the motivational structure of the individual volunteer. In the area of affiliation within the army, the transformation of the military from a group-oriented, fraternalistic institution to an individualistic, contractual occupation has been paralleled by a decreasing emphasis on small-group solidarity in combat or in training (Moskos, 1970). This trend was recently criticized by military authorities, who have made various attempts to recreate a sense of community and improve small group cohesion within units (Segal and Segal, 1983; Ingraham, 1984).[7] As the material collected in the present study demonstrates, similar processes of change have not evolved in the Israeli army. The IDF still follows the institutional model, is largely based on patriotism and social responsibility motives (Azarya and Kimmerling, 1985) and, as seen in many of the examples above, is highly successful in creating and maintaining small-group solidarity in its units. The mere fact that Israel's army is based on mandatory service, while the American army is, at present, a volunteer system, makes many of the comparisons irrelevant. However, it may be interesting to note that several of the interviewees said explicitly that they would have volunteered to serve in the IDF even had they not been required by law to do so.

A basic question repeatedly posed in the literature is: What are the men's motives for fighting? In spite of the recent trend in the U.S. Armed Forces to attract people by stressing motives such as the attainment of an education, technical training, and upward social mobility, in the description of basic training which will be presented below it will be emphasized that the motivation for military service in peacetime always presupposes future participation in war. The motive for fighting has been one of the riddles of humanity. It may be that we should approach the question of combat soldiers' motivation from the perspective of the unique attributes of the life stage at which most societies place military duty, namely the transition to adulthood. It is then that boys feel required either to earn or to prove their manhood, and the military role offers a means of meeting these requirements. On this assumption Shatan (1977) based his analysis of the willingness to volunteer for the Marine Corps, a topic that will be enlarged upon in the next section.

A parallel line of thought is expressed by Lifton (1973). The initial phase of military service, basic training, is a kind of initiation process, a symbolic form of death and rebirth that coincides with the attainment of adulthood. In that rite, the recruit's "civil identity, with its built-in restraints, is eradicated, or at least undermined and set aside in favor of the warrior identity and its central focus upon killing.'' (p. 28) By going through military training, ''a male youth earns a place in his society's immortal chain of manhood.'' (p. 244) Lifton emphasizes military training as a process of creating a model for identification, the image of the warrior-hero, with his superhuman skill, strength and courage. Lifton describes this myth as two thousand years old, and entitles it the ''warrior mythology.'' It leads people to believe that, in battle, all men acquire elements of the honorable hero, such as courage and male group loyalty or bonding. Only through this myth, according to Lifton, can they conquer their fear of death.[8]

Without reference to age, Bell (1976) has written of the concept of ''civitas,'' the spontaneous willingness to make sacrifices for some public good, and Hauser (1980) described the ''will to fight'' as a psychological impulse sustained by submission to legitimate military authority, fear of danger and punishment, loyalty, and pride. In a more recent work, Foster (1984) describes these conceptions as the ''military ethic,'' which he defines as the acceptance of the necessity for fighting, not a desire for it.

Segal and Segal (1983) address the problem of the job-oriented military force's willingness to fight, and cite some studies which found that about 20 percent of American soldiers reported that they would try to avoid combat or would even refuse it. One cannot ignore the fact, however, that the military mentality in peacetime is transitional, since in actuality the *raison d'etre* of the army is its availability for war. It is hard to conceive of the Marine Corps training, as an extreme example of military socialization, were it not for preparing men for combat. Again one notes easily the difference between the soldiers recruited by the U.S. military forces and the Israeli soldiers, who have no choice but to serve at this time of their lives; yet, as demonstrated in their personal accounts, they admit to having strong patriotic motives, based on their historical heritage and socialization processes throughout their childhood and adolescence.

In my former work (Lieblich, 1978, 1982, 1983), and especially as a Gestalt Therapy group leader, I gathered impressions concerning the effects of military service and the frequent experiences of war on the personality of young Israelis. Analyzing themes which came up spontaneously in the group work of students who had come back from service, I focused on the need to be strong and upon the price of heroism. My general conclusion was that Israeli men were struggling with, on the one hand, the need to be strong, and, on the other hand, their basic insecurity. Long before the Lebanon War, I noted that Israeli men had experienced severe moral dilemmas concerning their roles in the occupation of the West Bank and the Gaza Strip, and they had difficulty in integrating the contrasting values of strength, as soldiers, and of virtue, as taught by their Jewish tradition. I proposed that the price for the facade of the strong, decisive man is a certain emotional detachment, lack of sensitivity to oneself and to others, and a restriction of spontaneity—traits which several men in the groups I led had reported as bothering them.

A new book (Gal, 1986), written by the former chief psychologist of the IDF, recently presented a review, based on statistical evidence and military documents, of the vast majority of psychological research carried out in the Israeli army. In his discussion of the basic values which comprise the ethics of the Israeli Defense Force, Gal provides an excellent description of the system as, ideally, it should be. According to Gal the Israeli army is based on discipline centered around military performance and combat operations rather than on ceremonial discipline. For the mainstream IDF, high motivation and a strong sense of commitment serve as substitutes for strict formal discipline and blind obedience. Comraderie, often called "love sanctified by blood," along with unit cohesion and effective leadership, is the most important source of combat motivation for the Israeli soldier, although the basic sense of mutual responsibility is not restricted to wartime. Soldiers are instilled with the value of "the purity of arms;" this means the restricted and cautious use of arms, preserving humanistic values in combat, refraining from unnecessary bloodshed, avoiding harming civilians— particularly women and children, avoiding damage to sacred buildings, treating POWs humanely, and totally refraining from looting, raping, and other atrocities. Reactions to these values, and their effects during combat situations, were discussed frequently by the participants in the present research, especially in Ido's and Gad's accounts.

In discussing the fighting spirit of the IDF soldier, Gal presents a wider generalization: "The typical Israeli citizen is often seen as arrogant, aggressive and determined. When this same citizen dons a uniform, these characteristics are translated into military combat decisiveness. The IDF, by its very structure, leadership style, realistic training, and exacting performance standards, transforms the basic Israeli nature into a highly motivated, quite aggressive, yet distinctly moral, effective fighting machine." (p. 162) Another aspect of the soldier's motivation, according to Gal, relates to memories of the holocaust, which is part of the national heritage. Israelis bring their own memories into the service, and, at the same time, inculcation of an awareness of this heritage is part of the educational system of the IDF. According to the author, although there are currently very few Israeli soldiers who are actually survivors of the Holocaust, this combined collective memory is foremost in the mind of every Israeli soldier.

In the last chapter of his book, evidently appended after the Lebanon War, Gal presents several "faultlines" in the present military system in

Israel. The chapter focuses on four areas which pose a threat to the very foundation of the Israeli military during the decade of the 1980s, with the consequent possibility of altering the revered image of the Israeli soldier. These involve the areas of motivation problems, moral-ethical concerns, military competency, and quality of personnel. As supported by the present interview data, as in the stories of Ido and Alon, contemporary IDF soldiers may find themselves engaged in activities with which they have difficulty identifying, and they may be confronted with moral or ideological conflicts concerning their military duties, while lacking good leaders to follow and to emulate in these complicated matters. The real danger is that unit cohesion and morale may not be able to ward off situations where the military goals are profoundly questioned. As we will demonstrate in our concluding chapter, such experiences may leave the young soldier confused, rather than morally strengthened.

A different level of analysis of the topics of values and motivation can be found in the work of a group of sociologists of the Hebrew University in Jerusalem who study the effects of military service on the social system, rather than upon the individual (Azarya and Kimmerling, 1985; Horowitz and Kimmerling, 1974; Kimmerling, 1974; 1984, 1985).[9] Their work may provide a description of the social context within which the present study is embedded. Furthermore, in their empirical findings, they provide information about attitudes or reactions of individuals which are directly relevant to the present study.

The basic premise of this group of studies is that military service, including both mandatory service and the reserves system, is one of the most outstanding characteristics of Israeli society. In one of the earlier papers of this group, Horowitz and Kimmerling (1974) cite a saying attributed to a former Israeli Chief-of-Staff, which claims that the civilian in Israel is a soldier on eleven months' annual leave.

On the level of societal values, service in the IDF is anchored within the general consensus on the need to protect the collectivity from the permanent threat to Israel's existence. On the practical level, young soldiers and older reservists must always be prepared for an immediate call-up, and they must be adequately trained to perform their military role. While this could have resulted in a sense of victimization of the individual for the welfare of the collective, the authors claim that in Israel service in the IDF reflects the implicit assumption that participation in the security effort represents a kind of reward. In a sense, people who are required to serve in the army feel that they possess the ability to influence not only the course of crucial events, but perhaps the decision-making processes as well, by being attached to the common central goals through actual performance. Furthermore, they have access to restricted and classified information, a fact which adds to their status in society. This analysis demonstrates the centrality of military service in men's lives in Israel, and implies that their attitude toward it would be mostly positive—as has also been demonstrated in the present study.

A later study by Israeli sociologists (Azarya and Kimmerling, 1985) lends further support to the claims made above. In their attempt to investigate the cognitive permeability of civil-military boundaries in Israeli society, the authors collected data on draftee expectations from military service in the IDF. This paper is of immediate relevance to the present work, since it deals with the subjective individual perspective, focusing on the draftee's perception of linkage between military and civilian roles and purposes, and expectations regarding the use of military resources in civilian life and vice versa. Since Israel is a "nation-at-arms," extensive linkage between the two spheres is to be expected. At the individual level, this linkage would also mean a positive attitude toward the service and a tendency to volunteer for special roles and units.

Findings based on questionnaires administered to a large sample of soldiers at the military absorption base indicated that for the Israeli conscripts it was hard to distinguish between considerations related to collective goals or to personal benefits. This became especially apparent by comparing Israeli-raised soldiers to new immigrants. The first consistently showed greater willingness to serve in the IDF, but new immigrants were also positive. (For example: 72 percent of Israeli-born reported that they would volunteer to serve if service were not compulsory, *vs.* 61 percent of the new immigrants). Generally, Israeli-born draftees were very optimistic regarding their service, and in their expectation to gain personally from it. They did not envisage much difficulty in their adjustment to the army, and believed that the higher one's military rank, the higher his prestige in society.

The authors concluded that in the minds of young Israelis, it was difficult to separate military and nonmilitary spheres, or to differentiate between collective goals and personal incentives related to military service. These separations were more apparent to new immigrant draftees, who see the two spheres as exerting cross-pressures, hence lowering somewhat their willingness to serve in the IDF.

Another manifestation of the nonseparation of the two spheres is noted by Kimmerling (1984), when discussing the participation of the draftee's family in the experience of their son. The tendency to volunteer appears "also at the level of the entire family," he says, "which when its representatives serve in the armed forces feels itself contributing to and participating in a central task; a feeling which no doubt offers a certain amount of compensation for the risks and inconveniences involved in the duty to serve." (p. 23) The central role of the soldier's family in his military experience, noted also by Gal (1986), is of great significance for psychological development through the transition to adulthood, when, according to psychological theory, a major task of the young is separation from their family of origin! This point will be elaborated on in the concluding chapter of this work.

The Nature of Basic Training

Much of the research on life of soldiers in the army concentrated on the early phase of basic training. One of the recent American comprehensive descriptions of the subject was provided by Novaco, Cook and Sarason (1983). The authors developed a program for the improvement of coping skills among Marine Corps recruits, focused on cognitive intervention. Their intent was to help the recruit understand his reaction during the earliest phase of the training, which is known to be the most stressful as well as the most critical phase, to prepare him cognitively for future experiences, and to offer some coping strategies for the challenges he is about to face.

While focusing on their intervention, Novaco and his co-workers describe the 87-day basic training cycle in the Marine Corps, which is considered the most rigorous of all American military training, as "a period of rapid resocialization and enculturation occurring under conditions of relative isolation and confinement." (p. 380) This description seems to be similar in many aspects to the experiences of soldiers in the IDF, especially in combat units, as exemplified by the stories of David, Ido, Eitan and some of the others. The following analysis may, therefore, provide a theoretical framework for the cases presented.

The rigors of basic training are aimed, according to the authors, at preparing recruits for combat; *i.e.*, for the kind of unpredictable stressors likely to be encountered in combat. Each service assumes that the young soldier is unprepared for military life, that he is immature, undisciplined, and unkempt. The process of basic training is aimed at changing this initial situation by numerous techniques which were dramatically described by Goffman (1961) in his work on asylums. As training progresses, the recruit is expected to keep up with increasingly difficult physical demands. Psychologically, however, the recruit is going through a stage of "mortification" and "culture shock" resulting from the sharp distinction between the trainees' class and the supervisory class—what the participants in the present research called "distance." As in other total institutions, all aspects of life occur in the same place and under the same authority, each function is carried out in the immediate company of others, activities are tightly scheduled, and all are aimed at fulfilling the goals of the institution. The recruit finds that his autonomy is severely curtailed, his communication with the outside world greatly restricted, and his only identity in this setting is based on his conformity and performance. Furthermore, the system relies solely on negative reinforcements to shape recruit behavior.

While Novaco and his co-workers agree with many of the generalizations made by Goffman, they observe that as training progresses many recruits do have the opportunity to learn that significant rewards result from personal effort, and when graduation is in sight they experience an enhancement of their self-esteem and confidence. Those who have previously had few such opportunities often gain a sense of worth. At the end of the cycle, most recruits are extremely proud and feel that, in the eyes of society, they have now attained adulthood. Obviously, all these general statements, as well as the following, have numerous quotations to support them in the data collected in the present study, and in the cases of Part I.

In their own analysis, as in mine, the authors portray the stressful experience of basic training in terms of expectations and appraisals. All recruits experience a discrepancy between their prior expectations and the actual events, a condition which leads to physiological arousal, a state of shock, fear, and anger. Disappointment, "dazed apathy" (Bourne, 1967) and depression are among the stress-related reactions reported by many. For those recruits who successfully complete the training, these initial appraisals change as a result of exposure to the situation over time (Epstein, 1983), as well as through the active coping efforts which were utilized by them. Thus, they discover that drills that at first may have seemed senseless later turn out to have had a purpose. The drill instructor, who is initially immensely feared and hated, will commonly become a figure of admiration. Recruits learn to be task oriented, and to take each day as it comes.

Social support, according to Novaco and his co-workers, has a prominent role in the adjustment process. The support originates from family and loved ones at home, and from fellow platoon members. Letters are a major source of motivation, while the bonding between recruits gradually attains deep significance. Sharing of hardships and validating each other's experience is accompanied by the development of teamwork and a unit identity. *Esprit de corps* is instilled among unit members, and facilitates adjustment to stress.

While the above description presented a logical and humane framework for the experience of basic training in the Marine Corps (and in the combat units of the IDF as well), the authors seem to be aware of the controversy regarding some of the techniques used and the ambience of the "boot camp." They support their positive picture by citing recruits who remember their supervisors as exemplary individuals, and have fond reflections of unit cohesiveness. They comment that "it is often difficult for psychologists or social scientists, with little military exposure, to view recruit training as anything other than negative, aversive, and dehumanizing" (Novaco, Cook and Sarason, p. 386).

As our own data stands, the Israeli ex-soldiers recall their months of basic training with mixed feelings. For several of them, the positive aspects of mastery and coping with challenges are indeed dominant, while others, though a minority, retain bitter memories from this stressful stage of their service.

A completely different picture of the same environment, namely the basic training of the Marine Corps, is provided by Shatan (1977) and Eisenhart (1975). "The Marine Corps," according to Shatan, "provides the best illustration of the thesis that the military uproots and decivilizes young men, compels them to surrender, and then transfigures them. Along with their new military identity, they acquire a code of conduct utterly at variance with their civilian lifestyle. This code is dressed up as a 'code of honor' that conceals the true impotence of combat Marines." (p. 587) Shatan argues that military training, in particular that of the Marines, causes personality changes in the soldiers. He proceeds to describe the process, which he conceptualizes—following his psychoanalytical background—as a profound psychological regression that makes men into boys, and later allows these boys to win back their manhood by becoming unfeeling killers. As part of the same regressional process, men shed their individuality and acquire a new identity—of the disciplined soldier, a cell, a unit within a supreme organism, the army. While this process is engineered to achieve maximum results, it succeeds mostly with adolescents, whose identity is not well established, so that the anxiety-producing conflict they experience in the first phases of their training leads them to rebuild their personality and relationships on the basis of the images of the immediate authority figures around. The instability of the adolescent's superego makes conscripts especially vulnerable to the will and example of their leaders.

In a similar manner, Shatan is able to explain why young men are drawn to this kind of service. The authoritarian standards of fitness, stamina and endurance appeal to late adolescents who find difficulties in forging their masculine identity within civilian society. They feel that this military experience is the way to become men, and they learn that they can prove their masculinity only through violent aggression. However, by their abandonment of autonomy and of their own consciences, they become dependent upon an external power, thus becoming boys all over again.

The contradictory conceptualizations presented by Shatan versus Novaco *et al.* are each seconded by other, perhaps less well-known contributions (see Faris, 1976 and Eisenhart, 1985). While Shatan's thesis may, to some of the readers, sound extremely critical of the military, and profoundly true to others, one may question whether Shatan's description is typical of all military training or specific to the U.S. Marine Corps.

Gal (1986) describes the basic training of the IDF as highly demanding, yet much more humane than the Marine Corps Boot Camp. He refers to the period as a socialization into military life. The instructor frequently becomes an identification figure for the trainee, who, according to the author, begins as a confused and bewildered teenager and concludes as an assured, competent and highly motivated soldier. Furthermore, basic training involves the strengthening of the recruit's identification and familiarization with the nation, its history, and people. It enables the young enlisted men to establish personal relationships within a cross-section of different groups and to weaken their stereotypical ethnic conceptions. While all these may be desirable norms or *goals* set up by the military authorities, the cases of the present study demonstrate that in reality some of these goals have not been completely or unequivocally attained.

While most of the above focuses on basic training, especially in combat units, in other units of the army, however, and during more advanced stages of the service, one may find an altogether different atmosphere and lifestyle, as we will presently demonstrate.

Military Service as a Routine

For the Israeli soldiers whose accounts were presented above, military service almost always included skirmishes and direct combat involvement. Yet at different times, or if they have the "jobnick"[10] role, their lives follow a workaday routine, which has some rules of its own. "Military service," they say, "is not basic training." In the U.S. after Vietnam, far from the possibility of direct combat, we may also find a completely different military atmosphere and lifestyle, such as was recently described by Ingraham (1984).

In his book, *The Boys in the Barracks,* Ingraham (1984) provided a field report on the life and habits of a group of American soldiers below the rank of sergeant, living in a garrison in the U.S. Aimed primarily at studying drug use in the military, the report covers many aspects of the normal life of peacetime soldiers, ordinary men—medical and signal technicians, truck drivers, policemen, and mechanics—whose mission it is to maintain readiness for deployment, and who rarely receive public attention.

According to Ingraham's description, most of the men in the barracks see themselves "in the Army" for a short time, for the purpose of acquiring skills, or simply "getting it over with." (p. 25) They made a clear distinction between themselves and "lifers," who are in the military service for a career. They expressed an explicit antimilitary norm, disapproving of everything "military." The worst name to call a fellow was "lifer"—a person who talked and acted as if he liked the army and was willing to emulate its leaders.

Garrison duty, according to this ethnographic study, is not terribly demanding and provides considerable free time. As their typical duty day ends at 4:30 in the afternoon, Monday through Friday, men tend to view their day as divided into military work and their own free time, and behave quite differently within each of these settings. However, even during duty time the researchers noticed a relaxed atmosphere with highly informal relationships between the men. Stretches of idle time were quite common. Leadership at the platoon level was found to be personal and face-to-face, with very little 'commanding' style. The biggest bone of contention between the leaders and the men were haircuts and shoeshines, but compromises were often made. Reasoning, cajoling and moral persuasion were the chief means of supervising work in the various work groups, and horse-play and continual banter were standard routines among the men.

The researchers paid special attention to the social network of the men, and observed that the "army buddy," somewhat more than an acquaintance but less than a friend, was part of the temporal reality of the barracks life. The classic function of buddies, namely to take care of one another, to cover for each other when in danger, continued to operate in the garrison conditions. This was manifested when waking each other up in the morning, when sharing the job of loading a truck, and in other such daily routines. When the workday was over, at 6:00 at the latest, many of the soldiers left the garrison to be with girlfriends, to attend evening college classes, to work out in the gym, or to drive around the post and the immediate area. With the exception of occasional weekend guard duty, soldiers in the garrison were free every weekend and many of them went home to their families and hometown friends. Most first-tour soldiers affiliated only with others from the same work group, rank, residence and race. Their primary allegiance remained to their families and their hometown friends.

Within the social network of the barracks, certain norms were prominent. First, as mentioned above, was the antimilitary attitude, followed by the requirements of the 'squealing' norm and the 'stealing' norm. On their own time, barracks residents insisted on handling disputes in their own way, using from verbal abuse to physical assault as means of enforcement but never referring conflicts to officers ('squealing'). Regarding theft, the norm was that stealing from a soldier in the same barracks was always condemned, while theft from a soldier in another barracks was acceptable (as long as one did not get caught). Theft from the Army, however, was never stealing, but simply exacting one's due.

Some of the above descriptions may remind the reader of aspects in the stories of Gil, Yochanan, and Danny, the noncombat soldiers. But even in the lives of the combat soldiers, there are times during service which may resemble the above. It seems that, due to the high initial motivation to serve as combat soldiers, Israelis are usually displeased and quite critical of the routine life on military bases, especially the life of the "jobnick." The youngsters interviewed in the present study rarely chose this kind of military service of their own free will. From the totality of the picture depicted by Ingraham, one finds it unlikely that profound personality changes should occur as a result of a tour of military service under these conditions. Yet even so, according to Card (1983), in studying the retrospective accounts of non-Vietnam veterans—as in the evaluations of the Israeli noncombat participants in this research—one finds frequent reports of an increase of maturity, self-confidence and independence, and a general sense of growing up.

As the above picture of a leisurely military service emerges in comparison with the demanding experience of the Marine Corps (at least during basic training), one is reminded that military service has many faces for different Corps, units or individuals. Although military service in Israel is probably less heterogenous in its nature than that in the U.S., the personal reports of Israeli soldiers reveal striking similarities to both the more demanding and the more relaxed atmospheres of military service as described above.

We may conclude that arriving at a simple rule regarding the course or effects of military service during peacetime (in contrast to wartime, which will be discussed in the next chapter) is far from feasible. Service during peacetime is a term covering a multitude of unrelated experiences, from the ambient atmosphere of the barracks life to the incredible hardships of the Marine Corps basic training. Motivation to serve is profoundly connected with societal values, and with the differences between societies under greater or smaller threat of survival. Personality changes and growth patterns will take different courses for different individuals under varying circumstances.

Notes

1. For additional discussion and démonstration of these norms, see section below on "basic values and motivation for service". Former publications on this topic include Lieblich (1978, 1983) and Gal (1986). The tendency to volunteer has also deeper, universal roots in the special characteristics of adolescence and the pas-

sage rites to adulthood. Hall (1904), Eisenstadt (1962), and Gould (1978), each one from a different perspective, argue that individuals of this age group tend to search for outstanding deeds and actions, which extend beyond personal self-interest. It is probably due to the characteristics of this age that young people of this age group are able to withstand the extreme hardship of the military initiation stage (Shatan, 1977).

2. Two kinds of quotations will be used to demonstrate the proposed ideas in the following chapters. First, there are some quotations from the accounts or evaluations of the men whose cases were fully presented in Part I of the book. These will appear with the name of the participant, as in the chapters of Part I. Quotations from the remaining interviewees, whose stories were not included in this volume, will also be used when appropriate. These will appear without names, as here.

3. Similar factors facilitating adjustment were reported in research conducted in other armies. For example, see Gray (1959); Segal and Segal (1983); Wilson (1980).

4. The same learned skills or norms of behavior were also described by Janis (1945) and, more recently, by Ingraham (1984).

5. Most cited are the works of Janowitz (1964) and Moskos (1970). Janowitz analyzed the changes in political behavior and military doctrine of the American military since the turn of the century. He depicted the army as a professional system, with a body of ethics and standards of performance. His major point is that the growth of the destructive power of warfare increases the political involvement and responsibilities of the military. Moskos tries to provide a more concrete yet comprehensive view of the life of the enlisted soldier. For a more recent review of the sociological work on the military forces, the reader is referred to Segal and Segal (1983). The authors review the literature in the context of theories about increasing rationality on the part of societies, organizations and individuals.

6. For some of the research on these problems, the reader is referred to Bachman, Blair and Segal (1977); Bachman (1984); Dale and Gilroy (1984); Faris (1984); Fredland and Lille (1984); Johnston and Bachman (1972); Segal (1981); and Thomas (1984). A collection of papers on several problems of similar contents appeared in Goldman and Segal (1976).

7. More information about the trends in unit cohesion in the American military can be found in Meyer (1982) and Manning (1984).

8. Lifton's theory is not far from Eisenstadt's (1962) formulation of the outstanding impact of culture on youth. While numerous cultural symbols or myths may be acquired at this stage of man's life, the myth of the hero is certainly one of the most common. Regarding the motive for fighting, one should again mention Gray's classical autobiographical work on World War II (1959). His attempt to provide an answer to the problem of why men fight is perhaps the most profound in modern literature.

9. For a general sociological description of the Israeli Defense Force, two comprehensive studies, although somewhat dated, are Rolbant (1970) and Luttwak and Horowitz (1975). For a detailed description and a discussion of the educational role of the military in Israel see Lissak (1971).

10. A term used in Hebrew to describe soldiers who have a desk job in an office during their military service.

10

PSYCHOLOGICAL ASPECTS
OF
PARTICIPATION IN WAR

All the participants in this study had been in active service in the IDF during the Lebanon War. This chapter will present their reactions to that war (which took place in the summer of 1982) as well as to the military service for the following two years in occupied Lebanon, which involved constant skirmishes and other war-like conditions.

All the personal accounts contained some reference to the war, representing a great diversity in content and attitudes. Let me remind the reader that my primary focus of attention was not reconstruction of the historical events. The participants were keen to detail their experience of the war, but even I, who am neither a historian nor a journalist, could easily recognize that many of the stories were confused, lacked time and space continuity, and were often affected by the political attitudes of the narrators. Moreover, the interviewees experienced the war as privates, NCOs or junior officers, their awareness of the more general military plans was, at best, fragmentary, and their personal recollections were only of limited local events. However, since my major concern is the impressions of the actual events on the participants, the above "biases" or "inaccuracies" have different meanings in the present context.[1]

Like the former chapter, this chapter is divided into two sections, one based on the material collected in the present study, and the second on previous literature in this field. The first section will deal with three inter-related topics from the personal accounts: namely, attitudes and feelings prior to the outbreak of the war, during battle, and during later security duty in occupied Lebanon.

The Lebanon War as a Chapter in the
Soldiers' Accounts

Attitudes and Feelings Prior to the War

Almost all the men reported that they had known about the plans to invade Lebanon, and that they had participated in training for the war. Descriptions of the waiting period were salient in the men's accounts. During this period, many of the men participated in false alarms. Their units were repeatedly advanced to the North under orders to be ready for the invasion—orders that were postponed, cancelled, and changed again and again. As in the famous fable about the boy who cried wolf, the participants reported that, as a result of these false alarms, their psychological readiness for the actual event gradually diminished. When the real attack actually started, many of them were unable to believe that this was the "real" thing.

The atmosphere is well described by one of the paratroopers: "That night we were ordered to the landing vessels and we sailed up north. It felt like a vacation, we called our boat 'love boat,' and the next day we were all tanning ourselves up on board. You deny what could come next. Nobody on the boat tried to prepare himself mentally for combat. On the second evening, as we approached our destination, my squad leader said to me, 'You know, I am scared.' It startled me. He was the only one to think about what was coming."

This repeated practice, whether the authorities intended it or not, created an indifference toward the war, and, as a result, several of the men reported that they had no fear or worry about their future. The same man continues his account: "People in my battalion had never experienced a real war. We were briefed, we understood our orders, but none of us thought that somebody might be killed or wounded." This might also have been the result of the soldiers' belief in the IDF's military superiority in comparison with the enemy. Says David: "On Saturday I was on furlough at home. In the morning, I received a phone call. We were taken in buses to the Golan. There was an atmosphere of festivity and confidence. The farther north we drove, the more we were impressed by the tremendous forces which were ready for deployment, like an iron fist."

The Lebanon War was the first one they had fought, and the participants' sense of invulnerability and relative indifference resulted, perhaps, from their lack of former experience. Several soldiers related that older men who had served in former wars had a different attitude. For the participants, too, when they were later sent to the second round of combat, or to security duty in Lebanon, apprehension became much more common. The following is David's account of his feelings after six days of active combat, in which a good friend of his had been killed nearby: "At night the shooting stopped. We were told to prepare for battle against the Syrian commando forces at dawn. Each one of us went separately to check his weapons and ammunition, to prepare the gear. I prepared myself psychologically as well. I knew that I would be right at the first line, and that my chances to be hit were high. This was—" Here David finds it difficult to express his feelings, and leaves off. After his silence he resumes his account: "Later that night, we heard on the radio that a cease-fire would take place in the morning. Nobody hid his relief."

A different feeling that dominated the men's accounts of the period prior to the war was tension, which resulted from the long waiting period and the uncertainty. Many men described an increased intolerance of the waiting, a resultant nervousness, and the wish for action, any action, as a way out of the suspense. This was accompanied by the need to perform in actuality what the men had been training for. Whatever the political outlook of the soldiers, this was a dominant mood, as expressed directly by Ido: "The feeling that you have all the time, which people find hard to understand, is frustration. Because you practice a lot, and you never get the chance to perform even the smallest part of what you have been training for . . . As a soldier who has put so much effort into training, even the most ardent pacifist wants to apply his skills. It is a matter of being professional . . . The state of waiting is the worst of all. You want to start action just so that you'd not have to wait anymore. Politically I was one of those who had violently objected to the attack on Lebanon, but as a member of the team, I wanted the war to happen. This ambivalence was characteristic of many of us."

Among the motives for war, the men mentioned the importance of unit cohesion and "buddy" relationships. Many of the men were on leave on the Saturday prior to the invasion (which took place on Sunday), and some were in transfer between units. All expressed their urgent need to join their friends for the battle, as expressed in the accounts of Alon, Eitan, and others. Soldiers who had to fight in other units, removed from their buddies, expressed deep feelings of bitterness and regret. This motive was undoubtedly stronger in the men's accounts than expressions of loyalty to their leaders, or their agreement with the political act of declaring war.

The willingness to fight appeared in all of the men's stories, and especially in those who had trained for combat but had not been called for the war. They felt frustration, guilt and resentment for "not being where I belong." Says Gil, who had prepared the logistics for his battalion to move north, but was not ordered to participate, "We're waiting. Sitting with our heads between our knees. Eating our hearts out. We miss the war. I wanted to be there, like everybody else . . . All the first week we were frustrated and worried, but we had not been ordered to move. On Friday I was sent home on leave . . . I went to the Scouts. It was empty. Only kids showed up. I felt as if I was the only man in town, and was dying to return to the army.'' Similar feelings were expressed in their accounts by Yochanan and Danny.

When discussing their feelings before combat, several of the men mentioned the appeal, or joy, of combat, described also by Gray (1959). This was not often disclosed, probably because such feelings would not be positively reinforced in a peace-oriented society. Alon was, in his account, open enough to disclose such feelings, and, at the same time, he expressed difficulty in accepting them. "It wasn't heroism or anything like that,'' he said. "All I thought of at that moment was that I wanted to join my buddies, and perhaps that I wanted the experience of combat, just for myself.'' For another of the soldiers in Lebanon, the battle of Beirut was already the second experience of combat during this war. When I inquired about his eagerness to endanger his life again, he said: "First of all, it is the result of my upbringing. Secondly, all my buddies were there, inside. And thirdly, there was this tremendous attraction. It is difficult to explain. If war could be enacted without casualties, it would be the best possible game. There is this animal-like exhilaration in combat, and I felt it personally in all the battles that I experienced.''

At the beginning of the war, it was rare for the men to express unwillingness to participate in combat. Only one of the interviewees, who objected to the military system in general, reported his satisfaction at the fact that he was not sent to the northern front. As the war continued, and the general public split in its attitudes toward the war, soldiers also expressed the full gamut of opinions and concerns. Men who objected politically or morally to the war, yet were called upon to perform their duty, were, of course, in a difficult position. However, all the men continued to compartmentalize their opinions from their performance. They reported that their negative attitudes did not interfere with their action. As expressed with great clarity in the account of an Armored Corps man: "At that time, the argument about the war swept the country. I identified with the leftists, but I cut myself off from this level. What we were going through in actuality was a massive experience. If you thought about what was going on, you could not perform and survive under the circumstances. We didn't know everything, of course, but I think that even had I known, it wouldn't have made any difference. I am the type of person, who, for example, if ordered by the IDF tomorrow to invade Turkey, would, right or wrong, do what I was told. Later on, at home, when I took off my uniform, I'd join a demonstration against the war. I believe that the IDF is one thing, and politics another.''

The Experience of Combat and the Early Stay
in Lebanon

In describing their feelings during the war, the participants reported a
wide array of experiences. The only thing that they all have in common is
the intensity of their accounts, and the level of excitement that permeates
them. Since each one had experienced a different slice of reality, like parts
of a puzzle, their combined accounts may create a totality of the psychological phenomenon of the war.

Referring first to the form of the accounts, some of the participants
provided vivid descriptions, as if watching their own experiences on an inner screen during our interviews. Others presented vague and confused accounts. Frequent changes of mood and style were evident during the
interviews which dealt with the war, when the narrative shifted from descriptions of extreme stress, to relief through humor, noting the absurdity of
situations, or depicting strange coincidences. These were common in Alon's
account, as, for example: "Once some foreign reporters came down to take
pictures and found us all fishing, using the APC's antenna for a rod. That's
what Israeli soldiers looked like." And later on, during the combat in
Beirut: "I remember looking up to try to locate the window where this
RPG fire was coming from, and I saw a woman standing there, beating her
carpets. How bizarre." Shifts between the description of serious moments
of confronting death, and the light-hearted atmosphere of the "gypsy
convoy of APCs," the visits to the cemetery or the pubs, punctuate his
account.

David, whose story lacks almost any humoristic style, says, following
the description of the death of one of his buddies: "We joked about it. We
said that at least we would be killed as first lieutenants. We would have
quick promotion through death." Evidently, the inclusion of the funny or
the ordinary in the war accounts serves to release the tension of the war for
many of those men who were telling their stories for the first time since
they had experienced them.

A similar function is served by the description of the Lebanese landscape, which was greatly admired by the men, and described in detail by
many of them. All the men reported a sense of personal safety, or of invulnerability, on their first "visits" in Lebanon. This was partially the outcome of the warm reception of the Israeli soldiers by the civilian
population. The participants spent time at beaches, in coffee shops and
markets, met with local men and women of the same age, and experienced
again and again the gratitude of the Christian inhabitants who felt "saved
from the cruelty of the PLO." However, their image as noble rescuers
changed rapidly during the IDF's stay in Lebanon and, as was well demon-

strated in their accounts, a permanent sense of danger and of mutual resentment were characteristic of the following stages of the Lebanon episode.

In telling the story of their participation in combat during the first days, many of the men expressed pride and satisfaction in their performance. Several of them reminded me that they had fought "in the very front line," "in the leading tank," "in the first APC to enter Lebanon," etc. Stories of outstanding heroism and bravery are prominent in five of the accounts, in spite of the fact that in later perspective one of them—Alon—was very critical of the war in Lebanon. In Alon's account, the war is described as a peak experience (Maslow, 1954): "That's when I saw severely injured men for the first time in my life. I reacted . . . outstandingly. I was cool. Professional. A leader in the situation. I acted as if I were a different person there, with a fantastic ability not to panic, to cope under stress. I think that never before or afterwards could I be that man."

Other aspects of heroism appearing in the stories include descriptions of deprivation of both food and sleep, coupled with surprising successes in different missions. Several men recounted their discovery that they had been able to cope with stress much better than they had expected, as if drawing on a reservoir of power which was not available to them under normal conditions. "I discovered I was very cool, I didn't panic, and I knew what to do. I was in charge of the situation." This report appears in almost the same words in four of the accounts.

Gad's account demonstrates several of these feelings: a sense of adventure, pride, and satisfaction. The climax of his story occurs when, during one of the battles, he was wounded in the head. After being treated by the medic, he refused to go to the hospital and insisted on returning as soon as possible to the front. When I asked him to explain his decision, he said: "Look, as much as I was afraid, I felt that the events I experienced would never return, and I didn't want to miss anything." He also referred to the myth of the hero, saying: "One always hears all these stories about the wounded who escaped from hospitals to the front. So, I said, let me be one of those. I put my helmet on top of this huge bandage, and returned to my battalion."

In contrast to the sense of pride in battle, as described above, we find an expression of disappointment in a few of the stories of the combat soldiers, who felt that their contribution was marginal in comparison with their intensive preparations for the war. In some of these cases, as with Eitan and Alon, the men's frustration coincided with their placement in units other than the ones with which they had originally trained. These two factors are probably significantly related. The most severe sense of disappointment was expressed by Ido, from the reconnaissance unit. In our interviews, he discussed the events of the war both from the point of view of his experience as a soldier, and that of an officer examining the total context. About his feelings during the war, he says: "We felt that the army didn't need us, or our special skills. If I'd range our skills on a 100-point scale, they used only about 5 points of it . . . It was tremendously frustrating . . . What had we trained so hard for? This experience questioned our very existence."

The experiences of fear and ways of coping with it were also prominent in the participants' stories. All the men who had taken part in the war, or in service in Lebanon after the battles, referred in their accounts to fear, whether spontaneously or in response to my questioning. Their responses represent a wide range of experiences. Some of the men bluntly declared that they had no experience of fear, like Ido, who says simply: "There was no fear whatsoever."

On the other hand, some of the participants told me at length about their fears, describing moments or hours of intense fright. Says David: "Suddenly the bombs started to fall all around us. I remember this first feeling. You lie on the ground, the shells fall all around you, throwing soil in your eyes, you just lie there and feel like a tiny zero." Later on, when being shelled while in his APC, David remembers: "For a moment I thought—well, that's it, we're going to die . . . I remember this panic. As if in a moment we would be taking off into the sky." And, in his final evaluation of that day: "It was a nightmare. We felt like objects, caught up inside our vehicles. You don't see what's going on, and you're shot at all the time." Very similar is the story of another combat soldier, who was confined to his APC under shelling for nine hours. "It was frightening. When you sit like a duck inside the APC and the bombs fall all around you, you die of fear. You hear the awful din, the sound of shrapnel hitting the metal . . . It was horrible. After about two hours of this I decided there was no point in being afraid, and I started to write a letter, which I have never mailed. I was sure I would die, and it was tough, because only one of my close friends was with me in this APC."

While all this involves fear for one's own life, the participants also described fearing for the lives of others, whether friends or people under their command. Only a few of the men functioned in the war as commanders, but all of them expressed their concern for the lives and safety of their men. Again we may demonstrate this from the case of David, the last part of whose military service was spent as a young officer in Lebanon. "This time it was different," he says about the attack on Beirut, "because my trainees were following me in that street, and I was scared for them. An infantry commander is somewhat like a mother to his soldiers, you know."

The intense experience of fear had usually been brief, but recalling the events evoked it again. The participants did not specify how they coped with their fears. Only hints of this were given in their accounts. Thus, the importance of the radio in increasing panic, or in reassuring people in stress, was mentioned by several men. Gad and David talked about shooting as a means of relieving tension and fear.

Another coping device may be the belief in one's good luck. Several men, who did not report any fear, described moments of feeling lucky when a disaster was avoided. "It was my sheer luck that I entered the APC just a second before this shell hit us," says David. For one of the two observant soldiers, luck and God's grace are interwoven in the account of his escape from disaster. He summarizes his story saying: "Everything that happened to me was sheer luck, you know. Actually I could have been killed many times during that week." His experience in the war reinforced his religious beliefs. The opposite was true for another combat soldier: "After Beirut," he says, "there is no more God for me. If there were a God, my best friend would not have been killed, nor would the little kid we shot on the ramp." Both he and Alon, his buddy, celebrated the first Yom Kippur after the war at an eating and drinking party, in violation of the religious law.

Along with the other feelings described, two basic encounters are typical of the war: with the enemy as human beings, and with death. As might be expected, more of the participants referred to the second issue than to the first.

Often I had the feeling that the men described casually and coldly their part in the killing that took place during the war. This was probably due to the belief that the war was one of defense, as well as being a mechanism of emotional denial. Thus, one of the men describes his search for terrorist fighters in the Lebanon mountains almost like a hunting game. "It was almost like those video games. You see a head, and you aim at it. I don't know if I killed anyone, but I saw many fall down." Sometimes, however, the encounter with children in the enemy camp disrupted the emotional numbness. "We saw a child standing on a roof, he was signalling to someone below, and the shells kept hitting us right after he would signal. A friend of mine aimed at him, and he fell from the roof. He was about 10 years old, that's all. I can still see his mother as she emerged from the building screaming: 'My child! What have you done to my child!' For the first time I grasped what we were doing. It was tough." The difficulty in fighting against children was further complicated by the well-founded rumor about soldiers being killed as a result of taking pity on armed children.

Sometimes confrontation with the enemy took place immediately after casualties had been sustained, and some of the men described a feeling of revenge in such cases, replacing the sense of 'cool' performance described above. "At first we just did what we were trained to do, not feeling much. But after the first man from my unit was injured, I felt that they had to pay the price. We all fought like animals afterwards."

The confrontation with enemy casualties was usually described as unpleasant. Nobody rejoiced at the sight of the enemy's dead. All the men described this encounter as shocking at first, but, with its recurrence, they reported a growing indifference. Many of the men used the slogan "Life is cheap in Lebanon," referring to the frequent encounter with sights or events which, under different circumstances, would have shocked them.

On the other hand, there were solemn reactions to the death of their own buddies. For many of the men this was the first contact with death in their immediate social circle. They experienced profound pain, but expressed it in different ways. On his first encounter with death of soldiers in general, David says: "That's where I saw our dead for the first time. And the smell." But he goes on with his narrative. Later, relating how a close friend of his was killed right next to him, he says: "Levy fell, as if sitting on the steps, dying. The other cadet fell on top of me, full of blood. It wasn't easy." He describes how he evacuated the wounded, how he tried to clean the APC and get rid of the smell, but about his emotions, all he says is: "We were in a state of shock."

During the following days, David continued to bear his pain in silence. "On the radio they listed the soldiers who had been killed. Levy was among them. "Lieutenant Levy, promoted in death. I was silent." When visiting his parents, "I noticed that all the men who had participated in combat were unusually quiet. Me too. I smoked a lot, but didn't say anything."

On the other hand, Alon, who had also described an initial shock reaction, later on reacted violently to the death of his friend, Zvika. Alon described three stages—first the shock, the sense of emotional restraint. Then, at night, "we were lying on our mats on the floor . . . telling jokes. We passed the night laughing our heads off . . . We made a joke of death, a huge macabre joke." Finally, the breakdown at the funeral, crying and losing control. Later he describes a long process of mourning, a constant feeling of longing for Zvika, a sense of intimate closeness with his parents, and, on the other hand, a frantic attempt to cope with pain via humor, entertainment, alcohol, and drugs. Among the long-term reactions described by Alon is also a profound attachment to the small unit of fighters who had survived the same events in Lebanon.

Finally, let us examine the attitudes of the young men toward this war in the context of the growing political arguments about it. Did some of the soldiers feel strongly antagonistic toward the war, were they alienated while fighting it, what kind of conflicts did they experience? These questions are difficult to answer. Obviously, my material was retrospective, so that later reactions and attitudes may have affected the description of earlier feelings and events.

About half of the participants claimed that the war was just and unavoidable, while the other half believed it was wrong and that Israel should not have initiated it. The participants' opinions concerning the war at the time of its occurrence focused on three issues: doubts about the justice of the war, about the conduct of the battle, and about the morality of the IDF.

The great majority of the men said that they had obeyed their orders, as they had been taught to do, and did not remember any doubts or arguments about the justice of the war. They stressed that they were "too busy to think," or that such doubts would probably have interfered with the efficiency of their functioning. Only a few were critical of the war from its beginning, like Ido: "We had plenty of free time, and we used to argue about the political value of the planned attack . . . I was one of those who violently objected to the attack. I felt that the existing situation was far better, and that there was no sense in risking our lives for this operation." Likewise Alon: "I remember saying even then that the war was going to become a catastrophe for us all. Nobody realized this so early." In fact, for some of the soldiers, doubts started to arise after several days at the front.

Several men criticized the leadership of their commanders and the vagueness of their orders, and the general lack of specific directives during the battle. Says Ido: "Our task was performed quickly and perfectly, without any special stress. We felt anxious only when we had to interact with other forces . . . They seemed to be in a huge mess . . . No coordination, no overview." And a little later in the same interview: "A sense of not knowing why, what for, and what will be the end . . . We were in a fog, an information blackout on the wrong side." This confusion is perhaps normal in combat, but the events experienced by several men, in which Israeli forces mistakenly attacked IDF units, reinforced a more critical view of the situation.

Most profound was the criticism which concerned some of the sacred myths of the IDF. One of them is the belief in an army "of the people," about which one of the interviewees said: "I was educated to think that the IDF is the army of the people, a liberating army, with responsibility toward the people. What I saw was a smooth power-oriented organization, in which generals were competing with each other. Often I felt like a mercenary. This was a blow for me, as if the image of the IDF had been corrupted, and I felt exploited by the army." The same view was expressed by Danny: "After the war, I was not sure anymore of all the values that people were always advocating. For me, the war destroyed the myth of the virtue of the IDF." And finally Ido, in describing how he watched a night of heavy bombardment of Beirut, where he estimated that many civilians were hurt: "This was the night which shook me out of my senses . . . It was a city of many innocent bystanders, not an enemy post! That night it was bombed out . . . I felt disillusioned. My beliefs in the IDF virtues, in the 'purity of our arms,'[2] were demolished together with the city.''

Security Duty in Occupied Lebanon

Many of the accounts described at length the men's service in Lebanon after the termination of the early battles, during 1982, 1983 and 1984. Almost all the men participated in some way in the tasks of maintaining the occupied territory, carrying out functions like patrolling, guard duty, and security activities within the Arab population. The period was described as being characterized by constant danger, scattered but frequent clashes with the enemy, and difficult routines of physical work, in cold weather, with little sleep and relatively rare leaves. Fatigue and constant fear are described by most of the men, regardless of their political opinions about the war. Several of the men emphasized their sense of degradation of human values, of the worth of private property (of the Lebanese), and of human life (on both sides). They talk about the loss of moral criteria for their conduct during their stay, and the feeling of being exploited. All of the men reported their relief upon leaving Lebanon to serve within Israel, or to go on leave. For several of them, the knowledge that they might serve additional periods in Lebanon made them decide not to sign up for additional military service. These aspects were clearly demonstrated in the cases of Gad, David and Yochanan.

Emotionally, this was very demanding for most of the men. Several describe their reactions to the stay in Lebanon as depression; an example is an infantry soldier, who says: "It was a heavy feeling to serve in Lebanon under these circumstances. We were all depressed. I personally had another reason—my girlfriend had broken off with me, since we hadn't seen each other for so long. But that wasn't all . . . We used to sit in the tent, when we had a moment of rest, to drink something, and to listen to the tape-recorder. The music we all liked then was actually the American protest songs of the Vietnam era. To me, they meant a lot. I had similar feelings. I'm in a foxhole at the ends of the earth, and my duty is turning me into an animal.''

There were some positive sides to life in the strongholds in occupied Lebanon, too. Men became very close to each other. Commanders also were closer to their men in the crowded posts, and the formal distance between ranks often vanished. "We didn't feel like an officer and a sergeant any more,'' says David, "we were just two close friends who had these men to take care of.'' Many of the men talked about the good meals they used to cook for themselves, "as a means of preserving sanity under these conditions." Several managed to read and to write. Alon and his unit "used to sit on the veranda every evening, playing cards, drinking coffee, and watching the magnificent sunsets." Some soldiers described the holidays celebrated under these circumstances as especially moving events.

This lifestyle in the isolated posts often was considered "unmilitary." Officers saw it as a potential danger to security, and often tried to introduce more discipline into their soldiers' lives. Says David: "Men tend to disregard discipline when they are at the front . . . It might start with minor details, like forgetting to put on your flak jacket, and end with disaster. I tried to maintain discipline, and my men discovered that even under these conditions, in the middle of Beirut, I was capable of getting them to run and exercise." Although such attempts are recalled by several of the men, they all considered the period in Lebanon as relatively permissive, and experienced a sudden increase in military discipline when returning to their bases in Israel.

A departure from this background of daily life in Lebanon were the frequent tragic events in which men were injured or killed. Fear was evoked again, as during the battles—some of the men felt afraid, as Yochanan did, while others according to their reports remained indifferent or invulnerable. Several of the soldiers spoke about nightmares that kept bothering them after their service in Lebanon. "I used to see all these mutilated bodies in my dreams . . . Things I'd rather forget." Worrying about one's men is another aspect of fear. David: "What frightened me most was the responsibility for my men." This included not only his concern for their safety, but also his sense of responsibility for their moral conduct and military discipline.

Several soldiers spoke about their stint in Lebanon as belonging to another culture, "the Wild West," with completely different moral norms. Says one of the men: "There was no other way. We terrorized the population, so they stopped bothering us." Alon described an incident in which his unit threw a bomb at an abandoned building "simply out of boredom." The bomb missed its target, Alon says: "But who could care about one more bomb. There were explosions around us all the time." And Yochanan described the behavior of his superiors as "the realization of some childhood fantasies about cowboys and the Wild West—as if we were all in no-man's land." Men were frequently aware of the attrition of their human values during this period, as expressed by one of the participants: "Look, you're an ordinary soldier in this big army, and we all feel that life is cheap in Lebanon. Nobody takes life too seriously, and if someone is hit, even killed (on the side of the enemy)—you learn to take it quite easily. This awareness gradually affected us all."

If life was cheap, so, in some cases, was the property of the Lebanese population. Gad describes his struggles to prevent his men from looting, and so does Yochanan. David, however, feels puzzled by the situation, when he frequently faces a dilemma: to choose between blowing up a suspicious vehicle, or possibly risking the lives of his men. Confusion of this sort is apparent in his description of the later stages of his service in Lebanon. "In every patrol we blew up some civilian cars. It was crazy," he says regretfully. "That's what Beirut was like. Amusing on the one hand, and sad on the other . . . A terrible loss of control. We tried to survive among those civilians, and our attempts to guard our lives were a constant disaster for the population around us. I remember that I sat in my room and said to myself: This is life on the verge of insanity. I felt bad. I felt exploited."

All the soldiers reported a tremendous sense of relief every time they left this dangerous and hated territory, even on a short furlough, or for service at a base in Israel. "After about a month we were ordered to return to Israel . . . We decorated our vehicles with olive tree branches as symbols of peace, we made posters on the front . . . When we passed the point from which we had gone out to the war, we opened a bottle of champagne."

Avoidance of further service in Lebanon was so prevalent that many of the men reported that they would have signed up for additional service, or for officers' training courses, but decided against it because they would have had to serve another period in Lebanon. Obviously, the total experience of Lebanon in the life of the participants is largely negative, in spite of their initial motivation to be there and to take part in the war.

Psychological Aspects of the Experience of War: Recent Literature Review

In presenting the experience of war from the point of view of the research participants, I emphasized those aspects which may have psychological effects on personality formation during the transition to adulthood. This will also be the focus of the following literature review, which will concentrate on the psychological aftermath of the Vietnam War. The specific interest in this war is directed by our attempt to limit ourselves to recent psychological studies.[3] Furthermore, the Vietnam War may in several respects be considered similar to the Lebanon War. Without going into the details of a political and historical analysis, one may easily point to a common denominator, and to many differences, between these two wars.

All wars have much in common in that they expose the soldier to the danger of death and demand of him extreme reactions and performance. Yet, the Vietnam War is particularly similar to the Lebanon War in its unpopularity. It is difficult to estimate the degree of unpopularity of these two wars, yet undoubtedly the Lebanon War was the most controversial war in Israeli history, and opposition to it was widespread both at home and among the soldiers who fought there. Furthermore, because of live TV broadcasts, the soldiers' awareness of the protest at home was much greater, even though public opinion polls indicated that a substantial majority of the civilian population did support the war. Other similarities are that both wars were fought by the youth, with high technology, in situations where it was often impossible to distinguish between civilian and foe, and where soldiers were often attacked by women and children.

In many respects, however, the two wars did differ. The central issues were that since in Israel almost all the young men serve in the army, the question of who participated in combat and who avoided the draft is almost nonexistent; the prestige of the Israeli army is far greater than that of the U.S. army; while the Lebanon War lasted less than three months, with later military involvement in occupied Lebanon lasting only two years, the war in Vietnam lasted more than a decade; due to the short distances, Israeli soldiers regularly visit their home and friends, typically at two or three week intervals, even in times of war, whereas the American soldiers in Vietnam were usually separated from their homes for 12 months or more; primary groups and unit cohesion, which were reported to be lacking in the American forces in Vietnam (see Stretch and Figley, 1984; Figley and Leventman, 1980) are highly maintained in the IDF; despite the controversial nature of the Lebanon War, it was never blamed on the soldiers who fought in it, and they were not stigmatized as were many of the Vietnam veterans; men who shared the experience of the war in Lebanon remained in service together after it and were not lost to each other as reportedly happened to Vietnam veterans; drug abuse and soldiers' opposition to their commanding officers were far less prevalent in Lebanon than in Vietnam (Gal, 1985).

Keeping the above factors in mind, as well as the personal accounts presented in Part I of the book, some of the psychological impact of the Vietnam War will be described in the following section. Although most of the Vietnam literature is based on follow-up and later developmental effects, while our study is focused on immediate reactions, the reader will note that many of the effects noted regarding the Vietnam War were also experienced by the Israeli soldiers who fought the Lebanon War, although, due to the factors listed above, in a greatly mitigated manner.

From the beginning, and to a growing extent as the war continued for more than a decade, the Vietnam War was covered and accompanied by psychiatric, psychological, and sociological research.[4] Three concerns were at the focus of these attempts: Who were the soldiers in Vietnam, how did they cope, and what were the personal outcomes for each of them back in the United States?

The most extensively investigated aspect of the Vietnam War was the psychological health of its veterans. The majority of the earlier studies, as well as many which have recently been published,[5] were conducted on small clinical groups, with no adequate controls. Their general conclusions were that the Vietnam War veterans returned to civilian life with a host of physical, social, and psychological problems, ranging from drug and alcohol abuse, through violent and criminal behavior, nightmares, and insomnia, to chronic guilt feelings and difficulty in forming intimate relationships. There has been disagreement, however, as to the prevalence, severity and permanence of these and other problems.

While some psychological aftereffects have been known to plague a proportion of veterans after every war, the psychiatric terminology for describing these effects has changed with time and fashion. The term "shell shock" was used in World War I, the term "battle fatigue" in World War II, and the current term is "Post Traumatic Stress Disorder" or PTSD. This is defined in the official psychiatric manual, the DSM III (1980), by four indicators:

1. "Exposure to recognizable stressor or trauma."
2. "Re-experiencing of trauma through flashbacks, nightmares or intrusive memories."
3. "Emotional numbing to or withdrawal from external environment."
4. "The experience of at least two symptoms from a list including hyperalertness, sleep disturbance, survival guilt, memory impairment, and avoidance of situations that may elicit traumatic recollections."

The history of the concepts of psychiatric casualties has been recently described by Mareth and Brooker (1985).

Most of the disagreement in the area centers around two models for the long-range effects of the combat experience. The stress-evaporation model, advocated by Worthington (1977, 1978), claims that the problems of the veterans are short-term. In cases where the problems persist, they are attributable to adjustment problems prior to the military stint. Proponents of the other model, the residual stress model advocated by Figley (1978a, 1978b), claim that the problems persist many years after the experience. In the following review we will find more support for the latter than for the former model. Again, one should be reminded that the present research was concerned with short-range effects, while much of the American research is based on long-range development.

We will represent the field by focusing on three major contributions, differing in their methods and approach, which all provide descriptions of phenomena also experienced, to some extent, by our research participants. The first is Lifton's (1973) research, among the earliest and most influential works on the subject, which was based on an in-depth study of a small group of Vietnam veterans. The second is probably the most carefully designed follow-up study on a large sample, conducted by Card in 1981, and published as a book in 1983. The third is a collection of papers edited by Figley, one of the leaders in the field, in collaboration with Leventman (1980). This collection presents both objective and clinical research, and points to the general agreement among findings and conclusions reached by different methods.

Lifton's work was conducted as a study in psychohistory, work which combines a description of psychological development with a historical analysis of the events causing it. His basic thesis is that military training, combined with the special conditions of war, make every individual capable of violence, killing, and even atrocities. People who return from such an experience carry the scar of "survivors' guilt" which they need to resolve. As long as the veteran can believe that his war had purpose and significance, or that the horrors he witnessed can be placed convincingly within a meaningful system of symbols and values, he may come to terms with his experience and make a relatively successful transition to the civilian role.

Lifton found that as a result of war, several personality changes take place in the soldier. Unresolved guilt about death can be expressed by rage and impulsive violence. Violence may become a habit, an accepted means for the solution of any problem. It may be expressed randomly, against relatives, friends, or strangers. Another form of rage is the veteran's feeling of betrayal, of being victimized or badly used.[6] Veterans often expressed fantasies of revenge against those who abused them. Bitterness and the internal struggle to subdue their violence may effect a chronic personality change.

The amount of energy invested in violence and its control may lead to an "inability to feel alive," which has often been termed "psychic numbing" in the psychiatric literature. According to Lifton, psychic numbing already starts in the training for combat situations, when the enemy is dehumanized, in order to make it easier for the soldier to attack and to kill him/her.[7] This psychic numbing has, however, far reaching consequences, and is considered one of the reasons for the frequently observed phenomenon that war veterans tend to withdraw from relationships and to have difficulties in forming intimate contacts. In the antiwar veterans, Lifton observed another personality change, namely a profound mistrust for the older generation and for the totality of the "counterfeit universe," accompanied by a growing attraction toward an alternative, youth culture.[8]

While describing the negative psychological consequences of the war, Lifton details how this very experience may turn into a stepping stone for personal growth for some of the men.[9] Confronting a personal threat may open a route to greater awareness of the falseness, inadequacy, and lifelessness of previously unquestioned values, assumptions or symbols, and to the possibility of forming an alternative system. This may be followed, on some new level, by making the experience meaningful, and by the attainment of a new integrity. Thus, in a certain sense, war is an opportunity for growth.[10]

As an extreme contrast to the clinical, impressionistic nature of Lifton's work, I will present the recent work of Josefina Card (1983), whose study is based on a careful empirical investigation conducted in 1981 on 500 Vietnam veterans, who served in the war zone during the 1960s, 500 non-Vietnam veterans, who served in the military during the same period but were never assigned to Vietnam, and 500 nonmilitary controls.[11]

Of the many important conclusions from the Card study, I will concentrate on those which are relevant to the present study. Regarding physical and mental health, the most controversial area in the academic literature, Card reported that at the age of 36 the three groups did not differ significantly in self-reported cigarette smoking, alcohol, or drug consumption, although Vietnam veterans reported slightly greater usage. Vietnam veterans reported significantly more nightmares, social interaction problems, and antisocial behaviors. Alienation, anxiety, hostility, and depression were all slightly more prevalent in Vietnam veterans, although only anxiety and depression produced significant differences. The careful design of Card's research allowed her to conclude that while educational and occupational deficits were shaped by the military experience in general, personal-social problems could be traced directly to service in a war-zone. Vietnam veterans also reported more than others that they attributed their difficulties to their military experience and the war, and they rated their present and expected life as significantly less favorable than did the non-Vietnam veterans and non-veteran groups.

Based on the current definition of PTSD (see p. 137 above), Card developed two scores of the intensity of the syndrome, and was able to show that the more severe the soldier's exposure to combat and injury during the Vietnam war, the greater the number of PTSD-related problems at the age of 36. Thus, Card's follow-up 17 years after the war indicates that those who experienced heavy combat became especially vulnerable to long-term psychological consequences, lending support to the Figley model of residual stress.[12] When asked an open-ended question specifically about the effects of their service in Vietnam, Card obtained extremely emotional and bitter responses, in which veterans talked about PTSD symptoms and feelings of guilt and grief.

On the other hand, Card discovered that all veterans rated their military service as more positive than negative, with non-Vietnam veterans slightly more positive than Vietnam veterans. When asked to explain in their own words the influence of the military service, the dominant aspects they described as positive were: personal growth, increased social and psychological health, increased maturity, independence, self-confidence, opportunity to see the world, appreciation of other cultures, and improved sensitivity and ability to get along with others. Individuals who had served in the war mentioned among the positive results of their experience an increased appreciation of the value of life and things which are "truly important." Veterans who expressed more positive aspects were usually those who in the first place had been willing to serve, who later had less direct combat experience, and who came from cohesive units and had good officers. Yet, summarizing the open-ended part of her research, Card concluded that "overall, one is impressed not by the commonality but rather by the variance in the men's reactions to a common experience." (p. 141)

Although in both Lifton's clinical theory and Card's empirical work the reader could possibly discern many aspects which are similar to the experiences of the participants in the present research, most relevant to what concerns us here seems to be the work summarized in Figley and Leventman's *Strangers at Home* (1980).

Outstanding in this collection is Waller's chapter, actually written in 1944, demonstrating that the reactions of all war veterans are predictable and remarkably similar regardless of the circumstances of the war in which they fought. Central to this universal experience is the wish to come home, anger at being singled out to fight, see horrors, kill and die, bitterness toward civilians and soldiers who were not in combat situations, and, in the end, almost always the feeling that the combat soldier's sacrifices had not been fully appreciated.

Smith, in his chapter on oral history, expressed the belief that obtaining the individual accounts of the veterans in the form of an oral history may be a form of therapy for the above-mentioned conditions of bitterness, anger, and isolation. He reported that most of the veterans had not divulged to their family or friends the nature of their war experiences, and that when the pain of the experience was shared it was also partially alleviated.

Oral histories of the Vietnam war were also obtained by Norma Wikler, another contributor to the Figley and Leventman collection. Wikler points to the fact that the military service occurred, for many of the veterans, at the transition to adulthood, and that their experience may have become the context in which to work out questions of identity and directions of growth. In the same vein as Lifton, and using some of Erikson's concepts,[13] she claims that since the military is so different from his previous life at home, especially in wartime, the young man—who often joins the army in order to "become a man" or to "grow up"—may discover aspects and capacities that challenge former notions of himself. The range and depth of emotional response, of hate, love, guilt, courage, and terror, cannot be imagined. The awareness of acts one would or would not commit is often dramatic. Fortunately, most civilians are spared the opportunity of discovering within themselves the capacity for actions which are extremely dissonant to previously held conceptions of the self. Once these experiences are lived through, they may become parts of a new self-concept.

Some of the self-discoveries reported by the veterans possibly enhance the quality of their future lives. Wikler calls this personality change a "new self-knowledge" (p. 94). Citing Gray (1959), as well as her own interviewees, Wikler concludes that the most striking fact in the war accounts is the wide range of the veterans' responses to killing or violence. Some were shocked, others saw it as an exciting game, and some simply obeyed orders. Violence easily became a habit for some, while others found their capacity for brutality disconcerting, creating doubt, confusion, and guilt.

Another significant aspect, according to Wikler, is the question of "will" in war—the confidence in one's ability to control and direct one's behavior, which is vital to the formation of personal identity. In the military, endless drills and maneuvers insure automatic, reflexive responses. Acting like a "robot," or the sense of the overpowering of one's will, was often reported by the veterans, who obeyed orders and later regretted their actions. Such issues may create problems in forming the young adult's identity, and in his transition to the next Eriksonian stage of forming intimate relationships. It seems that Wikler, like Lifton, sees in war a potential for growth, yet considers it as frequently causing the opposite trend, which she terms the "hidden injuries of the war" (p. 105).

A third proponent of similar views is Wilson (1980), whose work is also based on in-depth interviewing of veterans. His interviews were specifically designed in order to understand how war in Vietnam changed the personalities of the veterans, and to investigate problems of identity formation, interpersonal intimacy, alienation, and intrapsychic conflicts in the process of personality integration. The model used here, again, is the Eriksonian scheme of development, taking ego-identity as the focus of analysis. Moratorium is an essential concept in this theory. Because most of the Vietnam veterans spent part of their late teens and early adult years at war, away from home, they were denied the normal period of moratorium from adult responsibilities, which is so essential for growth. Thus, the experience of war deeply affects the entire crisis of identity formation versus role confusion.[14]

Wilson tries to demonstrate that the experience of war may facilitate the formation of identity under certain conditions. This will be the case when the young soldier has good role models, a sense of purpose or mission in the war, a moral or political cause worthy of commitment, trustworthiness of authority and leaders, and a collectively shared experience with peers. Wilson reported, however, that most of these conditions did not exist for the Vietnam soldiers, as opposed, for example, to the former experience of World War II veterans.

On the other hand, the Vietnam veteran often encountered stressful situations which may have produced, according to Wilson, one of two forms of disrupted personality development. The first is termed retrogression, which brings back mistrust, doubt, guilt, and inferiority from former developmental stages. The second and more interesting form of maladjustment is an acceleration of development which leads the person prematurely into stages normally typical of an older age. While retrogression is often manifested in the various aspects of the PTSD syndrome, acceleration may produce acute existential anxiety and the awareness of ''marching to the beat of a different drummer'' (p. 147).

It is evident that although reports vary in their estimates of the severity and prevalence of long-lasting combat effects, the balance of opinion is that these were substantial.[15] Since, as we said in the beginning of this section, the Lebanon War was shorter, less controversial, and less extreme in the experiences it produced than the Vietnam War, it is probable that its effects, too, would be less devastating. However, in their accounts of the war, the participants in the present study reported similar reactions. On the negative side, they talked about reexperiencing traumatic moments through flashbacks in dreams and memories, about grief and survivors' guilt, about depressive moods, bitterness and hostility, and about a feeling that their sacrifices had not been fully appreciated. On the positive side, they reported a growing self-knowledge, pride in extraordinary performance, deep friendships as the outcome of their encounter with combat, enemy, and death, and greater appreciation of the value of life. These subjects will be elaborated upon in the following chapters, dedicated to the special aspects of transition to adulthood as it occurs in the context of military service during peacetime and at war.

In concluding this chapter, a few comments should be made regarding former Israeli research on the psychological effects of participation in war. As much as the reality of war is prominent in everyday life in Israel, published academic works on the subject are not as numerous as one might expect[16] and almost no previous research exists on the effects of war on personality changes or the transition to adulthood. This lacuna is outstanding in two volumes which appeared in the 1980s (Spielberger, Sarason and Milgram, 1982; Breznitz, 1983), dedicated to the study of psychological aspects of the stress of military tension in Israel. Both of these books were based on international conferences on war-related stress which took place in Israel in 1975 and 1978. Most of the work reported in these volumes deals either with the general stress level of life in Israel, or with the aftereffects of specific events, particularly the 1973 Yom Kippur War. The Yom Kippur War, being unquestionably a defense war, was quite different from the Lebanon War (for a historical reference see Schiff, 1985), but that is not the only reason why the material of these volumes is not highly relevant for the present purpose.

An exceptional study in these volumes is Yarom's (1983). The author interviewed men who had served in the front lines in the Yom Kippur War, trying to discover the range of possible effects of a life-threatening war on a person's subsequent life history. As in the American studies on the oral history of wars, the author reports that most of the interviewees considered narrating their story to be psychologically beneficial. She describes a wide range of positive and negative subjective outcomes, and focuses especially on the reassessment of the soldiers' values and relationships with others. Realizing the possibility of death, according to Yarom, may be a source of existential change, even of personal growth and psychological well-being. While these issues are close enough to the subject of the present work, Yarom does not take into account the life stage of her participants, while the span of their age range, from 22 to 42, makes any developmental generalization quite difficult.

A central question dealt with by theoreticians in Israel concerns the cumulative effects of stress, tension, or the salience of the threat of war. Two current approaches to this issue appear in the literature (Breznitz, 1983). The first may be termed the exhaustion model and it claims that the longer one lives under the influence of chronic stress and frequent outbreaks of acute threat, the more severe the psychological damage to the functioning of the personality. Therefore, adults in Israel who personally have experienced tension for more than forty years of their lives, and/or participated in up to six wars, would experience a decrease in their ability to cope with the situation, whether practically or emotionally. In the lives of eighteen-year-olds (and this is what concerns me in the present study), this approach would claim that being drafted into a dangerous military role is a traumatic experience for anyone, but will become even more so for youngsters of the 1980s, who were brought up with the cumulative memory of previous stress and an awareness of the price of repeated wars.

According to the opposite view, which may be termed the immunization model, people become stronger as a result of the repeated experience of stress. Evidently, it is essential to consider the results and circumstances of an ongoing stress situation. For example, a threat one is able to cope with and resolve successfully may indeed immunize the individual against the severe experience of future stress. On the other hand, when faced with an uncontrollable state of stress, when one is made to feel helpless, the psychological outcome may be completely different.

On the sociological level of analysis, a similar duality may be discerned. Kimmerling's (1984, 1985) approach is that as a result of the cumulative effects of the Israeli-Arab conflict, Israeli society has made the conflict routine. In other words, the Israeli social system has undergone a process of adaptation to the external conflict through making it partly routine. Reality in Israel is organized around two completely different yet substantially interconnected phases of activity: "routine" and "interrupted." From the organizational point of view, the transition between these two phases can, by now, take place without too much friction or difficulty, since social mechanisms and institutional arrangements were created for coping with the erupting conflict with maximum efficiency and minimum cost. From the individual point of view, the existence of the two phases includes the development of a mentality which sees the conflict as permanent, and keeps people in a chronic state of alertness for an emergency. In general, when the sociological literature on the subject is summarized, it seems that the conclusion from this point of view is that adaptation to the continuous stress situation, rather than exhaustion, is the rule.

Keeping in mind the descriptive material (derived from the present study) about the Israeli experience of military service both in peacetime and in wartime, and the previous literature summarized in the last two chapters, we will now turn to the discussion of personality changes and the transition to adulthood as they unfold from the point of view of the participants' reports.

Notes

1. For an objective description of the Lebanon War, the reader is referred to Gabriel (1984) and Schiff (1985).

2. This phrase refers to the central value in the education of the IDF soldiers, see Gal (1986).

3. Among the classical psychological works on the effects of war, and other related aspects, are the book by Grinker and Spiegel (1945), and the accumulated studies of Stouffer *et al.*, which appeared in 1949. These studies were based on the experiences of American soldiers in World War II. An outstanding book on the subjective experience of war, bringing up many of the emotional reactions and dilemmas, which will be considered later in the present study, is *The Warriors*, by Gray, first published in 1959, and based on the author's four years of service in the American army in Europe in World War II.

4. Card (1983) considers the Vietnam war to be the most studied war in U.S. history. The earlier publications about this war, especially those which appeared in books, are reviewed in Chapter 2 of Petersen (1974). Among those early works, an especially interesting book is Polner's *No Victory Parades* (1971), which describes in detail the impact of the Vietnam war upon nine veterans from the working class, three 'doves,' three 'hawks,' and three 'haunted.' This study also belongs to the oral history genre, as does part of the present book.

5. Even as late as ten years after the formal termination of the Vietnam War, one finds many new studies on the mental health of its veterans. Recent studies are, for example, Levenberg (1983) and Stretch and Figley (1984) on long-range mental health problems of the veterans, Yesavage (1983) on schizophrenia among veterans, Brende (1983) on character pathology in combat veterans, Pardeck (1982) and Pardeck and Nolden (1983) on the subject of veterans and aggression, Glover (1984) on survival guilt, Atkinson *et al.* (1984), Fairbank *et al.* (1983), Lipkin *et al.* (1983), and Mullis (1984) on several aspects of the PTSD syndrome, Van der Kolk *et al.* (1984) on nightmares, Starker and Jolin (1982) on imagery, Wilson and Zigelbaum (1983) on criminal behavior of veterans, Remer (1983) and Roy (1983) on alcoholism, and Keane *et al.* (1983) on substance abuse.

6. The most influential—and highly critical—report on the return of the Vietnam War veterans to the U.S. and the institutional organization (especially through the Veterans Administration) for their absorption in society was prepared by Ralph Nader. A book based on this report is *The Discarded Army*, by Starr (1973).

7. Interestingly, Lifton found that an encounter in which children were the "enemy" could play an important role in resensitizing the soldiers' "numb" feelings. A similar phenomenon will be described later for Israeli soldiers in the Lebanon War.

8. This, of course, is similar to the phenomenon observed by Kenniston (1965) in his study on alienation. In a study based on objective research based on a large representative sample, Segal and Segal (1976) totally rejected this point. They reported that Vietnam veterans did not, in their political views, differ from civilians who had not served in the army, and that veterans from the Vietnam era did not, in this regard, differ from veterans of other wars. Bachman and Jennings (1975) reported similar results concerning trust in the U.S. government.

9. A difficult problem related to Lifton's and other investigators' proposition that integration of the combat experience *may* lead to growth, is: Who are the

ones who grow and profit from their experience, and who are the ones who do not? Lifton did not discuss this question directly and he seemed to imply that all the antiwar veterans in his groups finally went through the growth process. It seems that he was deeply moved and changed, as he admitted, by the veterans he got to know in his groups, whom he described as prophets of their time. It is unclear whether Lifton believes that political commitments per se transform the war experience, or that psychotherapy is the essential factor. Anyway, he seems to have been dealing with an elite group with an outstanding pattern of development.

10. An interesting aspect of the growth process observed in the antiwar veterans in Lifton's study involves the changing image of masculinity in the eyes of these young men. With the loss of the hero myth, men repeatedly discussed their changing attitudes toward maleness. They described themselves as gradually softening, becoming more tender and vulnerable. From Lifton's point of view, this is understandable, because "caricatured maleness" is closely related to war and killing, so by rejecting one aspect of the male sterotype, these men also transformed other aspects of their former "macho" personality.

11. The only other large-scale research on the subject is a study conducted on 1400 Vietnam veterans and their peers by the Center for Policy Research. It studied their adjustment nine years after the war experience in areas such as education, occupation, mental health, coping with stress, marital status, friendships, drug abuse, criminal behavior etc. (See Egendorf, Kadushin, Laufer, Rothbart and Sloan, 1981.) However, one should be reminded that Card's is the only study including comprehensive preservice data.

12. Card, whose study is written in neutral, scientific terms, calls her results on the psychological effects of the Vietnam war "overwhelming" (p. 114), supporting many other studies conducted before hers. In particular, she cited data from a recent study commissioned by Congress (Laufer, Kadushin and their colleagues, 1981), who showed that the psychological problems of the veterans persisted over time, and that the intensity of combat experience was significantly associated with the incidence of stress symptoms such as hostility, drinking, and arrest. Furthermore, these correlations were higher for those men who fought after 1968, when, on the home front, there was little social support for the war effort.

13. Erikson is a major theoretician of life stages and development throughout the life span, his particular contribution being the understanding of adolescence as a stage of the acquisition of identity through a phase of psychological "moratorium." A fuller presentation of his theory, as far as it is relevant for the present research, will appear in the following chapters.

14. One should notice that the concept of moratorium implies several independent phenomena. One is the ability to experiment freely in various roles and activities—an aspect of the moratorium which is denied the young soldier. On the other hand, since military service demands of the soldier some highly specific functions and forms of behavior, he may delay making choices about career or family, which are otherwise typical of this age. Furthermore, the soldier is taking over an

adult function—defense—but is allowed to postpone other aspects of the transition to adulthood. Similarly, in the area of autonomy from parents, military service produces geographical distance and some economic independence, but from another perspective increases the emotional dependence of the soldier upon his family. We will return to this central issue in the discussion of our results.

15. Lifton, Wikler and Wilson each tend to attribute most of the veterans' problems to the war itself, other researchers blamed the reception of the veterans back at home for their problems (Camacho, 1980). While most of the clinical evidence presented in this chapter about the effects of the Vietnam War is indeed devastating, the results of surveys and more objective research are not so clear cut. While also reporting long-lasting combat effects, Card's study—in a representative and controlled sample—did not obtain the same dramatic results. Figley and Southerly (1980), another objective survey (in the Figley and Leventman collection of papers), report that the majority of a large sample of veterans adjusted well in most areas of life. Results concerning drug and alcohol abuse were far less alarming than in some other reports (see also Stanton, 1980) and except for some residue of combat service in nightmares and sleep disturbance, the results indicated that Vietnam veterans were apparently coping well in mainstream America, in spite of inadequate government programs and negative stereotypes. On the other hand, in a later report, Stretch and Figley (1984) review the recent research literature saying that psychosocial adjustment problems were not restricted to those veterans seeking psychotherapeutic help. Their report indicates that combat experience in Vietnam is correlated with an orientation to violence, indices of depression, political alienation, adjustment problems and substance abuse.

Finally, the most recent work I found on the subject (Hearst *et al.*, 1986) presents statistical evidence on the delayed effects of the military draft on mortality. Specifically, the investigators report that military service during the Vietnam War caused an increase in subsequent deaths from suicide (65 percent more than expected) and motor vehicle accidents (49 percent more than expected). Whether due to physical handicaps from the service, psychological or economical difficulties after return to civilian life, or greater familiarity with firearms, the authors concluded their report by stating that "the casualties of forced military service may not be limited to those that are counted on the battlefield" (p. 623).

16. Most of the psychological literature about the effects of military service in Israel also deals with combat stress reactions and their treatment (see for example Alon, 1985). For an updated reference list on combat stress reactions and their treatment in Israel, see Gal (1986). In Hebrew, a recent study of post-traumatic stress disorders among soldiers of the Lebanon War was published recently by Solomon, Schwarzwald, Weisenberg and Mikulincer (1987).

11

PERSONALITY DEVELOPMENT DURING
MILITARY SERVICE

How were the participants changed by their military service? This was the basic question which guided the present study. The experiences of three or four years, during the transition to adulthood, must make a difference in an individual's life. Could some of the patterns of change be attributed to the military experience per se? Would they have occurred anyway, due to the passage of time, in a college environment or at a place of employment?

Let us examine, before going into these questions, what is considered the "regular" development for this age group, namely the developmental tasks of young men at the transition to adulthood, as described in previous literature. In comparison to these, the next two sections of the chapter will present special areas of development which are characteristic of young men within the military context.

The Transition to Adulthood as a
Developmental State: Literature Review

Age and age differences are among the basic aspects of life and the determinants of human destiny. This is true of all cultures, but perhaps especially true of modern western civilization (Eisenstadt, 1962; Fry, 1976; Brandes, 1985). The period covered in this study, the 'spring of one's years' (18 to 22), has been referred to, variously, as late adolescence, post-adolescence, youth, young adulthood, or the transition into adulthood. According to Eisenstadt, this period is defined in all cultures as a stage of life because it is characterized by basic biological changes. Generally it is defined as the transition from childhood to full adult status in society.

In modern Western society, 18 is often the age of finishing high school, leaving the parental home, and entering institutions of higher education or the labor force. It is also the age at which individuals become eligible to vote, marry, and drink alcoholic beverages, and simultaneously become legally responsible for their actions. In some societies, this is also the age at which one begins military service, which is what this book is all about.

What are young people between the ages of 18 or 22 like, and what are some of their main concerns? Mitchell (1979) describes late teenagers or young adults as people who are biologically, psychologically and emotionally ready to assume adult roles, but, for personal reasons, choose not to do so, or are prevented from assuming adult roles because of social circumstances. Once physical growth has been largely completed, there is a stabilization of ego identity. In other words, one is likely to come to grips with "the way I am," assimilating one's negative as well as positive qualities. The older adolescent becomes more self-directed, and less influenced by parents or peers. There is a deepening of interests, a greater awareness of the concerns of society, and a growing understanding of the unique personhood of other individuals. At this age, people demonstrate increasing empathy and caring for others. Their new need for intimacy is united with a growing sexual drive, giving it both more force and meaning. Mitchell's account corresponds with White's (1966) outline of five characteristics of healthy development in young adulthood: the stabilizing of ego identity, the "freeing" of personal relationships, the deepening of interests, the humanizing of values, and the expansion of caring.

Although young adulthood is rarely discussed as a separate stage, several theories have been proposed on the more general, somewhat overlapping, stage of adolescence.[1] Hall (1904), one of the first to describe adolescence as a separate stage, was inclined to see the adolescent as "superhuman material." According to Hall, adolescents pass through a period of storm-and-stress, and are, at this time, more susceptible to cultural influences than at any other time in life. Following his general scheme, Hall claimed that adolescence reenacts a transitional phase of evolution in the development of the human species. He viewed the adolescent as the best candidate for advancing the species, and argued that society should offer the elite adolescents of each generation incentives and opportunities to develop both themselves and the entire human race.

Presenting adolescence as a culmination of human development is somewhat characteristic of Piagetian theory as well (Elkind, 1970). Piaget emphasized that the adolescent is a thinker. During adolescence the individual finally comes into possession of flexible, far-ranging cognitive abilities—arriving at the stage Piaget called "formal operations." Influenced by Piaget, Perry (1968) proposed a theory of intellectual development that characterizes the transition to adulthood in a college environment. Studying undergraduates for four years, Perry noted a general progression through several stages of development. From the earliest phase of dualistic thinking and placing responsibility for knowledge on authority figures, such as teachers, the students moved next toward diversity of opinions and uncertainty, then toward relativistic thinking, and finally they reached a stage of commitment which involved the taking of responsibility for one's opinions and choices.

Early adherents of psychoanalytic theory were always more concerned with the young child, and depicted the adolescent as reliving the oedipal stage, torn by inner drives and external pressures. In more modern versions as well (*e.g.* Blos, 1962, 1979; Deutsch, 1967), psychoanalytic theory describes adolescence as a time of psychological imbalance. Unresolved childhood conflicts are revived, and intense erotic and aggressive impulses strive for expression, with a frightening impact on the adolescent. Since these incestuous drives endanger the family, disengagement of the adolescent from parents and siblings eventually takes place near the end of this stage. Young people experience great inner turmoil during adolescence, but, towards its end, they learn to cope with their drives and feelings, and begin to crystallize an identity. At the same time the adolescent establishes meaningful, intimate heterosexual relations, and his or her choice of a career represents an acceptance of a system of societal values as well as of external constraints and internal limitations.

From the point of view of object-relations theory, Blos (1967) proposes viewing adolescence in its totality as the "second individuation process," the first one having been completed toward the end of the third year of life with the attainment of self and object constancy (Mahler, 1963). Mahler described a process of 'separation-individuation' as consisting of "two intertwined, but not always commensurate or proportionately progressing, developmental tracks. One is the track of individuation, the evolution of intrapsychic autonomy, perception, memory, cognition, reality testing; the other is the differentiation, distancing, boundary formation, and disengagement from mother" (Mahler, Pine and Bergman, 1975, p. 63). Regarding the comparable process occurring at adolescence, Blos (1967) writes: "Individuation implies that the growing person takes increasing responsibility for what he is, rather than depositing this responsibility on the shoulders of those under whose influence and tutelage he has grown up" (p. 168). In addition, Blos described the process as one of withdrawing emotional cathexes from parents as significant others and reinvesting these cathexes, first in the same-sex peer relationships and eventually in a more intimate heterosexual association.[2]

Undoubtedly the most famous psychoanalytic writings on adolescence are those of Erikson (1950, 1968, 1975), who saw the central crisis of this age as one involving identity formation versus diffusion. In Erikson's view, the adolescent is a person in search of a new and more encompassing identity. Experiencing the dramatic biological changes of pubescence, and moving into new realms of activity and opportunity, the adolescent is no longer a child, although not yet an adult either. Adolescence is a time of psychosocial moratorium, which cushions the young person's transition to adulthood and provides latitude for the search for identity. This moratorium allows the adolescent to make useful experiments without having to make definitive commitments. Thus adolescence, according to Erikson, is characterized by a "selective permissiveness on the part of society and a provocative playfulness on the part of youth" (1968, p. 157).

Sociological analyses present a slightly different view of this period of life. According to Eisenstadt (1962), youth, from a psychological point of view, is the age at which the individual constructs an identity and achieves self-control. However, from a sociological point of view, it is also the stage at which the young person is confronted with some of the major role models, symbols, and values of his or her particular culture. Paradoxically, because the young may play various roles without compromise or limitation, the image of youth is often the purest manifestation of cultural and societal values. "It may be, then, regarded as the only age in which full identification with the ultimate values and symbols of the society is attained—facilitated by the flowering of physical vigor, a vigor which may easily become identified with a more general flowering of the cosmos or the society" (Eisenstadt, 1962, p. 31).

In the work previously reviewed, youth and adolescence have been studied as a terminal phase of childhood, as a separate stage in life, and, less frequently, as one part of a more or less continuous process of human life span development. Often, in these writings, separation from childhood has been the dominant theme. In the 1970s, however, a different approach appeared in the literature, namely, the study of late adolescence as a first stage in adulthood. This important shift may be found in three influential studies by Gould (1972, 1975, 1978), Vaillant (1977a, 1977b), and Levinson et al. (1978; also Levinson, 1978).[3] Although the three formulations stress somewhat different aspects of the developmental process, they all convey deep respect for the 18-year-old as a young adult in an extremely important formative stage of life.

Vaillant suggests, as did Erikson, that the period from age 18 to 22 is dedicated to the achievement of intimacy and real autonomy from one's parents. Gould adds that youth is also a time for living without limitations, questioning every axiom of life, throwing oneself into wild adventures, taking extraordinary risks, testing the tolerance of the body for sleeplessness, hard work and ecstatic sensations. "In short," he says "we are condensed energy waiting for a direction" (Gould, 1978, p. 55). People at this transitional stage often live between two equally false and opposing realities—believing that they can be completely free, or feeling that they are totally controlled. This wavering continues until, during adulthood, a commitment to a more stable lifestyle develops.

Levinson, however, claims that the project of finding one's place in adult society and committing oneself to a more stable lifestyle may take as much as sixteen years, from 17 to 33. This period is not really adolescence, not even a delayed adolescence, but is rather an intrinsic part of adulthood, which he calls the "novice phase." Generally, for the novice, four developmental tasks are most crucial: He has to form The Dream—a vision of one's place in the world—find a mentor relationship, choose a career, and experience a love relationship. First steps towards accomplishing these tasks are taken during the early part of the novice phase—during a period from 17 to 22, which Levinson calls the "early adult transition."

If we examine the whole array of theories concerning youth and early adulthood, some of which have been presented above, it is obvious that they tend to agree on the issue of inconsistency, or lack of stability, of personality at this age. For example, psychoanalytic theorists, including Erikson, propose that youth is a time of much intrapsychic conflict and turmoil, a period of many compelling and conflicting role demands, and a growing number of opportunities and dangers. It seems inevitable, therefore, that the personality of the adolescent or young adult will be marked by change, instability, flux and much redirection. Erikson and others have suggested, however, that this kind of turbulent experience would generally be beneficial for later personality development. Keniston (1962), too, agrees that a lack of turmoil in adolescence has negative consequences for adult development.

On the other hand, research based on objective studies with representative samples seems to indicate that the personality changes that occur at the end of adolescence are neither stormy nor very surprising in their direction (Block, 1971; Offer and Offer, 1975). Most of the longitudinal data suggest consistency rather than crisis. The Berkeley longitudinal studies (Mussen *et al.*, 1980; Eichorn *et al*, 1981), for example, indicate substantial stability of personality and cognitive traits—conclusions based on more than 40 years of research. Changes occur, but they are slow to evolve, and continuity is the dominant group—if not individual—trend.[4] Thus, many modern scholars question the familiar notions of the "storm-and-stress" and "rebellion-against-parents" which seem to linger in the common beliefs about this age.

Among those who expect personality changes during the transition to adulthood, all theorists agree that specific cultural circumstances, or individual variations, might result in different developmental patterns.[5] There is substantial anthropological evidence of cross-cultural variability in the experience of similar age groups in different societies. Eisenstadt (1962) speaks about similar elements which find very different expressions in various cultures. Thus, while some cultures articulate the transition to adulthood in elaborate rites of passage, other societies are characterized by less dramatic transitions. Similarly, Opler (1971) claims that the remarkable differences around the world in adolescent character point to the need for a more central appreciation of cultural relativity. Youth in urban or rural settings, in the inner city or the suburbs, in authoritarian or permissive societies, may experience adolescence in a strikingly different manner. While specific cultural or social contexts have powerful influences throughout the life span, these influences are perhaps especially powerful at adolescence and during the transition to adulthood—an idea Honzik (1984) calls "plasticity in the early adult years" (p. 327).[6]

The present study may be conceptualized, therefore, in the framework of former theories, as looking at youth during military service from three perspectives: a) the developmental tasks of this age group, namely the formation of identity, finding one's place in society, separation from the family, establishment of new relationships and the beginning of a career; b) the special personality traits of individuals in this age group, such as the needs to rebel, experiment and risk oneself; and c) the assumption of the plasticity of personality at this age, which allows for maximal influences of particular cultural values and experiences.

Keeping these perspectives in mind, an attempt will be made to specify the prominent themes which appeared in the participants' accounts regarding their personality changes during their military service. It seemed useful to divide these themes into two general areas: one related to active coping with hardships and difficulties, the various skills needed to master the situations involved in military service, and the self-esteem related to such coping; and the second related to the widening of the men's horizons regarding various aspects of their life-experience (e.g., moral dilemmas, social and cultural variety, death). These two general areas of personality development constitute the Israeli version of transition to adulthood, each area with its own potential for growth or pitfalls and danger, each with possibilities for success and failure.

Before the discussion of the changes, however, a comment should be made regarding the nature of the material used for our presentation. At the beginning of the final interview, which was dedicated to a summary and evaluation of the service, each of the participants was faced with the following question: "How do you think you were changed by your military service?" As the conversation regarding this issue evolved, I introduced a second formulation, saying: "Do you see the period of time since you were a high school senior to the time of your release from the military as a period of growth and progress, as a time of standstill, or as a period of regression in your development? Where would you place yourself on this continuum, and why?" Both questions were answered at length by the participants, with additional probing for clarification introduced as seemed necessary.

Let me say right at the beginning that all the men reported that they were changed by their military service, although they differed in the contents and the intensity of the changes. The majority spoke of "drastic" or "far-reaching" changes, while a few said that the service had not changed them significantly, only strengthened some of their previous tendencies. As will be demonstrated below, this developmental effect was evaluated by the majority of the men as positive.

The Development of Active Coping

The most frequent and widespread reaction of the participants to my questions regarding change as a result of their military service involved development in terms of their ability to cope with difficulties. It seems that the experience of three or four years of service in the military provides young men with the opportunity to encounter a variety of unusual and stressful circumstances, and, as a result, they may emerge from their service with an enhanced sense of their ability to cope with various problems and master hardships, which they consider to be a central component of their adult personality. Most of the men seem to have profited from this opportunity.

In their first attempt to answer my complex question about personality changes during military service, a large number of the participants specified a trio of interrelated traits they felt they had acquired. They described the changes that occurred in them due to their service as an increase in independence, self-confidence, and responsibility. Often they referred to this trio as "maturity," or "manhood." This can be demonstrated in the following quotations. "The fact that I served four years in a combat unit made me into an adult. I became stronger, I learned to be responsible for myself, for my professional duties, and for the men I was in charge of." Or: "The main thing which has changed in me is that I have become independent. I learned to be on my own and to cope with problems as they occur all by myself. This is something I wasn't capable of before my service." And a detailed response: "I don't know if it's the age or the army, but I feel that the army is what has really produced the change. I have changed completely. The military service uncovered my real nature. Before I entered the service, I lacked confidence, I was full of inferiority complexes. In the army, I chose the hardest course, and in that way I made a man of myself. I made it by applying my will, and it gave me tremendous satisfaction. I grew up and built my self esteem. Now I know that if I make enough of an effort I'll be able to achieve any goal I may set for myself. The army is a real test for adulthood. If you complete your service honorably, you're a man."

Several men reported that the major contribution of their military service was the acquisition of methods for coping with stress and hardship, which is naturally central in the broad area of competence. While some of this concerned the physical level, other men emphasized emotional difficulties, social adjustment, or facing failure as the major stress-conditions they learned to master. "I have grown in the emotional sphere. I lived through many crises during my service. If you cope with such crises, you emerge stronger and more mature. It forges you. I feel sort of immunized now. Often, when facing a new challenge, I tell myself: It cannot be worse than basic training, and you succeeded in that. So I feel more secure." And similarly: "Perhaps every person has to go through a difficult time between childhood and adulthood, and that's how you become an adult. In my case, this was the military service. It was terribly hard, but it made me stronger." Or: "On the mental level, my service in the Infantry gave me the ability to withstand hardship. I think that the military is a great school, teaching you to cope with adverse conditions of various kinds." Finally, from Alon's summary: "I have built up my will power, and the ability to go on in the face of stress. It helped me tremendously this year in my studies. I could go through walls to achieve my goals—that's what I learned in those hikes in basic training, and during the war."

The sense of coping with difficulties as an initiation into adulthood is not limited to those who had experienced great physical difficulties. Organizational or intellectual tasks were also mentioned as providing similar outcomes. Said a man from intelligence: "I acquired a lot of self-confidence. I managed to succeed in demanding and responsible positions. I became an earnest and meticulous worker. I managed other men and was able to act as a leader. Before my service, I didn't realize that I was capable of all these."

In addition to the three traits specified above, the participants also mentioned several similar traits which they acquired as a result of their military service, and which may be considered as components of the central trait of competence. Several men, mostly those who had served in combat units, emphasized physical attainments, while for others, competence covered a wider area of traits and skills. The following are several quotations about physical achievements: "I was far from being an athletic guy before the service. But what can I tell you? The service changed me completely. Physically, you find that you're capable of much more than you thought." And David added: "Regarding fitness, I have learned that physical accomplishments and coping with lack of sleep can be acquired. I realized that there was no limit to what I could achieve in this respect, and therefore to what I should expect from my men." Eitan reinforces this view: "You can always go one step beyond what you considered to be your limit. You think that you're going to break down, but if you continue, you discover that you can attain new limits, that you have a huge range of abilities you weren't aware of. This is a great lesson for life." While most of these answers stressed physical achievements, some of the men also included survival skills, which they were able to apply in various situations after their service.

In reference to other, nonphysical skills: "As a student I used to be rather careless. In the army (in the Intelligence) I learned to respect the written word. I became a dilligent worker, thorough in my investigations and reports. I like this aspect, which is certainly a product of the army service." Or: "I learned to conduct a logical analysis of a situation, and I discovered that I am a careful, hardworking person." "I used to be absent-minded, my things were always in a mess. In the army I had to keep my gear in order, and I became much more organized as a result." And finally: "Before the army I didn't care much about things, I was irresponsible, all I cared for was travelling and amusing myself. The army has made me into a serious person. Now I want to settle down. I feel that time is short, and I have to make something out of my life."

Some of the men considered their boost in confidence to be related to their promotion to positions of command in the army. They mentioned that this step improved their self-image, as well as their social status. Most interesting was David's comment: "As a member of Israeli society, I learned in the army right away that your origin doesn't make any difference. If you're talented and willing to apply yourself, you will be rewarded. If you jump from an airplane, you receive paratrooper's wings on your chest. If you work hard, you'll get the silver bars (of an officer) on your shoulder. Everybody can do this, it doesn't matter if your parents are from Iraq, Morocco, or wherever."

Responsibility for others was mentioned by many as an experience which produced a sense of growing up. Says Gil: "You grow up, undoubtedly. You start to understand other people's problems. You have to make difficult decisions involving them. I remember a driver who came to me and complained that he couldn't perform his job that day, and when I ordered him to go anyway, he said that he felt he might have an accident. I decided to ignore his threat, and repeated my command. He never knew that I trembled inside, but I had my reasons and I used my authority. Such experiences were common, and they made an adult out of me.''

Several men who had held positions of command described ''skills'' which they had acquired during their service, mostly organizational skills and leadership. Achievements in these areas were described as contributing to the development of maturity—the trio of responsibility, independence and self-confidence. Said Gad: ''Everyone who served as an officer in the army gained something from it. You gain in leadership skills and practice. Today I can face a group of four hundred men and command them, or give them a lecture. I wouldn't hesitate at all—and I was never capable of doing this before my service.'' Later he also stressed an added understanding of others: ''I learned a lot of psychology in the army. How to talk to a man with problems, to make him feel better, to boost his morale, to help him cope with his fears. This is real leadership, I think, and I know it is something I'll use as a civilian too.'' Or: ''The army provided me with an unusual workshop to learn about people and how to manage them. When I was released, I felt that I had lost in terms of my authority. Today I'm a nothing in comparison to my former status, but at least I know what I'm capable of. I wonder if at any future time I will have as much power as I had at 21, during my service.''

Other human relations skills were also mentioned, often as an aspect of leadership. Said Ido: ''When I was in charge of the selection process for our reconnaissance unit, it gave me a rare opportunity to observe people and to learn about their nature. One of the main things I have learned was never to form an impression right at the beginning, according to external clues, but to remain flexible and open, and see the cumulative impression.'' Or: ''I simply learned to sit with my men and listen to them.''

For a few, the attainments described were in the intellectual or technical sphere. The descriptions in this area often referred to outstanding achievements, similar to those in the physical sphere. For example: ''In the Intelligence, I learned to think, to organize material and to present it in a clear report. Moreover, in the army I had the chance to become the best man in my area in the whole world. I know I was in this position, for sure. This is a pretty unusual opportunity that one rarely gets in life otherwise.'' Although this participant's comment on his exceptional status is not common, the skills which he acquired are not typical only of the Intelligence Corps. Said a man who had served in the Artillery: ''I learned to think: to take a goal, analyze it down to its components, and plan separately how to achieve each component. I learned to plan my steps, not to act impulsively. Make a plan, and include an alternative in case it doesn't work. All these help me tremendously outside the army.''

The material presented above dealt with the various positive achievements related to that aspect of development which I have called 'active coping.' Although this was the predominant attitude, not all the participants experienced positive achievements in this area, and some felt that their capacity to cope had been impaired as a result of their military service. These men referred to the fact that in an authoritative, hierarchical system, individuals are prevented from applying their own judgment, acting according to their own decisions, or initiating activities according to their own planning. This feeling leads to a completely different description of the military experience and its contribution to the transition to adulthood. But common to both groups of men was the emphasis on the theme of active coping, whether attained or impaired, as a central aspect of their transition to adulthood. It was this emphasis that led me to delineate active coping as a central theme in the Israeli version of transition to adulthood.

The following are some of the negative experiences mentioned by the men. Most critical is the following: "I think that personally I managed not to be affected by the military service, but in general I see it as highly destructive. The most destructive aspect is that it trains you to adapt rather than to fight for your own values. People don't struggle in the army, they learn to adapt, and come out thinking that you can adjust to anything. Later on, as civilians, they are willing to conform to anything . . . This is very bad, it is development-in-reverse, and may eventually lead to a disaster.'' While these objections were more philosophical, Yochanan admitted that he himself suffered from the negative consequences of the service. "I am a very independent type," he says, "and the army oppressed me. There is no place for individuality in the army, you learn to sit still and adjust.''

In a letter that he sent me several days after our final conversation one of the Nahal soldiers said: "I gave your questions a great deal of thought, and I arrived at the conclusion that there were three interconnected traits that I think I have acquired in the army. First is the avoidance of responsibility. In the army this was my attitude toward our commanders, but now, as a civilian, I continue to behave like this in my relations with any authority, any responsibility. I simply don't bother. Next is forgiving. We forgive others, our men or our buddies, for their inefficiency and lack of reliability. We also tend to forgive ourselves. Even now I continue to forgive myself easily when I have not tried harder and therefore have failed. But the third trait, indifference, is worse of all. The army made me apathetic and numb . . . This is the whole syndrome we all suffer from . . . I think that every army, or perhaps every large compulsory system, ends up destroying personal involvement and conscientiousness, and leads to some kind of withdrawal in people.''

Related to the claim that the army does not encourage independence is Ido's comment that the military service does indeed make men into more competent persons, but at a price: ''The army makes you into a one-sided, determined individual, a trait very typical of Israelis, which I personally dislike.'' A different kind of ''price'' was the following: ''In the military a person learns to steal, to be violent, to take advantage of friends. That's the way to survive. Now, as a civilian, I feel these traits in all of us, and it upsets me. We are all living under terrible pressure and we lack tolerance for each other.'' And in David's words: ''The army is a cruel system. You tend to judge people according to their performance, not according to who they are. In normal life, I don't want to use such criteria, but it's hard to change.''

It seems that the military service provides most men with the opportunity to achieve self-confidence and independence, or in more general terms the capacity for active coping. However, for a minority of the men, the experience is exactly the opposite, and is detrimental to their confidence, initiative and sense of self-direction. This was particularly the case for men who were assigned jobs which were below their potential, and were therefore not required to apply coping skills and develop personal responsibility, as in the case of Danny. ''My three years of service,'' he says in his final evaluation, ''were three years of complete deterioration. In all respects. Mentally, I didn't have to make any intellectual effort, and worked with people with whom I couldn't exchange any ideas. Socially, it was like a desert. I felt bad. I couldn't even study in this atmosphere, because I felt depressed most of the time. For long periods I had no motivation to get up in the morning. I only wanted the day to end and to go home. That's how it was for three solid years. It's not just that I didn't develop, but I really felt I was going backwards. In high school I did much more than during my service. I was head of the student council, I managed our sports program, I was a leader. The army didn't provide any challenge for me. I did what was expected of me, but all I was in charge of was my own work, and there was nothing to it.''

Furthermore, men who failed (at least in their own eyes) in meeting the standards of high competence during some stages of their service, remained with a sense of failure or a flaw in their personality. Said one of these men: ''Basic training remains a trauma for me, it's really a scar . . . I emerged from the army feeling imperfect, as if I were flawed. I have a sense of disrespect for myself. I would have felt better had I served in a combat unit, in the Infantry.'' However, even this is not totally negative. In a different context, he said: "In the army I often failed. Sometimes I had to cope with severe blows. I'd say that I have learned to fail. I learned to accept it and to cope with it as a part of life.''

At the time of our interviews, all the participants were struggling with their first year of academic education. Many of them experienced difficulty in returning to study habits and refreshing their previous knowledge. Although, as cited above, a few men did feel that their service had contributed to developing their intellectual skills, several participants, both officers and ordinary soldiers, attributed their academic difficulties to the military service, which had interrupted their education and channelled their energies in a different direction. In the present context, it seems to me that the military demands for active coping and 'doing' may have cast a shadow on mental functions such as studying and thinking. This, then, is another negative aspect of the norm of active coping.

David: "An army is something which blocks the individual. You live under strict constraints, and you're not allowed any liberty. So you are lucky if you maintain a certain level of mental functioning, but you certainly do not go forward, as would be normal for your age." Although I do not have evidence about the "intellectual deficit" and its effects, I would dare to speculate, based on years of work with Israeli students, that the academic difficulties mentioned above are temporary, and may characterize the transition period between military service and the period of higher education.

The excerpts presented in this section together form a wide array of coping capacities that all the men interviewed felt they attained (or failed to attain, or damaged) as a result of their military service. It was this aspect of development that the men experienced as defining their transition to adulthood. The majority of those interviewed, in fact, felt that they had succeeded during their military service in coping with considerable difficulties, an experience which enhanced their confidence in their further abilities to master hardships. This positive process was not, however, experienced by all the participants, and some of the men emerged from military service with the feeling that their coping capacities had been impaired. Now we will turn to a description of a second general area of personality development prominent in the men's accounts—the expansion of personal boundaries.

The Expansion of Personal Boundaries

In response to my questions about change, the participants reported a variety of new encounters during their military service which led to a widening of horizons in various areas. From a relatively homogeneous, protected home environment the young men joining the army embarked on a

journey traversing new experiences and meetings with people of greatly differing cultural backgrounds, opinions and values. Such encounters provided
individuals with new components for their developing identity. In their transition to adulthood, they were facing the task of integrating these components into a coherent self. In many cases, this produced a feeling of
enrichment on the part of the soldiers, a feeling of 'growing up' and gaining maturity. In others, this process was not easily completed, and, at the
time of our evaluation, several men seemed to linger in the stage of search,
doubt, or confusion while they had not yet integrated their experiences. The
following excerpts will demonstrate these phenomena.

As an introduction to the general contents of this chapter, we may use
an excerpt from Alon's final evaluation of his personality change in the
army. As in many other cases, his initial reaction focussed on the war.
"After the war," he says, "my self-image changed. During battle I felt that
a program of which I had been unaware was activated in my brain. I
found that I could behave unexpectedly, for better or worse. I acted like a
different man. The good side is the clarity, precision and awareness that I
was able to effect under extremely difficult conditions. During this stress
situation, I became a leader, better able to cope with the problems than all
the officers around me. I was amazed, but it came naturally to me, and the
men recognized it and followed my decisions. On the bad side, I see this
thrill of violence about which we have talked so much. How easily a man,
including myself, can become a beast. So now, when I think about my
personality, I have to encompass all these experiences as well."

It seems that many others had similar views, which they often summarized quite prosaically in presenting their military service as an enrichment. They said repeatedly that in the army they gained "an experience,"
and it was enriching, regardless of its specific contents. Said David:
"People who don't serve in the army are missing a fantastic experience
which they cannot have elsewhere. I see military service is an immensely
complex experience which enriched me. I finished it full of new questions
to explore, and it will be a long time before I answer them all."

While the above quotations seem to discuss mainly external events,
the following stress the opportunity for self-knowledge. Said Ido: "My military service contributed to my self-knowledge. Now I am aware of my
limits. I know that I can undertake a whole lot before I break down. I
learned techniques to cope, resist pressure, and calm myself. But most important, I have learned what might break me down." Similar responses
were given by all of the men who had served in elite combat units. Like
Eitan: "As a result of my service, I know my strong and weak sides. I
learned that I'm too lenient with people under my command, for example,
but that I'm good at negotiating, at dealing fairly with people. When I

undertake new roles as a civilian, I know what to expect of myself, and what to beware of.''

In trying to organize the references that fall under the heading of expansion of personal boundaries, we will concentrate on three main subjects: encounters with death, people, and values—and their effects on the development of the personality.

I. Encounters with death. Many people faced death and injuries for the first time during their military service, most frequently in war, but sometimes also during normal military training, and these encounters were mentioned by several of them as changing their approach to life. ''The primary outcome of my service is that I have learned to appreciate life. Everything is a matter of life-and-death here, everything is serious.'' And another participant: ''In the army I met death for the first time. This makes you grow. You're both hurt and strengthened by seeing death. I saw many wounded men, and I knew some who were killed. This will remain with me for ever. You see life for what it's worth. It's not paradise, not everything is rosy, as I used to think as a child. On the other hand, I'm so grateful that I'm well and alive. All this has changed me profoundly.'' Or: ''In the army I learned that life is the highest value. To save a man is the noblest deed. To me this also meant to be kinder to people, to act more humanely to others. It also taught me to appreciate the small things—being home for Saturday, meeting friends, going out on a date. All that used to be self-evident before.''

David, who had started his response to my question by announcing that he had not changed much during his service, later on provided the following long comment, focusing on the war as the most influential part of his military service: ''War changes people. It has changed me, but it's hard to share this with others. What can I say about death, about a friend who was killed—I'm afraid I'll just distort the truth, so I keep still. Only once a year do I feel that I'm being understood without any words, and that's on Memorial Day, at the military cemetery. A meeting of the eyes is enough there on that day. Moreover, I cannot discuss these things with people who haven't experienced the war. I have become sentimental, I can be all excited by a poem, a photograph of a place. On the other hand, I have developed this tough exterior. I know death, and therefore what else is there to be excited about?''

While a positive outcome of the encounter with death may be a better appreciation of life and humanity, a complementary, negative outcome is expressed in anxiety, depression or—rarely—rage. Several men talked about nightmares as a manifestation of anxiety. This was the case of one of the interviewees, an instructor of combat medics. ''Look,'' he said to me, ''they all may die. I have 'killed' my trainees in an endless number of situations. In my dreams I saw them mutilated on the battlefield. I received messages that they were killed in action. Especially those whom I liked the most . . . Look, if one of my trainees is killed while treating a soldier in a mine-field, then that's exactly what I was teaching him to do! And if they die, part of me will die with them.''

Another man discusses his nightmares related to combat memories, a well-documented effect of war. ''During my service I was mostly indifferent to what I saw. Now, however, these sights are returning in nightmares, like a flashback. They may come up suddenly even when I'm awake. It disturbs me, especially when I'm with a girl.''

A tendency toward depression is another emotional reaction that has been discussed in the literature. Alon often calls himself ''depressive,'' referring to frequent sadness or moodiness in his life. ''I received several severe blows during my service. What happened with my girlfriend, and the fact that Zvika was killed, and all the events in Beirut. I know that these events left their mark on me. I had a difficult time as a student, after my release. Often I think that all my moods and problems are the result of the war.''

II. Encounters with people. A different kind of new encounter occurs in the social sphere. As the men emerge from their family and school environment into the social reality of the military system, they experience a set of positive and negative events.

A highly popular response about the social sphere referred to the wider context, of getting to know ''all of Israeli society.'' Many men said: ''You get to know the whole country in the army,'' or: ''I met all kinds of people that I never knew before,'' or: ''The people I met in the army are what gave me a proper perspective on Israeli society.'' This broadening of horizons was perceived by many as a positive outcome of their military service.

The discovery of the wide spectrum of subgroups of Israeli society had different effects on the participants. Most general is the following comment: ''In the army I felt that we formed one society. In spite of our great differences and the variety of our backgrounds, we were willing to sacrifice a lot for each other and for our common goals. This gave me a good feeling, and much hope for Israel as a nation.''

Other men said more specifically that in the military they discarded some of their former prejudices concerning other groups. ''People say that the army is a great melting pot. This was certainly true for me. When I started my service in the Artillery, I was alone in the midst of people that had a completely different mentality than mine. They were mostly Sepharadic, with a relatively low level of education. At first I had many prejudices, and I resented these people. I acted like a snob, looking down on soldiers who had bad table manners . . . Gradually, we became friends and my prejudices started to dissipate. You learn to evaluate a person for what he is, not by the group he belongs to. I have become more tolerant in the army, and also more aware of social problems I hadn't understood before."

These two elements, greater awareness of the social gap and the replacement of stereotypical views by personal judgment, appear in about half of the participants' reactions. As in the case of Gad: "I used to make home visits at my soldiers' homes, and I discovered things I had never known to exist in reality. A family of 15, all cramped into a one-room apartment, whose father tells me that they used to be very affluent in Iraq before they fled. Naturally they hate everybody and are deeply bitter. They hated me too, but I have become their spokesman just the same. It bothers me that we do not deal with this problem, and I plan to contribute to its solution in any way I can."

While these statements seem to strengthen hopes for social integration through military service, this was not the conclusion for all the participants. About half of the men emerged from their service highly critical of the lower classes. Many of those who voiced their criticism were themselves of Oriental origin. Said David: "I met everybody in the army. Many Orientals would say to me: 'I don't have a chance because of my origin.' I hate this attitude, because I'm from the same background, and I know that it's not true. These people have the mentality of the chronic underprivileged. They don't want to give, just to receive all the time. From my own experience I know that in the army, if you want to, you can apply yourself, and you get your rewards. But these people refuse to work."

These findings support the claim that people become socially more aware during their military service, and in that sense they seem to have matured by their exposure to others. However, it was not always the case that intergroup contacts produced greater understanding. Apparently, about half of the men emerged as more tolerant adults, willing to bridge the social gap, while the other half became more extreme in certain of their prejudices. The data seem to indicate that combat soldiers and officers became more open-minded, while the opposite occurred for men with administrative roles. This tendency is not surprising, especially because it is in the administrative and service units that the more problematic social groups are concentrated. Those who reach combat units are, *a priori*, of a higher level and with more motivation. This, however, is not the only factor, and it does not account for all the differences of opinion, which were probably affected by a multitude of factors in the personal experience of the participants both during service and before it.

Before concluding the presentation of the expansion of boundaries as demonstrated in the social sphere, let me mention a surprising finding. The encounter with commanders as role models was expected to be one of the major factors in the development of personality during the military service. In contrast to my expectations and widespread Israeli beliefs, very few of the participants mentioned meaningful relationships with their superiors either in their summaries or their accounts. Several commanders were described as sadists or very distant figures, others as worthless. Only two of the participants mentioned the relationship with a commander among the factors which had contributed to their growth. One of these men was David, who said: "In my service I met some highly influential figures, and this is more important than the skills I acquired. The man who had been my squad leader during basic training, and my company commander when I became an officer, was someone I could really look up to and he influenced me a great deal."

III. Encounters with values. The third area in which a significant expansion of horizons occurred during military service concerns the testing of one's values against a variety of situations. Almost all the participants spontaneously discussed situations in which their values were put to some test, or in which they had experienced moral uncertainty. Several of them expressed regret regarding some of their actions. Three sets of values were at the focus of the new encounter: the value of peace as a means for the solution of the political conflicts in the Middle East, the value of the just or moral behavior of the soldier as an individual and the Army in general, and the belief in the state of Israel as a continuity in Jewish history. Some of these will be demonstrated in the following excerpts.

Israel is a country in which, due to its repeated engagement in wars and the general feeling that its physical existence is still endangered by the Arab threat, political issues enjoy a degree of emotional involvement on the part of the population that is rare in most Western countries. Attitudes toward peace form the core of the political struggle between different camps and parties in Israel. A great majority of the participants reported that they were little involved in politics before their military service. They had often identified with one of the large political camps, but saw their youthful opinions as superficial. All the men said that following their military service they had much more to say about politics, although for several of them there was no clear-cut identification with any of the political parties. Thus, the most general feature of their growing understanding was often a simultaneous increase in depth of interest and involvement, which in some cases was accompanied by a sense of confusion. While this may have been the result of their age, most of the men attributed this development to their experiences in the army, whether to their exposure to the total spectrum of political views, or to their participation in war and the subsequent service in Lebanon. For all these reasons, the following developments in political thinking seem to demonstrate an additional aspect of the expansion of personal horizons.

Regarding the contents of their opinions, about half the participants reported that they had changed their views, shifting from an identification with the "right," which is identified with a pro-military view, to the "left," which is generally identified with the peace movement, or vice versa. The remaining half said that the military experience did not change their loyalties, although they became either more convinced or more sophisticated in their opinions. Slightly more men reported a move towards the "left" than in the opposite direction.

Some men found that the promise of peace seemed further from them following their experience in the army: "What I saw during my service made me change my views to the right. I feel that Jewish blood has lost its value in our eyes, and we have become 'more pious than the Pope' in protecting Arab interests." When a change of direction was reported, however, it was more frequently toward peace-oriented, leftist views. "I identified with the right-wing views before my service, but the Lebanon War opened my eyes. I saw people getting killed for nothing, and I started to understand the Arabs, who want a state of their own. Today I identify with the left. Let the Arabs get back their territories and solve their own problems."

While it might seem that a person who had experienced war, with its painful memories, would afterwards tend to the view that future wars should be avoided, such a simple direction of change was not typical. Several men emerged from their experience more confused and worried about the absence of a clear "truth." These men expressed their dismay, and often argued that the political problem is more complex than they had realized before. Said a man who had served in the Military Police: "My opinions today are more complex. In the army I learned to examine every problem from all possible perspectives. As a result, today I'm unable to tell you who is right in the political argument between the right and the left." David, who was highly introspective in other areas, found it difficult to respond to my question about political changes. After some deliberation, he said: "My political views were not well formed before the army, and now I'm even more confused. My opinions often contradict each other. I can't find any party I could whole-heartedly support. I'd like to learn more about this, because I hate to remain indifferent. When I find a viewpoint I like, I'll work for it."

A pattern which could be discerned in some of the men's responses on the subject involved a two-stage process. First, they began to recognize the complexity of the political issues, and as a result they developed a growing tolerance and understanding of the diversity of opinions. This is similar to the process noted above regarding attitudes toward social groups. But for some of the participants this ambiguity was confusing, and rather than feeling that they had gained a deepening of their understanding, they felt that they had emerged confused. Thus, as in the other areas, the expansion of personal boundaries in this area of political views was experienced by the majority as a process of maturation, while some felt impaired by this very same process.

The second area of confrontation between values and reality relates to the moral behavior of soldiers and of the IDF. Several major contexts were mentioned by the participants as creating moral dilemmas: routine service during peacetime, involving norms of behavior among the soldiers, or between them and their commanders; guard duty in the occupied territories in the West Bank and Gaza, which often aroused doubts about moral conduct vis-a-vis the Arab inhabitants, and the Lebanon War. All the examples cited were instances in which former values of the participants were put to test by complicated reality demands. On the individual level, they sometimes behaved against their beliefs. On the general level, they were able to judge and evaluate the behavior of others, and of the military system, vis-a-vis norms and values that had used to guide their lives. As a result of these experiences, the men were divided into a larger group, which claimed that military service tended to weaken or undermine norms of moral behavior, or to shatter deep beliefs about the military system, and a minority who reported that their experience in the army improved their moral behavior or produced an increase of their awareness of moral concerns. Violence, and the ease with which people tend to act violently, on the one hand, and obedience to authority on the other, are among the recurrent themes in the men's accounts.

Many men described the daily lifestyle on a military base as obeying norms which greatly differed from their previous standards as civilians, referring mainly to the norm of stealing to cover up for missing gear, or the norm of cheating one's superiors as a legitimate means of improving one's welfare. A similar means of survival is the development of a network of 'connections,' bribing the powerful for the purpose of obtaining better conditions for oneself. Following this frequent practice, says one of the men: "We got used to cheating. Mostly because others in the unit were so negligent and we forgave them and covered up for them. This became rather confusing. Is it immoral—or, rather, tactful? As a result, today I forgive myself quite easily for cheating, for smoothing things over."

On the other hand, several of the men who served in elite units, or who completed officers' training, attributed their standard of absolute reliability to their military education. The demand for complete personal credibility represents the opposite of the behavior described above. Several men described these military norms as making them more honest and reliable. Gil: "For me it was simply a reeducation . . . The lesson of the officers' course remained with me all through my service . . . It really changed me."

Responsible and delicate situations often presented the men with difficult temptations or conflicts, testing their moral standards. As in the story of one of the Intelligence men: "We were obliged to report everything, including our mistakes or those of our men. Simply stated, never to lie about our work. Once, I blundered, and for a moment I was tempted not to report it to my superiors. This temptation was just a momentary weakness, but I see it as a personal failure. Because the mistake was meaningful, and I had really considered keeping it to myself. It was one of the most difficult dilemmas that I experienced. After a few moments, however, I went to my superior and 'confessed.' He took care of the problem, covered up a little for me, and somehow the storm passed. But to this day I am ashamed of my thoughts."

Civilian and military norms were often contradictory in the area of human relations, and some of the commanders found this to be particularly difficult. Says Eitan, an officer in the paratroopers: "As a commander I was often in a dilemma in my relationship with my men. As a sergeant, I was often ordered by my commander to discipline a soldier, unjustly, in my opinion. I remember that I used to try to argue with my commander, but usually he would not listen to me. So there I was, facing the soldier, having to discipline or harass him against my conscience, and having to hide my own thoughts and feelings about it. There was one case of a soldier who had sneaked into the kitchen to take some food, since he was hungry. Our company leader ordered me to ground this soldier on base for the weekend. I thought that the punishment was unfair, since he was a good man. He had been disciplined often in the past, and just then he was starting to do better . . . but the company leader would not listen to my arguments. He said that I was soft, and he ordered me to obey. Well, I disciplined the man, and I felt terrible. I remember that I, myself, went on furlough that weekend, and could not stop thinking about that poor man. But that is the army. You have no choice. You have to carry out your orders, and you mustn't ever show that you disagree with them. It is a matter of loyalty. I couldn't go to the man and say: "Look, I would have released you, it was the company commander who made me punish you." The whole system is built on loyalty, and you can't break it."

When I asked Eitan what the effects of such experiences on his personality might be, he said: "I think that when you live through such situations, it makes you grow up. You must learn to take into consideration not just your self-interests, but the interests of the general system. In that specific case, I realized that the principle of loyalty between the commanding ranks was more important than my own bad feelings *vis-a-vis* my soldier.''

David experienced similar situations. In his case, his main conflicts were internal, rather than with his commanders. It was natural for him to be tough with his men, but even he felt that fair behavior was sometimes difficult to define. ''A commander is a very powerful figure in the army,'' he says. ''Sometimes I humiliated soldiers . . . You may tell a man to his face some very tough things, things you'll never be able to take back later on . . . You are together on a forsaken hill somewhere, and you have all the power in your hand. At the same time, you catch yourself thinking: But he is just two years younger than me. I am also a child, what do I know more than he? I remember such moments, but generally I don't remember an instance where I really behaved against my basic principles.''

On the fragile line between right and wrong, some found a rather simplistic solution for their dilemmas: ''In the army I learned that you cannot survive without stepping on others. If you don't step on them, they will step on you. There is no third way. Obviously, I didn't want to be stepped upon . . . The more I understood the military system, the more I fought with everybody. Only when I was shrewd or violent did I gain respect and achieve my goals. When I was fair and polite, I never got anywhere, and was taken advantage of by others. Now that I'm a civilian, I'm not so sure that these are the most useful or desirable patterns for me.''

As in the issue of honesty versus cheating, some of the men saw their experiences in the area of human relations in the army as greatly enhancing their development as social beings. ''My experience as an instructor in the medics' course was like an ongoing situation of moral dilemmas. I had all these problems with my trainees, and I was constantly searching for the most appropriate solutions. This constant concern changed my moral judgment and values. I was always flexible with my men, and tried to approach every problem with an open mind.''

While all the above deal with confrontations that are typical of the routine on military bases, many of the instances brought up by the respondents on this subject involved unusual, extreme circumstances. Eitan recalls: ''We were ordered to participate in the evacuation of Yamit.[7] This was a moment where I was commanded to do something that was really against my beliefs. I believe that it is a crime to destroy a Jewish settlement in the Land of Israel, it shouldn't be done. Furthermore, I had friends and relatives among the settlers of the area. What would I do? Luckily, I was spared the conflict. On the week of the struggle in Yamit, I was cadet-in-charge on base, so I wasn't sent out with the others. But I gave the situation a great deal of thought, and I'm convinced that, had I been in

Yamit with the other soldiers, I would have obeyed all my orders, and even fought my own friends. Clearly, when the military system issues a command, even if it is against my beliefs, as long as I am a soldier, my orders come first. Maybe I would even not have felt so bad about it, since I would have been acting under command, and not out of my own free choice. I know how to make myself obey even when I disagree with the task."

The subject of acting against one's own beliefs was discussed most often in the context of contact with the enemy. This was the case when soldiers served in the occupied territories of Gaza and the West Bank, and during the Lebanon War. Again, the participants often noticed that they had made a compartmentalization between their moral or political opinions and their behavior as soldiers. Gil's general comment may serve as a summary for this dilemma, which was greatly elaborated in the personal accounts in Part I. "Look," he said to me in our final interview, "in the military you often do things that you don't think are the right things. Just the same . . . I used to take good care of the battalion's agricultural outposts, rarely paying attention to the mere fact of their location. Our new outpost was built in the Hebron Mountains, facing right into this Arab village. It shouldn't have been there in the first place. Here we are, on the Arabs' land, plowing what used to be their fields. I felt that we were wrong, and it was against my basic convictions. But, most of the times I didn't give it any attention. I denied the whole conflict. When the Arabs threw a rock at my jeep, of course I was angry, declared a curfew in the village and arrested some kids. But actually I *knew* why they threw those rocks in the first place . . . Once I was driving alone in my jeep in the hills, and suddenly I stumbled onto a blockade made by the villagers. A flag of 'liberated Palestine' was hanging from the electricity pole. Just then a bus full of Arab workers passed by. I went down alone, stopped the bus, and ordered the men to clear the road, and to take the flag down immediately. They all obeyed, and I went on my way. The fact is, however, that personally I do believe that the Palestinians should get a land of their own. But as a soldier, you learn to withhold your human emotions. Even more, you learn not to think."

Several men spoke regretfully about their behavior during security duty in the Gaza Strip of the early 1980s. They were called out for emergency duty when riots occured in this tense area, dense with Arab refugees. Several participants related in great detail their memories of that task, focusing on their amazement at how violent they were under the circumstances—a feeling later repeated during the Lebanon War. Several men describe their experience in Gaza as a kind of depersonalization, in which they were surprised to discover that aggressive behavior was easy, even enjoyable, for them: "Most shocking was the fact that in the middle of all this wild action, you even enjoy the experience! You enjoy striking people, shooting, just running wild. But later on, when I was thinking about it, I said: "What have I done? For I had lost my human image for a while." Common to the men's stories is the ease with which they felt that they slipped into violence, and the later resentment and guilt feelings—a chain of responses highly similar to that described by Lifton (1973), although the Israeli soldiers interviewed never participated in atrocities similar to those described by the Vietnam War veterans.

When confronting the Lebanese population during and after the war, similar feelings were aroused. "I felt like a conqueror. It was unpleasant. I had to learn to act forcefully. But you know there is no choice, and this reduces some of the pangs. Afterwards, however, one gets adjusted. You lose your sensitivity. It doesn't upset you anymore to see a woman weeping, or children sleeping in the gutters. It startled me to discover that I wasn't touched by suffering as I had been."

All the men who had served in Lebanon, even those in whose opinions the war was justified, described similar experiences. Often they expressed their dismay regarding these issues. None of the men considered disobeying their orders, however. Explained one of the participants, whose political views were very different from official government policy at that time: "The army made me into a conqueror, and there is no nobility in this role, none. But as much as I resent my position, I must obey my orders. Is there a limit to that rule? Perhaps I can see one. Perhaps I would have disobeyed an order to shoot at innocent civilians. Luckily I have never been faced with this choice. Up to this extreme point, however, I think that I would have obeyed anything."

A few of the participants were able to comment on what they considered the long-range effects of these experiences on their personalities. "During the war I lost some of my moral restraints. We lost the sense of value of human life—of the enemy, of course—and a respect for private property. We committed all kinds of sins, so what kind of morality remained? I do not blame our commanders, or the orders that we received, because personally we were also responsible for the way we acted. Now, as a civilian, I feel that I have lost my moral standards. Yesterday I was annoyed by a bus driver, so I almost hit him. For a moment I felt that, had I owned a rifle, I might have shot the man. I suspect that even now I may become violent, and enjoy it. This frightens me to death. Sometimes it even seems legitimate, you know: The returning soldiers may be a little wild. That's what happened to us when we returned from Lebanon to the kibbutz. They forgave us everything, because we had fought in the war. So how should we behave?"

He goes on to describe his own dismay. "Today I feel like a nothing. I don't know how to behave. I would give everything for a clear system of values, that would determine my behavior for me from moment to moment. Could I find this in religion, perhaps? Right now I don't think so . . . [Because] if there were a God, Zvika, my friend, would not have been killed, nor would the little kid we shot on the ramp in Beirut."

Not all the men came out of their experience with a similar dismay. There were others who felt that their experience during the war strengthened their moral conduct and reasoning. This was the main point of Gad's summary of his long service in occupied Lebanon, which was characterized by control and restraint. As an officer, he felt that he had to serve as a model of conduct for his men. "A person has to be accountable in such a state," he started slowly. "Everybody may be swept by impulses, as I had been before [during his duty in the Gaza Strip], but the trick is to control them. During the long period that we served in the strongholds in Lebanon, I knew that I had to maintain order so that my men and myself would survive the hardships. It was perfectly clear to me what was morally right or wrong. I acted with authority, but never against my conscience. My men never looted or hit Arab citizens. In my contacts with the Arab population I tried to live up to the ideals of what an IDF officer should be. I felt I was serving as a model for my men, to the last one."

For some of the men, their confrontation with values concerned the behavior of others, or the general conduct of the IDF rather than doubts about their personal responsibility or actions. Ido was most general in his view, which was embedded in his memories about the war: "I remember one night in particular. The PLO had shelled our forces during the day from their positions in Beirut. During the night, I witnessed the retaliation of the IDF. It was something incredible. This was a night which shook me out of my senses . . . That night was my night of disillusionment. My beliefs in the IDF's values, in our 'purity of arms,' were demolished together with the city. It was a terrible night for me." As a result of his years of military experience, in his final evaluation Ido expressed profound doubts about most of the values he had believed in prior to his service—and seemed at a loss for finding new ones in their place.

Yochanan was somewhat less general: "Often I sensed that my commanders had no respect for human life when it concerned our allies from Zadal, the pro-Israeli Christian forces of Southern Lebanon. I witnessed how the Lebanese investigated suspects of terrorism—like in the Spanish Inquisition, I'm telling you. Our own officers knew what was going on, we all heard the screaming, yet we were not allowed to interfere. It made me so mad! What could I do personally? I was just an ordinary soldier, and had been considered a troublemaker throughout my service. At least as a medic I had the chance to behave in a humane way towards the Lebanese, and I played the role of the "good Israeli." This was the mentality in Lebanon, incredibly cruel. There was no pity there." In another context, however, Yochanan describes how he, too, was affected by the same atmosphere. "Gradually, these values affected me too. I remember sitting in Lebanon and waiting for something to happen so that I, as a medic, would be saved from the boredom. Once, when I caught myself thinking like that, I was really startled."

"From then on," he continues, "I have this heavy feeling all the time, because I could understand how people acted like the Nazis, and how any sane human being may get to that point. It happens in two stages. First, you become indifferent to what others are doing, and next, you join them. It's a very fragile line, that's all. On the other hand, I didn't see any alternative to the way we acted, and that's what upset me more than anything. In Lebanon I discovered that the world is cruel, and only the strong survive. We must be strong. At the same time, this may lead to immoral actions, or to becoming an accomplice of such, by not objecting to what others are doing. This has left a deep scar in me, as I believe it has in all of the Israeli soldiers who participated in the war and the occupation. When you take off your uniform and return to civilian life, you can't simply ignore what had happened. We must be influenced by the experience, although I can't tell you exactly how."

So far I have presented expansion of one's personal boundaries in two areas—the political sphere, focusing on the value of peace, and the moral sphere, concentrating on the issue of just behavior in the military context. We will now turn to the last system of values explored in the present study, namely the continuity of Jewish history, which is the essence of Zionism.

In exploring this area in my final interview with the participants, my original intention was to examine whether the experience of transition to adulthood included also a clarification of national identity in the wider historical sense. I assumed that during their service, men were exposed to events which might evoke associations with the previous history of the Jewish people, and I wondered whether these associations would be absorbed and integrated as part of the developing self. The reactions of the participants to the exploration of this area differed widely in contents and depth.

Some of the participants "discovered" during their service their sense of belonging to the country or the society. "After the army, I feel more a part of this country. If I pass by the places in which I trained or navigated, it gives me a special feeling. I simply feel that I belong here more than I used to." Or "The first thing that I received from my military service is an identity, in the sense that I know that I'm part of this country, and that I want to live here. My awareness of all that's around me has grown. I cannot ignore things, and I'm not alienated anymore."

Other men referred more directly to Jewish history and their understanding of its continuity or discontinuity in the events they experienced during their military service. It seems that for about half of the participants, their experiences in the army, especially during the war, created a close link between their personal identity and different components of the Jewish people and its history. For the other half, the opposite process occurred, and they developed an identity which separated them from these general issues. In other words, for half of the men their evolving identity as adults included wider associations and components, while for the remaining men it was primarily marked by separating them from the wider national-historical context, even to the point of alienation.

The following quotations demonstrate the development of a broader identity by encompassing Jewish-Israeli identity as part of the self. Several men became aware of this aspect during the war. Said Eitan: "I believe in the importance of a Jewish state, and I consider the mission of the IDF to be to prevent a national holocaust. I think that a holocaust may take place, even here. That's why our army has to be the best. When I go to battle, to kill someone, I have to think that I am fighting for the nation."

David experienced the same feelings: "I felt proud that I was fighting for a large entity that was right behind me. I knew where we had come from, and where we were heading. I knew what we were fighting for. As an army unit, we were fighting for our own lives, and that of our friends. But at the same time we know that we belong to the larger body of the State of Israel, which was established to give the Jewish nation a home, right after the holocaust—and I feel part of this whole process. This truth is blurred by daily concerns, but it shines through in moments like this, when you go out to war. That's my belief, and that's what I was trying to instill in my soldiers. We have to know these things, because they will sustain us: That we have our glorious history, which was often sad, and we are part of this history, and have to draw our conclusions from it. The conclusion is that we must be strong. We must be on our toes. This awareness can emerge only during military service, I believe."

Several men stressed their evolving sense of belonging both to the state and to Jewish history. "I'm a strange man. My family does not come from Europe, yet I often think about the Holocaust. I feel it personally. I'm part of this nation, and I live in a place where you cannot avoid feeling concerned. We are a people of a burdensome history . . . There wasn't a generation which didn't have to kill or be killed. You either have to kill or be the victim, and if so, I certainly prefer to be on the strong side. I'm not enchanted by this image. I'd like to be more noble, but we have to be strong so that a second Holocaust will not take place. Can I run away from this fate? I used to have this dream about an isolated island, with its little volcano, with women in straw skirts . . . In fact, I believe that here is the safest place for me. But I don't live here because of my fears. I was born here, I grew up here, and this is the best place for me."

And Alon: "Somehow, during the last couple of years, I have developed a deep realization that I'm not a free citizen of the world, who can live in Brooklyn, in Peru, wherever he may choose. Because wherever I will go, people will say: You're a Jew. That's why this state is so important. Yet, here we're surrounded by people who—I know for sure—don't want to live in peace with us . . . Before my service I didn't have all these weighty thoughts, you know. But after it, I became a Zionist. My Zionism is nothing but a profound sense of myself as a Jew, belonging to this land . . . It's tough. Some days I see very slim chances for our survival here. But during army service this developed as a clear basis for my life. I feel that every inch of soil here is worth gold for me. I know that I'll stay here, and that nothing is more important than this country. I cannot forgive anyone who leaves. A man who goes to cultivate fields of another land is no better than a husband who betrays his wife.''

The remaining men, however, delineated a narrower definition of their selves following their military service. This, for example was the case with Ido, whose response emphasized the sense of separation or even alienation *vis-a-vis* a national identity. Said Ido: "Look, I don't feel I belong to the nation, or to the army. I used to feel that way, but after the war, I don't anymore. I belong to myself, to my friends, to my family—only they are part of my identity. These views developed while I was in the army, and grew stronger during my trip abroad. I don't have any sense of continuity of Jewish history which might dictate my way of life . . . I live here because I like it here. That's my truth, although I realize it's not the only one possible." Actually, Ido's sense of disillusionment is quite widespread, and includes several systems of values which were discussed in this chapter. In his final evaluation he said: "But more than anything, during my service I lost faith, which I feel as a loss of power. I lost my faith in Zionism, and other nice phrases that I used to believe in. I lost my faith in the myth of the army, in the myth of the elite unit—in many myths that had guided my life. Now I'm not sure of anything. I'm not sure of what's right for the world, the country, or my own private self. I think that if I hadn't served in the army, and if the war had not occurred, I would not have been changed like this. I didn't say this before, but today I'm willing to say that I would gladly have foregone my military experience. I think that a year of traveling alone would have given me much more as an adult than a year of military service."

To conclude this section, I would like to point out a process of cognitive change that seems to be connected to many of the areas of change which were presented so far. When describing changes in their approach to values or to people, several of the participants delineated a process very similar to the cognitive development described in relation to the educational process in an elite university by Perry (1968). Similar processes were described by men when discussing their moral dilemmas or changes in the social sphere. In the political sphere, too, a two-stage pattern could be observed. First, they began to recognize the complexity of the political issues, and as a result, they developed a growing tolerance and understanding of the diversity of opinions.

Said Eitan: "In the army, you talk to different people and you hear different opinions. You discover that every question can be answered in a variety of ways, and there isn't any one simple truth out there. As a kid I used to see only one side of the matter, and couldn't understand how anyone could have a different view. Among the paratroopers I met men with opinions completely different from my own. I liked many of these men, and didn't reject them just because of their political views. That's how I learned to respect the right of everyone to their own opinions. This is in particular important for me, because I grew up in a kibbutz, where everybody shared the same views. Today I'm more flexible, more moderate in my opinions."

And, in a broader context, said another participant: "There is so much dogmatism in our society. The black is all black, the white purely white, with nothing in between. This is probably a result of the war, in which we face a life-or-death struggle. This is the essence of this country for me, the image of the Israeli. I, myself, try to avoid this polarity. I want to remain loyal to my doubts, to the open questions. I want others to understand that I'm entitled to it."

We have outlined in this section widespread changes undergone by the soldiers as a result of the expansion of personal boundaries. The three areas of expansion discussed here—death, social encounters and values—comprise a wide spectrum which the soldiers had to integrate. We have seen the difficulties experienced by the participants in this task, and, complementarily, the feeling of maturity reached in the process. This process, in combination with the mastery of active coping, is at the core of the personality changes during the transition to adulthood. In the next, concluding, chapter I will draw conclusions regarding our findings in comparison with previous understandings concerning personality change in the transition to adulthood, in the culture-specific context of military service.

Notes

1. A serious attempt to collect the major theoretical contributions to the study of youth was presented by the American Academy of Arts and Science (*Daedalus*,

1962). Separate journals deal with this age group (*e.g.*, *Adolescence* and *Youth & Society*) and numerous books deal specifically with adolescence as a separate stage (see, for example, Cole's classic textbook, which appeared in five editions before 1959; or Ausubel, Montemayor and Pergrouhi, 1977. For an example of a large empirical study on adolescents, see Douvan and Adelson, 1966. For more recent textbooks on the topic, see Santrock, 1984; and Lloyd, 1985). In spite of this multitude of publications in theory and research, Adelson (1980), the editor of a recent, impressive volume on adolescence, says in his introduction: "After a long, long period of intellectual sleepiness the study of adolescence has begun to stir itself awake . . . yet the revival has gone virtually unnoticed" (p. ix). This may indicate that the above research has not directly contributed to a cohesive body of knowledge regarding adolescence or early adulthood.

2. See Josselson (1980) for a discussion of the parallels between the dynamics of adolescent individuation and the four subphases of the early individuation process described by Mahler, Pines and Bergman (1975).

3. While these studies have been widely acclaimed, and popular versions of their findings have appeared in the media (see for example *Psychology Today*, 1975, 1977, 1978), they have often been criticized for investigating men only (see for example Reinke *et al.*, 1985; Lieblich, 1986). Levinson and Vaillant indeed studied only men. Gould had a mixed sample, but his theory seemed oriented to males, and he did not examine the data for men and women separately. Although this is a valid criticism, it need not be a major concern here, since the present study is also focused only on men.

4. The issue of change versus continuity in development is the central theme in Brim and Kagan (1980). Additional support for the stability idea may be found in the study of Bachman *et al.* (1978).

One may wonder if some of the conflict among the views outlined above could not be reconciled when the time and context of the research are considered. People often comment about the differences between young people who grew up during the "stormy sixties" and the changes in the youth or college students of today. Furthermore, there must be some very basic differences between the samples of youth selected at elite universities, and samples of young people at a similar age who were selected at junior high schools, but some of whom later dropped out of school, or never attended college. Finally, the studies described above have used a variety of methods, from open-ended interviews and projective tests to standardized, objective measures. It seems to me that the methods employed, or the historical period in which the study was conducted, have had less effect on the results of the studies than have the different types of samples selected, whether clinical (as at the basis of psychoanalytic theories), elite (as in Keniston's studies) or wider and more representative (as in the research of Bachman *et. al.*, or Offer and Offer).

5. This idea is central for theories of psychological development at all ages, and has recently received special attention in the work of Gollin (1981) and Scarr and McCartney (1983).

6. As mentioned above, a similar idea was expressed also by Hall (1904), who claimed that individuals are more prone to cultural influences during adolescence than at any other time. One of the interesting findings of the Berkeley longitudinal study (cited in Honzik, 1984; and also in Eichorn *et. al.*, 1981), was the increase in I.Q. of individuals from the ages 17–18 to 36–48. This was greatest among those individuals who traveled outside the U.S. or who married a spouse whose I.Q. was higher than their own. These findings indicate the plasticity of intelligence during young adulthood.

7. Yamit is a name of an Israeli-Jewish town in the Southern territories, returned to Egypt as part of the Camp David agreement. In 1982, the town was evacuated under the extreme protest of its inhabitants. In this process, IDF soldiers were mobilized to enforce the instructions of the government in the face of the opposition of the civilians living there.

Conclusion

TRANSITION TO ADULTHOOD IN THE MILITARY CONTEXT

How are the processes of acquiring coping skills and expanding personal boundaries so far described related to the central issues in psychological literature about late adolescence and the transition to adulthood? How does the military context affect these processes of change in both Israel and the United States? These will be the central subjects for this, the final chapter of the book.

First, let me point to some reactions which seem related to both areas of personality change described in the two previous chapters: namely, the attainment of active coping and the expansion of personal boundaries. Even those participants who felt they had gained from their military service in both these areas, often, in their final evaluation, included a negative connotation, focusing on the "price of growing up." Due to their personal development in the military being embedded in an experience of hardship, struggle and the encounter with death, they seemed to emerge with a sense of loss, together with the more dominant themes of mastery and growth. It was, of course, self evident that the men had 'lost' a number of years of their youth. However, some of the men also complained about the loss of their childhood optimism and naivete. They described "grown-ups" as more able and sophisticated—but also as sad, aware of their limitations, and suspicious of their environment. In other words, the process of maturing was also a process of loss of previously held ideals and dreams.

Said Danny: "First of all, in the army I grew up. I became less naive. I saw things, how people achieve their aims, how much corruption there is everywhere. Give and take. Today I am much more skeptical about people and about values. The army has opened my eyes." And, as expressed by other participants: "Look, this is a period that should be the finest in one's life, the 'spring' of one's years. And here we dedicate it to military service. I feel that the military has taken away my energy, my vitality, all the impulsiveness that is so characteristic of this age. I'm unable to mobilize it again." "I became an adult. I understood that things don't happen just because you want them to, and that I have to make compromises." "Because of the army we lose the mood of our youth. I feel this as a loss, I know that I missed something here. I have skipped a stage in my development. I have become a serious adult and there is no way back."

Several men compared themselves with foreign students, mostly younger, since they had not served in the army. (Similar feelings were also expressed, however, toward foreign students of their own age.) Alon said this implicitly: "As a matter of fact, the army takes away three years of one's life. Often I think that I might already have graduated from the university, if I hadn't had to serve. Or perhaps I would have traveled around the world. So this is a loss as a result of my military service." David was more direct: "Often I think that I would like to have been a spoiled American college kid. They do have a good life at college, while I spent four years of hard service . . . I could have had my BA already." Finally, another participant: "Often I see foreign students, their happiness, their naivete, and I envy them. So we are more mature, but I would be willing to pay a lot to regain their spirit. Isn't it fun not to have to grow up? Those who do not have to serve in the army can grow up slowly, at their own pace, while here, at 18 we are all poured into the same mold and emerge as adults." Thus, several of the topics appearing in the psychological literature, such as the experience of "skipping" a developmental stage (Wilson, 1980), or the sense of the missed moratorium (Erikson, 1968), are directly expressed in the responses of the men.

Israeli and American Military Service

As explained before, my review of research on the military was limited to recent studies of the last two decades, focusing on two topics—the Vietnam War and garrison service. Surveying all the responses obtained in the present study, it seems that the early phase of military training is typically a period of crisis for all young recruits, who employ a host of coping mechanisms to adjust to the new demands and the strain. The chain of crises and reactions described by the participants is similar to those described in American literature, e.g., by Janis (1945), Bourne (1967), and Faris (1976), focusing on the initial stress response and the gradual building of a repertoire of habits adequate for dealing with the stressful situation. Factors which facilitate adjustment such as the "buddy system," family support or good commanders, were mentioned by soldiers both from Israel and from the United States. More significant for the Israeli soldier's adjustment is the support of his family and friends, while for the American recruit, who is usually more removed from his family, identification with role models, namely his commanders, is more important. The apparent lack of influence of the Israeli junior commanders on their men is possibly due to the small age difference between soldiers and their commanding staff in the IDF. The older, highly experienced drill instructor of the American recruit is, therefore, a more significant figure in the young soldier's adjustment. On the other hand, the Israeli's continuing dependence on the support of his family is a point of interest that, in relation to personality development, will be discussed more fully below.

It is hard to compare the atmosphere of basic training in different armies, since the various types of atmosphere within each army depend on the period of time, the kind of military unit, and the personalities of the recruits and their commanders. However, when taking as a point of reference the descriptions of basic training for the Marine Corps (Eisenhart, 1975; Shatan, 1977), my general impression was that the treatment of the new recruit is more humane in the IDF. It seems that producing regression is probably part of the ideology of basic training in the Marine Corps, but this is not the case for the Israeli army (see Rolbant, 1970; Schild, 1973; Gal, 1976). From the point of view of the participants, however, there was evidence of feelings of being oppressed, scorned, or punished for no reason. In evaluating these reactions, as in other aspects of the present study, it is not the objective reality but the subjective experience which is the main determinant of the individual's reactions. One should be reminded that Israeli men usually do not volunteer for the army, while the Americans do so out of free choice. Furthermore, at the present time, military service is a job or a career for the American soldier, while the Israeli recruit's perception of his role is a service which he performs out of his ideological convictions. (See Janowitz, 1964, and Moskos, 1978 for a comparison of these two basic attitudes toward the military.) These differing ideologies naturally influence the soldier's psychological reactions to his experience during basic training as well as later on.

As to the wartime experience, the reader of previous chapters has probably noticed the similarity of my findings to former literature on the Vietnam War. A comparison of some of the characteristics of the Lebanon War and the Vietnam War appeared above (pp. 135–144). Both wars were controversial—although the Lebanon War was significantly less so than the Vietnam War. In general, Israeli soldiers appear to identify with their mission more than do the comparable group of Vietnam veterans. The fighting forces in Israel are much less detached from society as a whole than are those of the U.S., due to the small distances between battle zones and the home, and because virtually the entire male population serves regularly in the army reserves. Thus, the alienation of the Vietnam War veterans from society (Camacho, 1980) had no parallel in Israel. In addition, the Lebanon War was much shorter, and did not separate from their homes those men who fought for long periods. Furthermore, as a rule, high unit cohesion was maintained in the Lebanon War, a factor often missing in the American fighting units in Vietnam (Moskos, 1970; Segal and Segal, 1983; Ingraham, 1984).

Both highly positive and highly negative emotions were evoked by the Lebanon War. People reported pride, exhilaration and even some kind of peak experiences (Maslow, 1954) on the one hand, and the common feelings of fear, anger and guilt on the other. The range and quality of feelings resembled those described by Gray (1959) in his personal report on World War II. Due to both political circumstances and the characteristics of the Vietnam War, the American literature on psychological aspects of the war stressed its negative effects. In reading the Israeli men's reports, many seem surprisingly similar to the experiences of the Vietnam veterans—or perhaps to those of all other wars—yet they lack the more extreme aspects of dehumanization and its revolting accompaniments. Thus, some encounters, as for example that with children as the enemy, were described as having similar effects on soldiers of both cultures. During combat in Lebanon and the occupation following it, some Israeli soldiers also complained of feeling exploited in fighting a battle with which they did not agree. There was no direct involvement in atrocities on the part of the participants, yet later on resentment and guilt feelings—responses deeply analyzed by Lifton (1973)—were experienced by some of the men. On the other hand, at least during the first weeks of the fighting (which constituted the main part of the war), the majority of the men did not feel alienated from the aims of the War. Cases of disobeying commands were entirely missing from the reports of my participants, and are considered to be very rare in the IDF in general (Gal, 1985). Thus, the extreme experiences and aftermath of the Vietnam War as described in Figley (1978a, 1978b), Figley and Leventman (1980), and Lifton (1973), for example, appeared to have been mitigated for the Israeli soldiers. Interestingly, later political opposition or alienation did not seriously affect the participants' feelings regarding their combat experience. In contrast to Card's (1983) findings that many Vietnam veterans remained bitter for years afterwards (at least in response to her open-ended question), Israeli veterans of the Lebanon War displayed a much lesser degree of bitterness.

War presented the soldiers with difficult moral dilemmas. Obedience to orders often clashed with personal beliefs. Common to both Israeli and American war experiences is the ease with which the men felt that they slipped into violence. Wikler's (1980) finding, noting the wide range of personal reactions to "new self-knowledge" regarding their own propensity for violence, is well borne out in the present study. The consequent moral confusion of some of the participants, or the resulant transformation of values for others, were similar for veterans of Lebanon and Vietnam. Here, again, the differences between veterans of the two wars is quantitative rather than qualitative. In comparison with the findings of the research on the Vietnam War, the moral pressures on the Israeli soldier induced regret, but not to the extent of provoking subversive behavior, such as disobeying or undermining orders, or of depersonalization, as in the 'robot-like' behavior described by Wikler (1980). Basically, the Israeli soldiers' trust in the decency of the IDF and its well-known precautions regarding civilian casualties (Gabriel, 1984) counteracted their personal doubts and dilemmas.

At the present time, there is very little available data to use as a basis for comparison between the Lebanon and Vietnam Wars in regard to their longer-range psychological effects. Interestingly, although none of the participants applied to mental health services regarding symptoms following combat, several of them reported reactions such as repetitive nightmares, survivor's guilt or hyper-alertness, which are considered as part of the syndrome of Post Traumatic Stress Disorder (PTSD) (DSM III, 1980). This concurs with the findings of Stretch and Figley (1984), who reported that many of the Vietnam War veterans were suffering from PTSD yet they did not receive, or even seek, any type of treatment. In his recent book, Gal (1986) claims that with regard to immediate combat stress reactions in the form of psychiatric casualties, the Israeli soldier apparently does not differ markedly from his Western counterparts in kind of symptoms or their prevalence. However, as far as long term ongoing effects of combat stress reactions are concerned, there is not enough data to provide an evaluation. Even in the American case, where an abundance of data was accumulated, the argument about the severity of the psychological aftermath of the war, and the extent of its effects, is still undecided. As will be presented in what follows, my impression is that the development of adult personality is profoundly affected by the experience of war (*e.g.*, the encounter with death and the resulting changes of priorities), but in Israel this cannot be easily distinguished from the total experience of military service and the social values associated with it, such as heroism and voluntarism.

While an attempt was made to make some generalizations, there are, of course, in each response or category, considerable personal variations. This conclusion is similar to that of Card (1983), who studied the effects of the Vietnam War. In spite of the many individual differences, it should be stressed that most of the men described positive change as a dominant trend. In their final evaluations they tended to agree that their military service, above and beyond the specific negative effects, was worthwhile. This finding is also supported by Card (1983) regarding American soldiers. According to Card's research, 17 years after their service, American veterans rated their military service as being more positive than negative. Among the positive effects, those which resemble the Israeli findings include: personal growth, increased maturity, independence, self-confidence, and greater sensitivity toward others. Only a few positive effects were attributed by the American veterans to the war itself, and among them, as for the Israelis, appeared the increased appreciation of the value of life.

Aspects of Transition to Adulthood: Israel and Western Society

We turn now to the central aspect of this study, namely the comparison of personality development in the Israeli military service with that of youth of comparable age elsewhere in Western society. If life is conceived as a series of stages, connected by unstable transition points (Levinson *et al.*, 1978), the three-year service at the age of 18 constitutes a normative transition period, the transition into adulthood. Its culture-specific nature as a transition period is marked by the fact that the vast majority of Israeli men undergo it in a similar manner, as institutionalized by Israeli society, namely through military service. In other words, military service in Israel, often including the experience of war, provides the specific cultural context for the Israeli transition to adulthood. This book demonstrates that, occurring as it does at a time of great plasticity in an individual's life, military service has a significant impact on the personality and the social perspective of young Israeli men. This impact may be evaluated by comparing their major characteristics with the attributes and developmental tasks of their age group as described in the psychological literature.

The reader should remember that we are dealing with the psychological development of men, rather than that of both sexes. Since in Israel military service demands much more time and effort from men than from women, it is probably especially men (and not women) who are affected deeply by this factor in their lives. To find out specifically about the personality development of women at the time of transition to adulthood, the effects of military service on their lives, including the fact that their menfolk—husbands, boyfriends and sons—serve in the military, another project is necessary. (A few of these aspects were presented in Lieblich, 1978.) Interestingly, studies about the transition to adulthood in Western societies have, in this important area, usually neglected gender differences. Among the few references to this subject one may mention Gilligan (1982) and Miller (1976), who both hypothesize that while men invest most of their energy at this age in their choice or preparation for a career, women deal more with the establishment of interpersonal relationships. There may be a better chance for young women to develop heterosexual relationships during their service in the IDF than for men to make progress in their careers. This, however, again requires a separate study.

Regarding the developmental tasks and experiences common to this age group, there are a number of themes prominent both in the present study and in the psychological literature. Gould (1978) described young men of this age as tending to throw themselves into adventures and risks, thus gaining experience in a wider spectrum of events and relationships, and testing their tolerance for extreme conditions. Furthermore, men of this age have also been described as confronting role models, symbols and values of their culture (Eisenstadt, 1962). This encounter, which sometimes takes the elaborate form of passage rites, serves to promote their socialization as adult members of their society. Thus, cultures take advantage of the natural plasticity of this age group to imprint upon their members their main norms and values before they become responsible, adult citizens. On the other hand, when military service is the focus of the discussion, it is probably due to the characteristics of this age group that young people are able to withstand the extreme hardships of the military initiation stage (Shatan, 1977). The participants' emphasis on their positive reactions to the strenuous conditions (often related to the experience of active coping) strengthens the impression that Gould's (1978) 'experimenting with extremes' played a significant role in the soldiers' motivation.

In the case of Israeli society, one central value which is instilled toward and during military service is the myth of the hero (Lieblich, 1978, 1982; Gal, 1986), which demands outstanding, altruistic deeds for the welfare of the country, and includes a superhuman capacity for solving all kinds of problems in reality. This myth underlies the norm of voluntarism (the willingness to volunteer for duties required of them by the country), and is often demonstrated in the stereotype of Israeli men as exceptionally performance-oriented on the one hand, and nonexpressive in the emotional sphere on the other. As I described in some of my previous work (Lieblich, 1978, 1982, 1983), Israeli men frequently repress their feelings of pain or inadequacy, and demonstrate instead a facade of omnipotence and invulnerability. Other Israeli men often experience conflicts between their commitment to be heroic and strong, and the natural tendency also to be weak and in need of support. These tendencies emerged in the present study as well, especially in the accounts of the participants about their experiences during the war. In some of the reports this tendency toward 'nonemotionality' was obvious. One of the few who had insight to his own conflict regarding this trend said the following: "I knew a couple of men who were killed in the war. To this very day I have not mourned for them properly. I don't know how to. I wish I could cry, but I'm not supposed to, I guess.'' In many ways it is apparent that Israeli men often experience an intense contradiction between the Israeli-macho norm of supressing tender emotions—and the underlying love, longing, anger, and guilt. Military service and repeated participation in wars obviously have a central role in reinforcing both authentic and artificial strength in the men's personalities.

White (1966) and Mitchell (1979) have stressed other aspects of social maturity. According to their views, young people may be characterized as deepening their commitments and concerns for society, and becoming more capable of understanding others. Social and political issues which were formerly outside of their interests become part of their adult identity. In the reports and evaluation of their military service, most of the Israeli participants indeed described a deepening concern for wider social issues, and a growing understanding of moral, political, and ideological matters. In the cognitive sphere, according to Perry (1968), young people emerge from earlier stages of dogmatic, one-sided beliefs into the more mature stage of acceptance of uncertainty and the diversity of opinions. In the present study, this trend of development was demonstrated in several spheres, indicating that both a growing tolerance and deeper convictions are possible results of the military service.

While these aspects are common to the Israeli experience and to Western literature, in several other important aspects the processes attributed to late adolescence or to the transition to adulthood were not experienced in the same manner by young men from the Western world as by the Israeli soldiers. Erikson considers the formation of personal identity to be the result of a moratorium in which role diffusion and experimentation are legitimate. This is considered to be the nucleus of that process whereby adulthood is attained (Erikson, 1950, 1968, 1975). In the case of Israeli youth, their military experience allowed them to test their limits and skills under various conditions, as long as they accepted the general military framework. They could not, however, experiment with roles and relationships outside the scope of the military system and its compulsory rules.

In this context, one should notice that the concept of moratorium implies several apparently independent phenomena. One is the ability to experiment freely in various roles and activities—an aspect of the moratorium which is denied the young soldier. Yet, in another sense, since the military service demands of the soldier some highly specific functions and forms of behavior, he may delay making choices concerning career or family— namely, he does enjoy this aspect of the moratorium. Furthermore, the soldier is taking over an adult function—defense—but is allowed to postpone other aspects of the transition to adulthood. Similarly, in the area of autonomy from parents, which will be dealt with below, military service produces geographical distance and some degree of economic independence, but, from another perspective, increases emotional dependence of the soldier on his family.

Thus, for the Israeli soldier permissiveness toward youth (Eisenstadt, 1962) was curtailed, moratorium restricted, and the opportunities for the expected rebellion of this age group (Kenniston, 1962, 1971) extremely rare. The participants experienced an abrupt change from their childhood life in high school to the adult responsibility of being soldiers in a politically tense area. The tendency of some of the men released from the army to go on long trips abroad, or to shift from one simple job to another rather than to pursue a "serious" career—phenomena mentioned by some of the participants as possibilities they had rejected but which some of their friends had adopted—may represent an attempt to recreate the moratorium at an age when most young men in the Western world are already past it. Our sample was, of course, selective regarding this tendency, in that all the participants were University students within half a year from their discharge from the army—*i.e.*, those who had not chosen a (late) moratorium. These men, who had opted to go to the university, reported a sense of loss at being denied the normal opportunity to exercise free experimentation for a period prior to entering adulthood; instead that time had been allocated to military service. They often expressed regrets about the loss of their naivete, and felt a sense of urgency in making serious choices. According to Erikson, this may interfere with the building of an integrated identity. This has not been found to be the case in the present study, in which lack of complete moratorium is part of a culture-prescribed pattern of development rather than an individual deviation.

The effects of military service, and of war in particular, may also be analyzed in terms of Erikson's scheme of maturational stages. Lifton (1973), Wikler (1980), and Wilson (1980) interpreted their findings about the American soldier as indicating a shift in the maturational process toward concerns which are typical of much older age groups. As demonstrated in the participants' reports too, men who experienced the war seem to acquire self-knowledge and an acquaintance with death far beyond the normal level of their Western peers. According to Erikson's scheme, they are grappling with dilemmas which belong to the period of Ego Integrity versus Despair, before they have tackled the earlier issues of Intimacy and Generativity. These struggles may be resolved and contribute to a rich and well-defined identity, but without resolution they may produce a state of confusion and doubt.

In addition to the different moratorium, the Israeli experience differs in a variety of ways from what, in American literature, is considered the norm for this age group. It is difficult, within a restrictive military system, to become self-directed (White, 1966), although men have experienced growing responsibility, independence and self-esteem within it. Developing deep heterosexual relations (Blos, 1962; Levinson *et al.*, 1978) was rarely possible in a predominantly male environment, but intimacy was frequently achieved with other men, one's buddies in the unit. Men in the IDF lived at a certain distance from their parents, but could hardly be described as attaining real autonomy from them (Vaillant, 1977). Military experience rarely provided the young men with an opportunity to choose a career, to form a dream, or to find a mentor (Levinson *et al.*, 1978), although they may have acquired useful skills in different areas. Little testing of freedom (Gould, 1978) was reported by the participants. Humanizing of values (White, 1966) was often experienced, yet, at the same time, war provided the participants with instances of dehumanized conduct and feelings. In the next section I will enlarge upon several of these aspects, which were central to the men's accounts.

First, there are a number of points requiring emphasis, regarding the culture-specificity of "independence" as exemplified by the Israeli group in comparison to other studies of this age group in Western cultures. Here we have a concept, independence, which did seem to be common to the two cultures, yet upon closer examination has different connotations within each specific cultural context. In other words, a number of characteristics of this age group in Western cultures were prominently absent from the Israeli group—occupational identity, economic independence (or making significant progress in that direction) and forming a meaningful heterosexual relationship. In spite of the fact that these aspects of "adulthood" had not been achieved, or even begun, the Israeli men felt themselves to have passed significantly from boyhood to adulthood.

Even more dramatic than these is the contrast between cultures regarding independence from parents, considered a major accomplishment at this age—a task postulated by psychological theory as essential. While responses stressing the various aspects of active coping and the expansion of boundaries were very frequent in the men's evaluations, one may be quite surprised to discover that this transition into adulthood is not accompanied by the breaking, or even the weakening, of family ties. According to the men's reports, military service in Israel often removes men from their parents' home, but emotionally they remain highly attached to their parents (see also Azarya and Kimmerling, 1985). Due to the hardships of military service, the men find great solace in their visits home, where they frequently become the 'spoiled boys' who deserve much attention and consideration. Many of the men praised their families for providing support and encouragement during their service. Fathers often identify with their sons' military experiences, and this results in greater closeness between them. While parents are indeed physically more distant from their sons, and their direct control and influence on their lives probably diminished, emotionally, however, the opposite is often the case.

The following excerpt is an extreme example of this trend: "We live far down South, and I have always had a long, long trip to get back home from the army for Saturday . . . For long periods, during basic training or difficult courses (and even later as an officer), I used to arrive home totally exhausted. My father used to wait for me at the central bus station. He drove me home, stripped me of my uniform, and put me in a hot bath. My feet were so sore, and I remember how he massaged them. He helped me into a clean shirt. I felt like a baby, but I didn't mind. At the same time he used to tell me about his own past in the army, what he had done in the War of Independence. Often I dozed off while he was telling his stories."

Among the interviewees, who often described the importance of family support, there was only one who referred to this paradox of both greater independence and greater dependence on family relations. (This is probably due to the fact that he had spent his high school years in the United States, where the norm of achieving independence from one's parents is very apparent.) He commented: "I think that service in the army prolongs your dependence on your parents, at an age when you could already have separated from them. You come home every weekend, and this is very important for you. You give all the laundry to your Mom to take care of, you want to be fed, to be patted on the head. Your parents are there to support you through every crisis. I myself have experienced this. I ran to my parents to cry about my problems . . . At the same time, in the army you're obliged to obey all the time. Every single step is determined by your superiors, or by a set of rules and regulations. Therefore, I feel that I have started to mature, to become an individual, only after my military service. Elsewhere, this process occurs much earlier in men of our age."

The Israeli experience of 'independence' in the army is, therefore, unique, in that it occurs without breaking the intimate family ties, in contrast to the findings of Valliant (1977), Gould (1978), and Levinson *et al.* (1978) regarding American young men of this age. This culture-specific aspect of Israeli independence seems to me to be of special interest in the context of the ongoing debate in psychological literature regarding the "rebelliousness" of adolescence (Offer and Offer, 1975). The material of the present study suggests that rebelliousness, especially the aspect involving separation from the nuclear family, which has been called (Blos, 1967) the "second individuation process," may be specific to a particular culture and period, rather than a universal process. In Israel, independence from the nuclear family seems to necessitate a much lesser degree of 'emotional distancing' and less strenuous efforts on the part of the young person to establish a differentiated identity. Referring back to Mahler's (1975) psychoanalytic theory of separation-individuation as applied to adolescence, it would seem that for Israelis the developmental track of 'individuation' is culturally enhanced in the military service, while that of 'separation' is (relatively to other Western cultures) delayed. Whether this difference has repercussions in later development is a matter for further study. It would seem, however, on the basis of the present study, that the Israeli version of development provides an alternative to the prevailing Western pattern of late adolescent development by allowing youth to achieve a widely respected adult role at an early age. This achievement, and the independence implied by it, allows young men to become 'adults' without having to sever their emotional ties to, and dependence on, their families.

An important aspect of the transition to adulthood in Western society concerns the development of intimacy with women. A central aspect in the Israeli participants' accounts, however, related to close relationships between men. Especially for those who had served in combat units, life in the military provided the opportunity for developing deep friendships. Said Eitan: "The main thing I gained in the army was the experience of kinship among men. I made very good friends in my team." And similarly Ido: "My friends from the unit will stay with me for the rest of my life." This was also the main gain reported by Shlomi and Alon, who served in the same unit. Said Shlomi: "The first thing I gained from my service were buddies. I have such good friends that if I need them and call in the middle of the night, wherever they are—they will come to help me." And Alon: "I developed such deep relationships that I don't believe would have been possible in another context. I love the people from my group even if I hate some of their traits. It's a result of the endless time we spent together at the blockades, drinking and fooling around. We are like brothers. This year in Jerusalem, I didn't have a room of my own. I bought an old car, in which I keep all my books and things, and at night I'd drop in at the apartment of one of my buddies and pull out my sleeping bag. This is a kind of brotherhood I don't think exists anywhere else."

The parallel between these deep relationships among men and relations with women was pointed out by several of the participants. For example Eitan: "At this stage you become very close to others in the unit. You have more time to sit and chat. You know them better and you love them more. This is the famous love between soldiers which is as much of a mystery as love for women." It seems that the psychological function of this close friendship may be its service as the only channel for warm and tender feelings available under the conditions of constant stress, the focus on competitive performance, strict demands and hierarchical relationships.

This deep friendship, or the tight "buddy system" which develops within the units, is known to be one of the major sources of support during military service, especially for the combat soldiers. As has long been known by social scientists who investigate the military, the army becomes worthwhile for the sake of your friends in the unit. Recent attempts in the American army to change this orientation have failed, and the present military system again encourages the development of tight unit cohesiveness and interpersonal relations (Moskos, 1970; Segal and Segal, 1983; Ingraham, 1984). But in the present context what was emphasized is the fact that all these deep relationships were among men. None of the participants saw the army as a good opportunity to meet women, in spite of the fact that women do serve on bases with men (Schild, 1973), and Israelis believe that the army is the country's greatest matchmaker. On the contrary, several men described their service away from home as causing an interruption of their former heterosexual relationships.

Another issue concerning the specific meaning of independence in the context of military service in Israel relates to self-determination versus obedience. While adulthood may be characterized as a life stage in which people are required to 'decide for themselves', all societies also demand obedience to certain norms and regulations. Adulthood, therefore, implies a certain balance between self-determination and conformity. In the case of the Israeli youth, many of the reports demonstrated that in some sense military service provided opportunities for individual initiative, especially for those men who became commanders, but, at the same time, it reinforced obedience without questioning orders. Our study cannot provide clear evidence as to whether one or the other of the above traits is especially reinforced. Rather, instances of both extreme self-reliance and conformity were experienced by men who had served as soldiers in comparison with those who did not. Again, the kind of developing independence is highly affected by such a mixture of experiences.

Summary: The Male Soldier Pattern of Transition to Adulthood

The general conclusion I have drawn regarding the influences of military service on personality development is that the pattern of transition to adulthood during military service in Israel is different from that described in Western literature. Rather than evaluating it in terms of acceleration or delays of development (as presented for example by Wilson, 1980, in his analysis of the psychological development of the Vietnam veterans), I consider it an alternative pattern. The former approach implies a deviation, or set of deviations, from a norm. In Israel, military service does not constitute a deviation from a norm, but rather it *is* the norm. Therefore, it should be studied as a culture-specific version of the developmental stage of transition to adulthood, with its own tasks and emphases. At the core of the Israeli pattern of development we may place the increased capacity for active coping and the mastery of difficulties on the one hand, and the expansion of personal boundaries in the encounter with death, and with a wide variety of people and values, on the other. The former is related to various skills, strengths and ego functions, in both the physical and the mental spheres, which the participants felt they had developed during their military service. As a result of the development of these, the men acquired the awareness and confidence that they were independent adults, capable of coping with a variety of hardships and problems.

The second area, the expansion of personal boundaries, refers to the development of greater understanding regarding the complexity of issues and life-situations. In their greatly expanded variety of encounters with people, values, and extreme situations, the participants felt that they had emerged as more mature in their views and attitudes. In these respects they seem to have lived through a rapid maturation process. At the same time it is apparent that they did not progress much toward personal careers or toward the development of meaningful heterosexual relationships, nor had they separated themselves or rebelled against their parents in the manner characteristic of Western society.

These two areas, one concerning 'doing,' the other 'being,' constitute the two major developmental tasks characteristic of the Israeli transition to adulthood. The military service provides young men with a challenge, or an opportunity. If their former personality and the military circumstances allow them to succeed in their developmental tasks, they may become more mature in both areas. For some, however, one (or both) of the tasks is not performed in the same manner, and they may emerge from their military service with reduced self-esteem due to a sense of failure in performing their duties, and/or in a state of confusion regarding their values and way of life. None of the men experienced this transition without a price, which is expressed in a sense of loss of time, energy, and naivete.

Comparing the military experience of Israeli men with that of American soldiers in training, routine duty, or war, we have found several similarities and numerous differences. Serving in a highly prestigious army, fighting within a supportive social climate, in highly cohesive units, where all men are drafted equally, provide the possibility, despite its hardships, for a highly rewarding service. On the other hand, feelings of alienation and existential doubt, as well as other negative features of the aftermath of combat and occupation experiences, were not entirely missing in the men's accounts of their military service in the 1980s.

It was my purpose neither to defend nor to condemn military service in Israel. Political and military concerns were not the focus of this book. Presently, Israeli young men must complete their mandatory service of three years, and this is, for better or for worse, their cultural context for the spring of their years.

References

Adelson, J. (ed.), *Handbook of Adolescent Psychology*, N.Y.: Wiley, 1980.

Allport, G. W., *Personality: A Psychological Interpretation*, N.Y.: Holt, 1937.

Allport, G. W., *The Use of Personal Documents in Psychological Science*, New York: Social Science Research Council, 1942.

Allport, G. W., *Pattern and Growth in Personality*, New York: Holt, Rinehart and Winston, 1961.

Alon, N., "An Ericksonian Approach to the Treatment of Chronic Posttraumatic Stress Disorder Patients," in: J. Zeig (ed.), *Ericksonian Psychotherapy*, New York: Brunner and Mazel, 1985, 307–326.

Atkinson, R. W., *et.al.*, "Diagnosis of Posttraumatic Stress Disorder in Vietnam Veterans: Preliminary Findings," *American Journal of Psychiatry*, 1984, *141*, 694–696.

Ausubel, D. P., Montemayor, R. and Pergrouhi, N.S., *Theory and Problems of Adolescent Development*, 2nd ed., New York: Grune and Stratton, 1977.

Azarya, V. and Kimmerling, B., "Cognitive Permeability of Civil-Military Boundaries: Draftee Expectations from Military Service in Israel," *Studies in Comparative International Development*, 1985–6, *20*, 42–63.

Bachman, J. G. and Jennings, M. K., "The Impact of Vietnam on Trust in Government," *Journal of Social Issues*, 1975, *31*, 141–156.

Bachman, J. G., Blair, J. D. and Segal, D. R., *The All-Volunteer Force*, Ann Arbor: The University of Michigan Press, 1977.

Bachman, J. G., O'Malley, P. M., and Johnson, J., *Youth in Transition*, vol. VI, Ann Arbor, MI: Institute for Social Research, 1978.

Bachman, J. G., "American High School Seniors View the Military: 1976–1982," *Armed Forces and Society*, 1984, *10*, 86–104.

Bell, D., *The Cultural Contradictions of Capitalism*, New York: Basic Books, 1976.

Bertaux, D. (ed.), *Biography and Society: The Life History Approach in the Social Sciences*, Beverly Hills, CA: Sage, 1981.

Bertaux, D. and Kohli, M., "The Life Story Approach: A Continental View," *Annual Review of Sociology*, 1984, *10*, 215–237.

Binkin, M. and Bach, S. J., *Women and the Military*, Washington: Brookings Institution, 1977.

Block, J. in collaboration with Haan, N., *Lives through Time*, Berkeley: Bancroft, 1971.

Bloom, A. R., "Israel: The Longest War," in: Goldman, N. L. (ed.), *Female Soldiers—Combatants or Noncombatants*, Westport, CT: Greenwood Press, 1982, 137–162.

Blos, P., *On Adolescence—A Psychoanalytic Interpretation*, New York: Free Press of Glencoe, 1962.

Blos, P., "The Second Individuation Process of Adolescence," *Psychoanalytic Study of the Child*, 1967, *22*, 162–186.

Blos, P., *The Adolescent Passage: Developmental Issues*, New York: International Universities Press, 1979.

Blythe, R., *Akenfield: Portrait of an English Village*, New York: Pantheon Books, 1969.

Borus, J. F., "The Reentry Transition of the Vietnam Veteran," in: Goldman, N. L. and Segal, D. R. (eds.), *The Social Psychology of Military Service*, Beverly Hills, CA: Sage, 1976, 27-43.

Bourne, P. G., "Some Observations on the Psychosocial Phenomena Seen in Basic Training," *Psychiatry*, 1967, *30*, 187–196.

Brandes, S., *Forty: The Age and the Symbol*, Knoxville: The University of Tennessee Press, 1985.

Brende, J., "A Psychodynamic View of Character Pathology in Vietnam Combat Veterans," *Bulletin of the Menninger Clinic*, 1983, *47*, 193–216.

Breznitz, S. (ed.), *Stress in Israel*, New York: Van Nostrand Reinhold, 1983.

Brim, O. G. and Kagan, J. (eds.), *Constancy and Change in Human Development*, Cambridge: Harvard University Press, 1980.

Bromley, D. B., *Personality Description in Ordinary Language*, New York: Wiley, 1977.

Burgess, R. G., *In the Field*, London: Allan and Unwin, 1984.

Camacho, P., "From War Hero to Criminal: The Negative Privilege of the Vietnam Veteran," in Figley and Leventman (eds.), *Strangers at Home: Vietnam Veterans since the War*, New York: Praeger Publishers, 1980, 267–277.

Card, J. J. *Lives after Vietnam: The Personal Impact of Military Service*, Lexington: Heath, 1983.

Chapkis, W. (ed.), *Loaded Questions: Women in the Military*, Amsterdam: Transnational Institute, 1981.

Cole, L., *Psychology of Adolescence*, 5th ed., New York: Rinehart and Co., 1959.

Cronbach, L. J., "Beyond the Two Disciplines of Scientific Psychology," *American Psychologist*, 1975, *30*, 116–127.

Dale, C. and Gilory, C., "Determinant of Enlistments: A Macroeconomic Time-Series View," *Armed Forces and Society*, 1984, *10*, 192–210.

Denzin, N. K., *The Research Act*, 2nd ed., New York: McGraw-Hill, 1978.

Deutsch, H., *Selected Problems of Adolescence*, New York: International Universities Press, 1967.

Diagnostic and Statistical Manual, Edition III, Washington, D.C.: Mercian Psychiatric Association, 1980.

Dollard, J., *Criteria for the Life History*, New Haven: Yale University Press, 1935.

Douvan, E. and Adelson, J., *The Adolescent Experience*, New York: Wiley and Sons, 1966.

Earl, M. M., *Bibliography of Women*, West Point, NY: U.S. Military Academy, 1976.

Egendorf, A., Kadushin, C., Laufer, R. S., Rothbart, G. and Sloan, L., "Summary of Findings," vol. I of *Legacies of Vietnam: Comparative Adjustment of Veterans and Their Peers*, Washington, D.C.: U.S. Government Printing Office, 1981.

Eichorn, D. H., Clausen, J. A., Haan, N., Honzik, M. P. and Mussen, P. H. (eds.), *Present and Past in Middle Life*, New York: Academic Press, 1981.

Eisenhart, R. W., "You Can't Hack it Little Girl: A Discussion of the Covert Psychological Agenda of Modern Combat Training," *Journal of Social Issues*, 1975, *31*, 13–23.

Eisenstadt, S. N., "Archetypal Patterns of Youth," *Daedalus*, 1962, *91*, 28–46.

Elkind, D., *Children and Adolescents: Interpretive Essays on J. Piaget*, New York: Oxford University Press, 1970.

Epstein, S., "Explorations in Personality Today and Tomorrow," *American Psychologist*, 1979, *34*, 649–653.

Epstein, S., "Natural Healing Processes of the Mind: Graded Stress Inoculation as an Inherent Coping Mechanism," in: Meichenbaum, D. and Jaremki, M. E. (eds.), *Stress Reduction and Prevention*, New York: Plenum Press, 1983.

Erikson, E. H., *Childhood and Society*, New York: Norton, 1950.

Erikson, E. H., *Identity: Youth and Crisis*, New York: Norton, 1968.

Erikson, E. H., *Life History and the Historical Moment*, New York: Norton, 1975.

Eshkol, E., Lieblich, A., Bar-Yosef, R., and Wiseman, H., "Some Correlates of Adjustment of Israeli Women Soldiers to Their Military Roles," *Israel Social Science Research*, 1987, *5*, 17–28.

Eysenck, H. J., "The Science of Personality: Nomothetic!, *Psychological Review*, 1954, *61*, 339–342.

Fairbank, J. A., Keane, T. M. and Malloy, P. E., "Some Preliminary Data on the Psychological Characteristics of Vietnam Veterans with Posttraumatic Stress Disorder," *Journal of Consulting and Clinical Psychology*, 1983, *51*, 912–919.

Faris, J. H., "The Impact of Basic Combat Training: The Role of the Drill Sergeant," in: Goldman, N. L. and Segal, D. R. (eds.), *The Social Psychology of Military Service*, Beverly Hills, CA: Sage, 1976, 13–24.

Faris, J. H., "Economic and Noneconomic Factors of Personnel Recruitment and Retention in the AVF," *Armed Forces and Society*, 1984, *10*, 251–275.

Figley, C. R. (ed.), *Stress Disorders among Vietnam Veterans: Theory, Research and Treatment*, New York: Bruner/Mazel, 1978a.

Figley, C. R., "Symptoms of Delayed Combat Stress among a College Sample of Vietnam Veterans," *Military Medicine*, 1978b, *143*, 107–110.

Figley, C. R. and Leventman, S. (eds.), *Strangers at Home: Vietnam Veterans since the War*, New York: Praeger Publishers, 1980.

Figley, C. R. and Southerly, W. T., "Psychosocial Adjustment of Recently Returned Veterans," in: Figley and Leventman (eds.), *Strangers at Home: Vietnam Veterans since the War*, New York: Praeger Publishers, 1980, 167–180.

Foster, G. D., "The Effect of Deterrence on the Fighting Ethic," *Armed Forces and Society*, 1984, *10*, 276–292.

Fredland, J. E., and Lille, R. D., "Educational Levels, Aspirations and Expectations of Military and Civilian Males, Ages 18 to 22," *Armed Forces and Society*, 1984, *10*, 211–228.

Fry, C. L., "The Ages of Adulthood: A Question of Numbers," *Journal of Gerontology*, 1976, *31*, 170–177.

Gabriel, R. A., *Operation Peace for Galilee: The Israeli-PLO War in Lebanon*, New York: Hill and Wang, 1984.

Gal, R., *A Portrait of the Israeli Soldier*, Westport, CT: Greenwood Press, 1986.

Gal, R., "Commitment and Obedience in the Military—An Israeli Case Study," *Armed Forces and Society*, 1985, *11*, 553–564.

Gilligan, C., *In a Different Voice*, Cambridge: Harvard University Press, 1982.

Glover, H., "Survival Guilt and the Vietnam Veteran," *Journal of Nervous and Mental Disease*, 1984, *172*, 393–397.

Goffman, E., *Asylums*, New York: Doubleday, 1961.

Goldman, N. L. (ed.), *Female Soldiers—Combatants or Noncombatants?* Westport, CT: Greenwood Press, 1982.

Goldman, N. L. and Segal, D. R., *The Social Psychology of Military Service*, Beverly Hills, CA: Sage Publications, 1976.

Gollin, E. S. (ed.), *Developmental Plasticity: Behavioral and Biological Aspects of Variation in Development*, New York: Academic Press, 1981.

Gould, R. L., "The Phases of Adult Life: A Study in Developmental Psychology," *American Journal of Psychiatry*, 1972, *129*, 521–531.

Gould, R. L., "Adult Life Stages: Growth toward Self Tolerance," *Psychology Today*, 1975, *8*(9), 74–78.

Gould, R. L., *Transformation: Growth and Change in Adult Life*, New York: Simon and Schuster, 1978.

Gray, J. G., *The Warriors: Reflections on Men in Battle*, New York: Harcourt Brace Jovanovich, 1959.

Grinker, R. R. and Spiegel, J. P., *Men under Stress*, New York: McGraw Hill, 1945.

Hall, G. S., *Adolescence*, New York: Appleton, 1904.

Hammersley, M. and Atkinson, P., *Ethnography: Principles in Practice*, London: Tavistock, 1983.

Hauser, W. L., "The Will to Fight," in Sarkesian, S. C. (ed.), *Combat Effectiveness: Cohesion, Stress and the Volunteer Military*, Beverly Hills, CA: Sage, 1980, 186–211.

Hazleton, L., *Israeli Women: The Reality behind the Myths*, New York: Simon and Schuster, 1977.

Hearst, N., Newman, T. B. and Hulley, S. B., "Delayed Effects of the Military Draft on Mortality: A Randomized Natural Experiment," *The New England Journal of Medicine*, 1986, *314*, 620–624.

Holm, J., *Women in the Military: An Unfinished Revolution*, Novato, CA: Presidio Press, 1982.

Holt, R. R., "Individuality and Generalization in the Psychology of Personality," *Journal of Personality*, 1962, *30*, 377–404.

Honzik, M. P., "Life Span Development," *Annual Review of Psychology*, 1984, *35*, 309–331.

Horowitz, D. & Kimmerling, B., "Some Social Implications of Military Service and the Reserves System in Israel," *European Journal of Sociology*, 1974, *15*, 262–276.

Howe, N. J. A., "Biographical Evidence and the Developing of Outstanding Individuals," *American Psychologist*, 1982, *37*, 1071–81.

Ingraham, L. H., *The Boys in the Barracks: Observations on American Military Life*, Philadelphia: Institute for the Study of Human Issues, 1984.

Janis, I. L., "Psychodynamic Aspects of Adjustment to Army Life," *Psychiatry*, 1945, *8*, 159–176.

Janis, I. L., *Psychological Stress*, New York: Wiley, 1958.

Janowitz, M., *The Professional Soldier: A Social and Political Portrait*, New York: The Free Press, 1964.

Johnston, J. and Bachman, J. G., *Youth in Transition*, vol. V, *Young Men and Military Service*, Ann Arbor, MI: Institute for Social Research, 1972.

Josselson, R., "Ego Development in Adolescence," in Adelson, J. (ed.), *Handbook of Adolescence Psychology*, New York: Wiley, 188–210.

Kagan, J. and Moss, H., *Birth to Maturity*, New York: Wiley, 1962.

Keane, T. M., *et.al.*, "Substance Abuse among Vietnam Veterans with Posttraumatic Stress Disorder," *Bulletin of the Society of Psychologists in Addictive Behavior*, 1983, *2*, 117–122.

Keniston, K., "Social Change and Youth in America," *Daedalus*, 1962, *91*, 53–74.

Keniston, K., *The Uncommitted: Alienated Youth in American Society*, New York: Dell, 1965.

Keniston, K., "Youth as a Stage of Life," in: Feinstein, S. C., Giovacchini, P., and Miller, A. A. (eds.), *Adolescent Psychiatry*, New York: Basic Books, 1971.

Kimmerling, B., "Anomie and Integration in Israeli Society and the Salience of the Israeli-Arab Conflict," *Studies in Comparative International Development*, 1974, *9*, 64–89.

Kimmerling, B., "Making Conflict a Routine: Cumulative Effects of the Arab-Jewish Conflict upon Israeli Society," in: M. Lissak (ed.), *Israeli Society and Its Defense Establishment*, London: Cass, 1984, 13–45.

Kimmerling, B., *The Interrupted System: Israeli Civilians in War and Routing Times*, New York: Transaction, Inc., 1985.

Kluckhohn, C., "The Personal Document in Anthropological Science," in Gottschalk, L., *et al.* (eds.), *The Use of Personal Documents in History, Anthropology, and Sociology*, New York: Social Science Research Council, 1945.

Laufer, R. S., *et al.*, "Post-War Trauma: Social and Psychological Problems of Vietnam Veterans in the Aftermath of the Vietnam War," vol. 3 of *Legacies of Vietnam: Comparative Adjustment of Veterans and Their Peers*, Washington, D.C.: U.S. Government Printing Office, 1981.

Lazarus, R. S., *Psychological Stress and the Coping Process*, New York: McGraw-Hill, 1966.

Levenberg, S. B., "Vietnam Combat Veterans: From Perpetrator to Victim," *Family and Community Health*, 1983, *5*, 69–76.

Levinson, D. J., Darow, Ch. H., Klein, E. B., Levinson, M. H. and Mckee, B., *Seasons of a Man's Life*, New York: Knopf, 1978.

Levinson, D. J., "Going Up with the Dream," *Psychology Today*, 1978, *11*, 20–31.

Lieblich, A., *Tin Soldiers on Jerusalem Beach*, New York: Pantheon, 1978.

Lieblich, A., "Living with War in Israel: A Summary of Gestalt Therapy Work," in Spielberger, C. D., Sarason, I. G. and Milgrom, N. A. (eds.), *Stress and Anxiety*, vol. 8, Washington: Hemisphere Publishing, 1982, 103–114.

Lieblich, A., "Between Strength and Toughness," in: Breznitz, S. (ed.) *Stress in Israel*, New York: Van Nostrand Reinhold, 1983, 39–64.

Lieblich, A., *Kibbutz Makom*, New York: Pantheon, 1981.

Lieblich, A., "Successful Career Women at Mid-Life: Crises and Transitions," *International Journal of Aging and Human Development*, 1986, *23*, 4.

Lieblich, A., *The Spring of Their Years*, Tel-Aviv: Schocken, 1987 (in Hebrew).

Lifton, R. J., *Home from the War*, New York: Simon and Schuster, 1973.

Lipkin, J. O., Scurfield, R. M. and Blank, A. S., "Posttraumatic Stress Disorder in Vietnam Veterans: Assessment in a Forensic Setting," *Behavioral Science and the Law*, 1983, *1*, 51–67.

Lissak, M., "The Israel Defense Forces as an Agent of Socialization and Education: A Research in Role-Expansion in a Democratic Society," in: Van Gils, M. R. (ed.), *The Perceived Role of the Military*, Rotterdam University Press, 1971, 327–339.

Lloyd, M. A., *Adolescence*, New York: Harper and Row, 1985.

Luttwak, E. & Horowitz, D., *The Israeli Army*, New York: Harper & Row, 1975.

Mahler, M. S., "Thoughts about Development and Individuation," in: Mahler, M. S. (ed.), "The Selected Papers of Margaret Mahler," vol. II, *Separation-Individuation*, New York: Jason Aronson, 1963.

Mahler, M. S., Pine, F. and Bergman, A., *The Psychological Birth of the Human Infant*, 1975, New York: Basic Books.

Manning, F. J., "Critical Commentary to the Boys in the Barracks," in: Ingraham, 1984, 205–232.

Mareth, T. R. and Brooker, A. E., "Combat Stress Reaction: A Concept in Evolution," *Military Medicine*, 1985, *150*, 186–190.

Maslow, A. H., *Motivation and Personality*, 2nd ed., New York: Harper and Row, 1954.

Meehl, P. E., *Clinical Versus Statistical Prediction*, Minneapolis: University of Minnesota Press, 1954.

Meyer, E. C., *The Unit Defense 82*, Arlington, VA: Armed Forces Information Services, Feb. 1982.

Miller, J. B., *Toward a New Psychology of Women*, Boston: Beacon Press, 1976.

Mitchell, J. J., *Adolescent Psychology*, Toronto: Holt, Rinehart and Winston, 1979.

Moskos, C., *The American Enlisted Man*, New York: Russel Sage, 1970.

Moskos, C., "The Enlisted Ranks in the All-Volunteer Army," in: Keely, J. B. (ed.), *All-Volunteer Force and American Sociology*, Charlottesville: University of Virginia Press, 1978.

Moskos, C., "The American Enlisted Man in the All-Volunteer Army," in: D. R. Segal & A. W. Sinaiko (eds.), *Life in the Rank and File*, Washington: Pergamon Brassey's International Defense Publishers, 35–57, 1986.

Motley, M. P., *The Invisible Soldier: The Experience of the Black Soldier in World War II*, Detroit: Wayne State University Press, 1975.

Mullis, M. R., "Vietnam—The Human Fallout," *Journal of Psychosocial Nursing and Mental Health Service*, 1984, *22*, 27–31.

Murray, H. A. *et al.*, *Explorations in Personality*, New York: Oxford University Press, 1938.

Murray, H. A., *Assessment of Men*, New York: Rinehart, 1948.

Mussen, P. H., Eichorn, D. H., Honzik, M. P., Bieber, S. L., and Meredith, W. M., "Continuity and Change in Women's Characteristics over Four Decades." *Internation Journal of Behavior Development*, 1980, *3*, 333–347.

Myrdal, J. *Report from a Chinese Village*, New York: Pantheon Books, 1965.

Novaco, R. W., Cook, T. M. and Sarason, I. G., "Military Recruit Training: An Arena for Stress-Coping Skills," in Meichenbaum, D. and Jaremki, M. E. (eds.), *Stress Reduction and Prevention*, New York: Plenum Press, 1983.

Offer, D. and Offer, J. B., *From Teen-age to Young Manhood*, New York: Basic Books, 1975.

Opler, M. K., "Adolescence in Cross-Cultural Perspective," in J. G. Howells (ed.), *Modern Perspectives in Adolescent Psychiatry*, New York: Bruner/Mazel, 1971, 152–179.

Pardeck, J. T., "Veterans and Aggression: An Empirical Test of Two Rival Theoretical Models," *International Journal of Social Psychiatry*, 1982, *28*, 223–229.

Pardeck, J. T. and Nolden, W. L., "Aggression Levels in College Students after Exposure or Non-Exposure to an Aggressive Life Experience," *Adolescence*, 1983, *18*, 845–850.

Perry, W. G., Jr., *Forms of Intellectual and Ethical Development in the College Years: A Scheme*, New York: Holt, Rinehart and Winston, 1968.

Petersen, P. B., *Against the Tide: The Argument in Favor of the American Soldier*, New Rochelle, NY: Arlington House, 1974.

Polner, M., *No Victory Parades: The Return of the Vietnam Veteran*, New York: Holt, Rinehart and Winston, 1971.

Reinke, B. J., Ellicott, A. M., Harris, R. L. and Hancock, E., "Timing of Psychosocial Changes in Women's Lives," *Human Development*, 1985, *28*, 259–280.

Remer, S. G., "The Prevalence of Alcoholism in a Veterans Administration Medical Center," *Military Medicine*, 1983, *148*, 735–739.

Rogan, H., *Mixed Company*, New York: Putman, 1982.

Rolbant, S., *The Israeli Soldier, Profile of an Army*, NJ: Yoseloff, 1970.

Roy, R. E., "Alcohol Misuse and Posttraumatic Stress Disorder (Delayed): An Alternative Interpretation of the Data," *Journal of Studies on Alcohol*, 1983, *44*, 198–202.

Runyan, W., *Life Histories and Psychobiography*, New York: Oxford University Press, 1982.

Rustad, M., *Women in Khaki: The American Enlisted Woman*, New York: Praeger, 1982.

Santrock, J. W., *Adolescence: An Introduction*, 2nd ed., Dubuque, IA: Wm. C. Brown, 1984.

Scarr, S., and McCarthney, K., "How People Make Their Own Environments: A Theory of Genotype-Environment Effects," *Child Development*, 1983, *54*, 424–435.

Schiff, Z., *A History of the Israeli Army, 1874 to Present*, N.Y.: Macmillan, 1985.

Schild, E. O., "On the Meaning of Military Service in Israel," in Curtis, M. and Chertoff, M. (eds.), *Israel: Social Structure and Change*, New Brunswick, NJ: Transaction Books, 1973, 419–432.

Segal, D. R., "Military Service in the Nineteen-Seventies: Attitudes of Soldiers and Civilians," in: Miller, A. R., and Trupp, A. F. (eds.), *Manning the American Armed Forces: Problems and Prospects*, Columbus: Mershon Center of Ohio State University, 1981.

Segal, D. R. and Segal, M. W., "The Impact of Military Service on Trust in Government, International Attitudes and Social Status," in: Goldman, N. L. and Segal, D. R., (eds.), *The Social Psychology of Military Service*, Beverly Hills, CA: Sage, 1976, 201–211.

Segal, D. R. and Segal, M. W., "Change in Military Organization," *Annual Review of Sociology*, 1983, *9*, 151–170.

Segal, D. R. and Sinaiko, H. W., *Life in the Rank and File*, Washington: Pergamon-Brassey's International Defense Publishers, 1986.

Selye, H., *The Stress of Life*, New York: McGraw-Hill, 1956.

Shatan, C., "Bogus Manhood, Bogus Honor, Surrender and Tranfiguration in the U.S. Marine Corps," *Psychoanalytic Review*, 1977, *64*, 585–610.

Smith, C., "Oral History as 'Therapy': Combatants' Accounts of the Vietnam War," in: Figley and Leventman (eds.), *Strangers at Home: Vietnam Veterans since the War*, New York: Praeger Publishers, 1980, 9–34.

Solomon, Z., Schwarzwald, J., Weisenberg, M. & Mikulincer, M., "Post Traumatic Stress Disorder among Soldiers with Combat Stress Reaction: The 1982 Israeli Experience," *Megamot*, 1987, *30*, 219–229. (in Hebrew)

Spielberger, C. D., Sarason, I. G. and Milgram, N. A., (eds.), *Stress and Anxiety*, vol. 8, Washington: Hemisphere Publishing, 1982.

Spradley, J. P., *The Ethnographic Interview*, New York: Holt, Rinehart and Winston, 1979a.

Spradley, J. P., *Participant Observation*, New York: Holt, Rinehart and Winston, 1979b.

Stanton, M. D., "The Hooked Serviceman: Drug Use in and after Vietnam," in: Figley and Leventman (eds.), *Strangers at Home: Vietnam Veterans since the War*, New York: Praeger Publishers, 1980, 279–292.

Starker, S. and Jolin, A., "Imagery and Fantasy in Vietnam Veteran Psychiatric Patients," *Imagination, Cognition and Personality*, 1982, *2*, 15–22.

Starr, P., *The Discarded Army: Veterans after Vietnam*, New York: Charterhouse, 1973.

Stephens, R., *The Female Column: Women in the Military*, Toronto: Nortwood, 1983.

Stiehm, J., *Bring Me Men and Women: Mandated Change at the Air Force Academy*, Berkeley: University of Calif. Press, 1981.

Stiehm, J., "The Generations of U.S. Enlisted Women," *Signs*, 1985, *11*, 155–175.

Stouffer, S. A. et. al., *The American Soldier*, vol. 1: *Adjustment to Army Life*, vol. 2: *Combat and its Aftermath*, Princeton, NJ: Princeton University Press, 1949.

Stretch, R. H. and Figley, C. R., "Combat and the Vietnam Veteran: Assessment of Psychological Adjustment," *Armed Forces and Society*, 1984, *10*, 311–319.

Terkel, S., *Hard Times: An Oral History of the Great Depression*, New York: Pantheon, 1970.

Terkel, S., *Working*, New York: Pantheon Books, 1974.

Terkel, S., *"The Good War": An Oral History of World War II*, New York: Pantheon, 1984.

Thomas, G. W., "Military Parental Effects and Career Orientation under the AVF: Enlisted Personnel," *Armed Forces and Society*, 1984, *10*, 293–310.

Thompson, P., *The Edwardians: The Remaking of British Society*, London: Weidenfeld and Nicolson, 1975.

Thompson, P., *The Voice of the Past: Oral History*, Oxford: Oxford University Press, 1978.

Van der Kolk, B. *et. al.*, "Nightmares and Traumas: A Comparison of Nightmares after Combat with Lifelong Nightmares in Veterans," *American Journal of Psychiatry*, 1984, *141*, 187–190.

Vaillant, G. E., *Adaptation to Life*, Boston: Little Brown, 1977a.

Vaillant, E. G., "The Climb to Maturity: How the Best and the Brightest Came of Age," *Psychology Today*, 1977b, *11*, 4, 34–49.

Wachtel, P. L., "Investigation and its Discontents: Some Constraints of Progress in Psychological Research," *American Psychologist*, 1980, *35*, 399–408.

Waller, W., " The Victors and the Vanquished," in: Figley and Leventman (eds.), *Strangers at Home: Vietnam Veterans since the War*, New York: Praeger Publishers, 1980, 35–53.

Wikler, N., "Hidden Injuries of War," in: Figley and Leventman (eds.), *Strangers at Home: Vietnam Veterans since the War*, New York: Praeger Publishers, 1980, 87–106.

Willens, E. P. and Rausch, H. L. (eds.), *Naturalistic Viewpoints in Psychological Research*, New York: Holt, Rinehart and Winston, 1969.

Wilson, J. P., "Conflict, Stress, and Growth: The Effects of War on Psychological Development among Vietnam Veterans," in Figley and Leventman (eds.), *Strangers at Home: Vietnam Veterans since the War*, New York: Praeger Publishers, 1980, 123–165.

Wilson, J. P. and Zigelbaum, S. D., "The Vietnam Veteran on Trial: The Relation of Post-Traumatic Stress Disorder to Criminal Behavior," *Behavioral Science and The Law*, 1963, *1*, 69–83.

White, R. W., *Lives in Progress: A Study of the Natural Growth of Personality*, 1st ed., 1952, 2nd ed., 1966, New York: Holt, Rinehart and Winston.

Worthington, E. R., "Post-Service Adjustment and Vietnam Era Veterans," *Military Medicine*, 1977, *142*, 865–866.

Worthington, E. R., "Demographic and Pre-Service Variables as Predictors of Post-Military Service Adjustment," in: Figley, C. R. (ed.), *Stress Disorder among Vietnam Veterans*, N.Y.: Brunner/Mazel, 1978.

Yarom, M., "Facing Death in War—An Existential Crisis," in: Breznitz, S. (ed.), *Stress in Israel*, New York: Van Nostrand, 1983, 3–38.

Yesavage, J. A., "Dangerous Behavior by Vietnam Veterans with Schizophrenia," *American Journal of Psychiatry*, 1983, *140*, 1180–1183.

Youth: Change and Challenge, Daedalus, 91, 1962.

Index